The Foundations of Islamic Banking

Theory, Practice and Education

Edited by

Mohamed Ariff

Professor of Finance, Bond University, Australia

Munawar Iqbal

Professor and former Chief, IRTI, IDB, Saudi Arabia

Edward Elgar

Cheltenham, UK • Northampton, MA, USA

Published by
Edward Elgar Publishing Limited
The Lypiatts
15 Lansdown Road
Cheltenham
Glos GL50 2JA
UK

Edward Elgar Publishing, Inc.
William Pratt House
9 Dewey Court
Northampton
Massachusetts 01060
USA

A catalogue record for this book
is available from the British Library

Library of Congress Control Number: 2010934047

ISBN 978 1 84980 792 0 (cased)

Typeset by Servis Filmsetting Ltd, Stockport, Cheshire
Printed and bound by MPG Books Group, UK

Contents

Contributors

Ibrahim Abraham is a doctoral student at a late stage of completion of his studies in the United Kingdom.

Syed Othman Alhabshi, PhD is professor and the academic head of the INCEIF, the global university for Islamic finance. He is a key scholar in the *takaful* field, and is currently the chief academic officer of INCEIF.

Syed Hamid Aljunid, PhD is a professor at INCEIF, a global accreditation university for studies leading to a chartered qualification to practice Islamic finance. His research is in the area of professional accreditation/training in Islamic finance.

Mohamed Ariff, PhD, CMA is a professor of finance at the Bond University in Australia, and holds an endowed chair as a visitor at the GSM of University Putra Malaysia. He is one of three researchers in receipt of an Australian government grant for Islamic banking research. His current research is on extending theoretical and technical financial details to the emerging field of Islamic finance.

Mohammad K. Badar, PhD is an assistant professor in the very old Alquds University in Jerusalem.

Ishaq Bhatti, PhD is an associate professor of finance at the Latrobe University, Australia: he also holds a professorship in UAE University. Prof. Bhatti is instrumental in establishing Islamic banking training at postgraduate level at his university. He is also involved in the industry.

Maria Bhatti is a postgraduate student at the Law School, University of Melbourne, Australia. She specialises in comparative legal systems, and is doing research on Islamic finance as well.

Eric Girard is a co-author of the chapter by Kabir Hassan.

Kabir Hassan, PhD is a professor at the University of New Orleans, USA. He is a mainstream researcher in banking and finance, and holds an endowed chair in his university. His publications in top-rated journals are well-cited in banking literature: he also specializes in Islamic finance studies. He is the editor of a new journal on Islamic finance.

Taufiq Hassan, PhD is an associate professor at the University Putra Malaysia. One of his research interests is in applied research in Islamic banking and *sukuk* bonds.

Munawar Iqbal, PhD is a professor at the International Islamic University, Islamabad, Pakistan: as the dean of the faculty of Islamic economics and finance, he was instrumental in the educational advancement of the people within the industry. Prior to that, he had significant research appointments at the Islamic Development Bank. He is an accomplished scholar in Islamic finance, having had decades of research and teaching developments in this field.

Mervyn K. Lewis, PhD, FASSA is a professor of banking and finance at the University of South Australia. He is an eminent researcher with notable publications on Islamic ethics and on banking in general. He has published books and articles on Islamic ethics. He is also the series editor of Islamic finance books for Edward Elgar Publishing.

Constant Mews, PhD is a professor of religious studies, and is director of the Centre for the Study of Religions at the Monash University, Australia. He is one of the award holders with two others of the Australian Research Council grant used in this project to work towards this book.

Abdullah Saeed, PhD is the endowed (Sultan Qaboos) chair, professor and director of the Centre for Excellence in Islamic Studies at the University of Melbourne, Australia. His writings on Islamic studies are well-known. He holds concurrently the directorship of the Centre as well as the Asia Institute.

Shaikh Hamzah Razak is a member of the teaching staff at INCEIF, Malaysia. He specializes in *takaful* studies.

Shamsher M., PhD is a professor of finance at the University Putra Malaysia while holding the deputy dean position at his university's Graduate School of Management. He is a well-published Asian scholar with a specialization on emerging capital market behaviour, especially of Malaysia.

Michael T. Skully is a professor of banking at the Monash University, Australia. He is a well-known educator in banking and his books on the subject are widely used. As a specialist in banking studies, his recent works on Islamic banking are becoming a good contribution to the field.

Adrian Walsh, PhD is an associate professor at the University of New England in Australia. His contribution to the book is in tracing the intellectual source to Bentham's work for the break in the historical tradition of opposition to usury in Western religious literature.

Raquib Zaman, PhD is a professor of finance at the prestigious Ithaca College, USA. He is a noted scholar in finance, and has contributed a very carefully researched scholarly paper on Islamic banking. His views are based on interpretations of principles in Islamic jurisprudence over historical times, which is in contrast to narrower interpretations that have come about over some 90 years. His carefully researched views in his writings bring a fresh perspective on the issue of usury.

Preface

In just under half a century as at 2010, an idea that started as interest-free banking has now transformed itself into modern niche banking called Islamic banking with about 500 organisations describing themselves as practicing this new form of pricing monetary transactions using profit-sharing or fee-based contracts instead of the conventional interest-based contracts. The total assets of Islamic banking is estimated to be about US$3–4 trillion as at 2010 – just about 3 per cent of conventional banking assets – held in about 370 banks spread across 76 countries. These banks have expanded the single banking product offered 50 years ago, the two-tier lending certificate called the two-tier *mudaraba*, i.e. the depositor's money, which a bank agrees to off-lend as production loans to firms for a profit share to depositors. Nowadays these new niche banks manage a large number of so-called Islamic banking products, which are structured on the principles of (i) avoiding interest, (ii) sharing risk, (iii) securing profit-sharing or fee-based contracts that meet the demands of customers, who have eschewed interest-based financial transactions in preference of profit-shared transactions. This form of finance also avoids funding productions of: alcohol and pork meat for human consumption; gambling; prostitution.

An additional 150 registered entities manage Islamic mutual funds, where the client's money is invested in shares of companies that are carefully vetted to ensure that these companies do not engage in prohibited economic activities (production of pork; gambling; prostitution; money lending on interest). Yet more companies are offering risk transfer (*takaful* insurance) cover as mutual insurance with the specific aim of redistributing each year the excess profits after costs to the premium holders instead of the shareholders. Another set of financial firms trade in securities known as Islamic capital market instruments such as the short-term money bills/papers and long term *sukuk*.

This book is about these new niche financial institutions that have become a viable industry after half a century. This book is thus a first one to engage in an inquiry into and report on the foundations of the Islamic financial institutions after a study was sponsored by an Australian grant to study the ethical foundations of financial transactions that underlie Islamic finance. The book, as will be seen in the introductory Chapter 1, brings to the readers a perspective from moral philosophy by examining the ethical bases of the practices that are shrouded in the jargon of this new form of banking/finance. Stripped of all its jargon and technical details, the offer of profit-shared–risk-shared contracts in financial transactions can be examined from an ethical angle by connecting the ideas and practices that have shaped human financial transaction ethics that has evolved over the last five millennia. At the foundation level of this niche banking are three branches of ethical thinking moulded over historical time.

The first thing to understand is consumption financing. The Roman Church started the practice of 'poor' loans a millennium ago and they gave the loans free of interest! All religions prohibit financiers from expecting an increase or a reward for lending to a fellow human in need. This prohibition is found in all religions, in fact in all secular societies as well with controls in place on pawnbroking and usury laws. Since the rich with a pile of money could use that money power to exploit those seeking consumption loans in times of need, all civil societies from the time of Hammurabi to Henry VIII had laws that prohibited usurious lending – lending at exorbitant rates (Islam defines it as doubling and quadrupling of the sum lent). These laws offered protection to the citizens of all civil societies in the Old World all the way to China – because the Ming and Tang dynasties outlawed this practice – and India (the Book of Manu prohibits usury), as did Islam by prohibiting the same (*ribaal jahalia*).

The second historical thread one finds in the history of human ethical standards as developed over the same time is that financing to produce an outcome (production loans) should be based on the sharing of risk of that enterprise, so that only if risk is shared should a profit share be demanded over and above the principal. This connotes that the lender may lose the principal for reasons other than fraud by the entrepreneur. This precept was in practice for a long time: think of sea voyages and the camel trains of the Silk Route and the financing of exploration by Spain, the Dutch and the English in the New World, all done by people with money. If the ship sank or the camels were stolen, the loan was not fully recovered!

Profit- and risk-sharing was the mode of production finance until about three centuries ago, when modern banks started to reduce such human financial transactions from formerly joint risk-and-profit shared contracts to a one-sided contract, whereby the bank was not interested in sharing the risk but offered a much reduced cost for financing a production loan by offering a low interest rate, which must be paid irrespective of the outcome of the risky enterprise. No doubt, the birth of the modern corporation around the same time with limited liability tended to make these one-sided no-risk-shared–interest-only contracts the mainstay of today's commerce after about two centuries. If we could wind the time back some 400 years or more, profit- and risk-sharing contracts were the mainstay of production loans in such diverse places as Amsterdam, Naples, Genoa, Germany, Italy, India, China and so forth. Today banks hold sway, and individuals can be charged in court for lending!

The third principle is this: lending and borrowing at interest was despised, but was practiced by some segments of society such as certain ethnic groups and kings going to war, or the very poor. Such interest rates were regulated as late as the last century to ensure that the interest rate was not excessive, meaning usurious. It appears from a careful reading of the history of money and interest that these three principles slowly got forgotten when modern banks – and in the last century deposit-taking firms – were the ones permitted to lend and receive deposits, and started to dominate human financial transactions.

The idea of interest-free banking evolved during the 1930s to 1950s as many thinkers during the period of revival of Islamic countries (in the face of impending decolonisation of empires) wanted to go back to earlier *Shari'ah*-based financial practices of societies in the pre-colonial era. Their ideas and the persons who spawned these ideas are described in the book, so we need not go into these details here. What the editors of this book wish to point out is that these ideas laid the groundwork over 30 years, then led to community banking in 1963 under the name of interest-free banking, which has today expanded to this new niche banking based on (i) eschewing interest, (ii) risk-sharing contracts between asset owner and borrower, and (iii) profit-sharing or fee-based financial transactions in banking. Thus, the interest-based intermediation so essential for the prosperity of modern civil society to secure economic growth is now being done via profit-shared and fee-based pricing mechanisms guided by financial ethics. The happy outcome of this is that the mainstream banks, especially the larger ones, are now adopting these ideas in order to serve those customers who wish to engage in profit-shared financial transactions. The stage is set for this experiment to expand wherever there are such customers, be they in London, Zurich, Cairo, Kuala Lumpur, Jakarta or Hong Kong.

We are grateful to the Australian Research Council for the financial grant (made to professors Ariff, Mews and Skully) in 2006–2010 to enable this study to be undertaken at the Monash and Melbourne universities. We thank the eminent scholars who answered invitations to join in this research and these are the contributors to this book. Several hundred people attended the three conferences/symposia and offered suggestions, and supported us in this effort: Kuwait Finance House and the MCC Ltd were our industry partners. Alongside this effort, the publisher of this book – Edward Elgar – encouraged this foundational work as an original contribution on this topic since his company had published several books on this topic. We would like to thank the publishing house representatives, particularly Alex Pettifer. Also, I wish to record my deep appreciation of the excellent copy-editing help of Joanne Betteridge, for the third time. As editors of the book, we wish to dedicate this book to the professionals in this niche banking area, who are likely to read this book as they avidly learn and mould this new niche finance in the decades to come.

Mohamed Ariff
Gold Coast, Australia
Munawar Iqbal
Islamabad, Pakistan
December, 2010

1. Introduction to Islamic financial institutions

Mohamed Ariff and Munawar Iqbal

1.0 INTRODUCTION

This book is a compilation of studies of eminent scholars in the field of Islamic finance to bring to the readers a book that can be termed a foundation source book on Islamic banking or financial institutions. The book aims to bring to serious students and professional practitioners of Islamic banking a single volume of writings on the theory, principles and practices by financial institutions operating in an already viable niche banking industry growing fast in some 76 different countries. We also add at the end of the book a chapter which is an outline of possible professional accreditation and tertiary level education in Islamic banking. The contributors are eminent scholars who, having identified a need for a carefully-structured book for tertiary level training of industry professionals, then got together and produced in two years a series of studies forming the core of this book.

2.0 ETHICAL PRINCIPLES OF PROFIT-SHARING INTERMEDIATION

We arrange the studies in five parts that constitute this book. Three chapters are included in Part I on the important questions of financial transaction ethics that have evolved over several millennia of mankind's history. Financial ethics appear to have evolved over four millennia going back to the Mesopotamian laws relating to usury and interest rates and for financial contracting/transactions. In the first chapter of Part I, we trace the essential ethics on financial transactions as is evident in the historical writings on money, interest rates and usury. It appears that there are seven fundamental ethical principles that underlie all Islamic financial norms governing profit–risk-sharing funding practices. For example, it is revealed that there is no lending of funds if there is no immediate ownership claim to a class of assets to back the lending: that is no assets to back lending, no borrowing should be permitted. Modern lending is based on a promise of payment and the funds lent are not backed by explicit access to a set of assets from the start of the contracting. Another principle evident from the historical review is that there is no reward to be had in lending activities if the lender and borrower are not sharing in the risk of the venture for which the funds are put to use. Modern bank lending is based on a promise to be repaid irrespective of the consequences of the investment of the funds as justified by the very low interest charged.

It appears, in the light of current practices, that borrowers are able to access funds of savers without necessarily giving ownership claim (explicit asset-backing) to a class of assets but merely by a promise to pay the interest. This encourages profligate access to funds leading to collapse of states and of investments unsupported by asset backing. It is worthwhile to examine these human financial ethics carefully, as is done in Chapter 2 of the book, with an open mind to see how modern finance is based on principles that are far removed from the financial standards that evolved in India, Mesopotamia, China and the lands around the Mediterranean, etc.

In Chapter 3, the reader will find the foundation principles of ethics clearly espoused as Islamic guidelines as brought to the reader in this chapter. It is found that, while usury is forbidden, so are financial transactions based on not sharing in the risk of the venture for which the funds are borrowed. Sharing in the risk is a prerequisite to earning a profit share, unlike under the modern interest rate regime, where the promise to pay is based on not sharing in the risk, indeed not even providing a set of assets to back the money borrowed. What we have in modern finance is a promise to pay from the profits (or from future borrowings) a low rate of interest unconnected with the actual outcomes of the venture. Today, the *sukuk* bond industry has evolved over the last ten years to correct the second of the missing links in borrowing contracts by asset-based lending.

An age-old issue, still smouldering with no consensus of opinion in Islamic banking, is the concept of usury (*riba*) and its connection to interest rates. The interest rate is the pre-agreed claim to be rewarded – obtain an increase – without sharing in the risk of the venture nor having a set of assets to which the lender has first claim prior to the bankruptcy of the firm. In Chapter 4, a clear elucidation is made on this vexing question. The reader will learn that it is difficult to equate usury and interest as interchangeable if one looks at the historical positions of Islamic or other jurists on this question. While interest existed for millennia, so did usurious lending, which alone was banned on fear of serious punishment by such different societies as the Sung Dynasty of China, Hammurabi of Mesopotamia, the God of Moses, Jesus and of Mohammad. Then there is the problem of the modern banking interest rate, which to all intents and purposes is not much more than the long-run inflation rates in an economy! This low modern interest rate is designed to maintain the *status quo* of the value of money, for fear that without this modern banking interest rate given by banks to savers, the value of money will erode over time. Readers will learn that there is a contemporary position, a sort of consensus among Islamic scholars today, to treat usury and interest as equivalent in order to make Islamic banking palatable or saleable. The historical position on this issue has been rather different, as pointed out in this well-researched chapter.

3.0   ISLAMIC BANKING PRINCIPLES, REGULATIONS AND GOVERNANCE

Part II of the book is devoted to selectively introducing the regulatory and governance issues confronting Islamic financial institutions. While cursory discussions on these issues are found in various parts of the book, we make an attempt to identify three related issues in this part. In Chapter 5, we trace the foundation principles of Islamic banking from its concept formation in the pre-1960s period to the present day. The writer traces the increasing sophistication of the products being offered today compared to those in the early period. From a simple two-tier bank deposit (two-tier *mudharaba* contracts), more sophisticated products have appeared in recent years as evidenced by the fast developing infrastructure financing vehicle of the recent Islamic bond market instruments in several countries. The foundation principles are clearly stated in this chapter for the reader to gain the essential character of Islamic banking as being one made on two premises: risk-sharing with profit-sharing and asset ownership before funds move to the counter party, not just a promise to pay as in modern finance: these two principles enable lending to be safer, and rewards potentially tied to the usefulness of the investments for which the funds are raised.

In Chapter 6, we examine the lack of development on the important question of governance of Islamic financial institutions. Governance is more important in Islamic financial institutions because the basis of financial transactions is on ethical behaviour and disclosure standards are much more onerous to comply with the principle of *gharar*, the idea that the risk in a venture has to be revealed clearly upfront before entering in the contract. Ethical behaviour also requires a set of good governance standards. This chapter explains the concept of *Hisbah* principles for good corporate governance. The reader will find an argument to develop standards consistent with the much-copied OECD model of corporate governance. There are other issues discussed in this chapter on enabling legislations needed in common-law regimes to make a level playing field for Islamic banking to be licensed along with conventional banking.

The extent to which Islamic financial institutions follow the already established accounting standards and financial standards is explored in the final chapter in this part (Chapter 7). An important point is made that the compliance and disclosure standards of Islamic financial institutions are still evolving, because most institutions are not disclosing compliance. Compliance needs to be fast-tracked to protect investor interests in Islamic banking, even if the *Shari'ah* board supervision provides a set of initial safeguards.

4.0   OPERATING ISLAMIC FINANCIAL INSTITUTIONS

In Part III of the book, the reader will find three studies covering the practice aspects of three types of financial institutions including banking. In the first of these chapters (Chapter 8), we examine the critical question of whether or not Islamic banks across the world are performing as well as the conventional banks. If Islamic banking is an alternative mode of financial intermediation, no doubt replacing the interest rate of the one-sided risk-based contract with profit-shared intermediation, then it follows that the Islamic banks should by now – after 47 years of experience – perform as well as the conventional banks. So, the test is done using a large sample of Islamic banks matched with conventional banks in the same countries across the world.

What the reader will find is that the new niche Islamic banking based on eschewing usury and interest is performing as well as the conventional banks if we are to believe the test results using 16 years of data of nearly 90 banks. This finding is reassuring in that the present day Islamic banks, though the total assets of this niche industry are no more than 1 per cent of the total assets of the conventional banks, are performing as well as conventional banks. The measures we use are (i) commonly used financial ratios on performance and (ii) economic efficiency indices based on factor productivity.

In Chapter 9, we examine the performance of Islamic Index-based investments. There are about 22 so-called Islamic Index stock market-traded shares. The principles governing the choice of these investment objects are explained, while also showing how such investment funds perform relative to the conventional investment funds. Given an efficient market for such funds, it is the risk of funds one trades, so the rewards to either type of the funds must be the same, provided the risk is the same. That is exactly what this empirically verified behaviour of the Islamic investment fund shows.

In the last chapter in this part of the book (Chapter 10), we provide a complete description of the very recently emerging Islamic insurance (*takaful*) institutions. There are few important differences in this form of insurance: it has to be mutual insurance, meaning that profits must be distributed to the insured after the cost is deducted; agents do not receive commissions; and the premium is invested only in permitted investments based on Islamic profit-sharing lending. The *sukuk* bonds that have appeared in the last ten years will form an ideal investment vehicle for premiums of insurance companies: there is already a total of about US$65 billion *sukuk* instruments. This chapter explains the different principles that govern the practice of *takaful* insurance.

5.0 WHAT IS THE RIGHTFUL REWARD FOR OWNERS OF CAPITAL?

A careful study of money shows that there has been a set of human ethics that evolved over several millennia on dealing with money. One is that exorbitant interest rates are considered as wrong by civilised societies, and by different societies as far removed as Mesopotamia, India and China which all developed laws to control usurious rates of interest until modern times. Second, interest was permitted to be charged for financial transactions so long as that interest was not usurious, that is excessive. The scriptures of the three great religions too forbid the practice of usury. Islam has a definition of usury as 'doubling and quadrupling' of the sum in a financial contract, which was a practice in ancient times: when a borrower did not return the funds borrowed on the due date, the lender would double it. Some nations legislated the rate of interest that was considered 'normal': it was fashionable to consider interest rates of 4–7 per cent as normal as recently as during the last century.

When parties to a contract charged excessive interest rates, laws were passed to annul such contracts, for example by the Sung Dynasty emperors twice, making such lenders suffer huge losses. What appears to be the human ethics in all these practices is to institutionalise protection for the borrower from the capital owners. Capital owners must not use their capital to exploit the weak, who needed money for living or for venturing. If that is the case – though Bentham would disagree – what is the right reward for parting with one's funds?

In Part IV of the book, we explore this very ancient issue by studying the religious doctrines of the three old religions: Jewish, Christian and Islamic. In Chapter 11, we show that the Catholic Church's position appears to have shifted dramatically after the Lutheran teaching and later by the writings of Bentham in England. Bentham is well known as a writer who campaigned to remove the usury law, and succeeded much later when England rescinded the law in the nineteenth century. In Chapter 12, we identify the scriptural prescriptions on usury and interest to show that the interpretation of usury was strictly as excessive interest (akin to Islam's prohibition of doubling and quadrupling the sum borrowed). We also come to realise that usury and interest has been equated by very recent-day scholars under certain strict reinterpretation of the principles, unaware of the historical tolerance of interest: modern bank interest is unknown to earlier scholars. The reader will note that this has been a thorny problem and has been adjusted by completely making interest as also forbidden in contemporary thinking in Islamic banking. In Chapter 13, we also examine the changing attitudes to usury and interest – in general, reward for money dealers – in Christianity.

6.0   PROFESSIONAL ACCREDITATION AND EDUCATION

After almost five decades of the development of Islamic banking, this ethics-based experiment has resulted in a niche banking based on a profit- and risk sharing mode of financial intermediation. One could describe Islamic banking as one encouraging strict codes of financial contracting thus introducing historical ethics to financial transactions. Though still having some faults as some critiques would decry this new industry, this niche banking has grown from nothing to a sizeable industry in 76 countries. There are about 500 financial institutions around the world bearing the description Islamic financial institutions with about 3 per cent (US$3–4 trillion) of the world's total assets in Islamic banks, about US$650 billion Islamic Index funds, about 40 insurance firms, and about 150 investment funds (mutual funds). Capital markets with publicly traded instruments have developed very fast in at least five locations in Malaysia and in the Middle East with products that are based on ethical principles ties to mankind's historical practices.

These developments mean that the industry needs trained manpower to manage this new industry. Chapter 14 traces what is available in this regard. Much more needs to be done by tertiary institutions to train such manpower as is needed for managing the Islamic banks, *takaful* insurance, mutual funds and capital markets. Chapter 14 provides information on what investment is being made in one country to provide professional accreditation to Islamic banking personnel as well as describe what needs to be taught to train people for this industry.

We believe this book provides the reader with the foundations on Islamic banking by examining the fundamental principles that constitute the theories, guide practices and provide the material for human resources training in this new niche industry.

PART I

Foundations of ethical financial transactions

2. Ethics-based financial transactions: an assessment of Islamic banking

Mohamed Ariff

1.0 INTRODUCTION

This is an analytical chapter with the modest aim of assessing a 48-year old experiment commonly termed Islamic finance, which describes the profit-sharing and risk-sharing contracting in financial transactions as being ethically consistent with human welfare. Profit-earning after risk-sharing in debt contracts (as has always been the case throughout history in equity contracts) has been practiced in financial dealings in settled societies for over four millennia, before the birth of modern banking practices which are debt-based on no risk-sharing, with pre-agreed fixed interest charges. In just 48 years, the ethics-based Islamic finance has gained a respectable foothold in some 76 countries, including seven major financial centers, as will be supported by evidence in this chapter. Its presence is felt in many countries. With the Bank of England's adoption of a landmark liberal regulation in 2002, after careful study over many years, to accept Islamic financial institutions as another niche in banking, the pace of growth of adoption of this experiment has substantially accelerated.

These two facets – foothold and wider recognition – have been hard-earned, and deservedly so, if one were to examine Islamic finance as an alternative ethics-based financial practice, which it is claimed to be. As we will observe later in the chapter the ethical moral-based financial principles, along with the human principle of equitable dealings in financial transactions, reconnects these financial activities of Islamic finance to the long-practiced wider belief in human history that financial transactions should be based on risk-sharing, and thus, also by the sharing of the *ex post* outcome of the risk, that leads to profit-sharing as morally correct in finance.

If, for acceptable reasons, profits do not materialize in a risk-sharing venture during the term of a debt contract, then the most a lender gets is the principal put at risk. Despite the widespread practice of safeguarding the principal borrowed in guaranteed contracts in this new finance, some authors (Iqbal, 2007) claim that guaranteeing the principal is also strictly not kosher in Islamic finance, but, in practice, is allowed. In publicly-traded debt contracts this is always the norm, as traded prices of bonds decline if the risk does materialize, leading to losses because of declining bond prices.[1]

In this sense, modern banking practice of exacting a pre-fixed interest charge in debt contracts, albeit not high enough to reach the legal limit of usury rate, introduces a one-sided contract with no equitable recourse for borrowings at risk. Some claim that this makes the moneyed, wealth-owning, capitalist class introduce an element of oppression of the borrowing class. Throughout history it is the entrepreneur without the money wealth who predominantly created inventions to improve society's progress. Indebtedness, due to non-risk-sharing, dents entrepreneurial benefits to society, which is a limiting factor for human welfare, despite the protection of limited liability laws available to a small sliver of entrepreneurs in large formal organizations.

This new form of ethics-based finance has been offered as a new financial invention, replacing the much older, very entrenched, financial transactions based on lender-favored pre-fixed interest payments with no risk-sharing, in debt contracts of conventional finance. While this much older modern finance[2] finds no strictures against lending on these bases to promote economic activities such as gaming, production of intoxicants for non-medical consumption, prostitution, etc., the new ethics-based Islamic lending prohibits such lending activities as being anti-social. Islamic financial institutions do not lend based on interest, nor receive interest (as it is considered non-risk-shared reward, and for reasons of canon law) nor lend to promote anti-social activities. Historical writings (Goetzmann and Rouwenhorst, 2005) suggest that Muslim communities in the 10th–13th centuries, and throughout Muslim communities thereafter, engaged in both formal and especially the more dominant informal lending via profit-sharing debt (and equity) contracts. Pre-fixed interest-based debt contracts also thrived at the formal end in Muslim, as well as in other societies. Even today much informal lending on a profit-shared basis is very prevalent, but is unrecorded based on zero interest or profit share. That is not to deny that in the over 15 centuries of Islam, there was no interest rate-based financing. Nor is it easy to argue that all interest charges are forbidden (El-Gamal, 2006).

The research questions addressed in this chapter are aimed at making a modest contribution to the ethics literature on a number of directions. What are the essential ethical principles, and how do these compare over historical time and against current modern practices? How successful is the penetration of this new form of profit-making with ethics-based financial practices? How is the ethical dimension overseen? What is the comparative assessment of Islamic finance and modern finance?

The following sections elaborate the contributions of the chapter. Section 2 provides a quick discussion and an important review of what this author considers as the seven ethical–moral principles of financial transactions as evolved over 5,000 years in many belief systems that are embodied in Islamic finance. We also discuss the contributions of the debate in the Islamic finance literature. In Section 3, the reader will find a discussion based on summary statistics on the incidence of Islamic financial institutions (IFIs) and modern banks, as at 2007. That leads to Section 4, which contains a quick review of the meaning of money, basic regulatory structures and performance of IFIs, mainly Islamic banks in comparisons with modern banks. There is little known about the performance of Islamic investment and insurance entities, so we discuss these items only tangentially in the same section. An assessment as to whether this new idea will further spread speedily is made in Section 5 as a conclusion of this study.

2.0 EVOLUTION OF FINANCIAL TRANSACTION PRINCIPLES: A LONG VIEW OF HISTORY

An examination of historical writings found in historical, finance and religious literature around the world suggests that pure financial transactions (meaning banking, finance and insurance that are to do with exchange of money wealth to be defined in a later section) may be surmised as being based on seven fundamental principles, as a summary of the many principles found in the Islamic jurisprudence (*fiqh mualamat*) about financial transaction.[3] Financial transactions in historical times were carried out mostly by savings of individuals (the modern day capitalist) who lent it directly to borrowers. These individuals had the power to dominate, and extract economic rent, even the labor of the borrowers, by lawfully taking the wives and children of the defaulting indebted into slavery. There were no formal organizations for intermediation, such as exist in the banking environment of our modern times,[4] which was only established in its modern form with fractional banking in the 18th century. The Catholic Church undertook some custodial functions of banking as far back as the 11th century, but these were not equivalent to fractional banking.

Three ethical principles of a total of seven that evolved over several millennia in borrowing–lending activities are discussed first.

1. For a participant in a contract to rightfully demand a return in a financial transaction when one party makes her savings available as a

loan to another party to carry out entrepreneurial economic activity by lending (or share ownership in the activity as part or full owner), the lending party first shares in the risk of the activity for which the money is lent (or a share ownership is taken if owned), and then take a profit share from the *ex post* outcome. So, the sharing of profits is *ex post* the sharing of risk. An historical example is the 2/3 share of profits taken by wealthy lenders financing voyages of the Dutch East India Company in the 16th century, or a '2 and 20' term (meaning 2 per cent of capital provided as fees, and 20 per cent of profit share) venture capitalists require to fund a business today. If the loan is made on a pre-fixed interest basis as agreed upon by a lending party and the borrowing party, then the interest rate charged, as regulated by societies over long historical periods, was limited to be non-excessive, that is not usurious. Usury as a moral compass has been around for nearly 5,000 years in different settled societies, as is discussed later (Nelson, 1969).

2. The return the lender (or part-owner) gets must be commensurate with the amount of risk undertaken. For example, a sleeping partner may get just a small share of the profits, whereas the active partner may get a larger share of the profits. On the other hand, the lender may get less than the sleeping partner, since the lender undertakes the risk only over the short period of lending, unlike the sleeping partner who carries the risk over an undefined period of time. These are consistent with the time-invariant principle of risk–return that has been enshrined as Nobel prize-winning theories in Economics: here reference is made to Markowitz's portfolio theory, and Sharpe's capital asset pricing theory, for example.

3. Where a return is demanded and agreed upon ahead of the financial transaction – this is the case of what modern banks practice as pre-fixed rate of return – the rate of charge could not be usurious. Usurious return is excessive return, and such contracts are proscribed by law and also by religious laws.[5] For an exhaustive treatment of how Christian and Jewish scriptures prohibit usury, see Homer and Sylla (2005) and Goetzmann and Rouwenhorst (2005).[6] Verses in Upanishad, the oldest Hindu scripture, suggest that excessive interest was forbidden by Manu (Creator).[7]

Laws existed in historical times and in many societies that specified usury as excessive interest causing 'excessive inequity' (Rusd, 1198). Hammurabi is reported as having set usury as a charge exceeding one-third of the amount in a financial transaction: see Homer and Sylla (2005); and for growth of money, see Chown (1994); in Sung Dynasty China, usurious contracts were cancelled thrice, and the usurious lenders were punished by huge losses. This also happened in Greece, too, at different historical times; debt forgiveness became news during the Bush (senior) and Clinton presidencies.

Medieval laws in the UK, now repealed, specified usury as a 24 per cent interest charge. Major religions, all of them, have specific restrictions on usurious charges as immoral earnings. Jewish scripture forbids usury among fellow religious folks, and makes it mandatory to charge interest on Gentiles. Islamic scripture specifies usury as a charge that multiplies the returns, doubling and quadrupling to benefit the owner of capital, and as having an element of exploitation, which the Most Compassionate Divine dislikes, so it is not advised. In general, the usury rate has been considered normally as a rate that is very high, ranging from 24 per cent and above, in legal literature. In contemporary times, laws, including common law recognition of a ban on this practice, exist in most societies that limit or regulate such practices under the class of laws and case laws applying to loan sharking or pawn shops.

It is difficult to specify a particular interest as usury, in that, in a country with rampant inflation, a high interest rate bordering or exceeding the specified usury rate may still be not usurious since the money value is being degraded by high inflation: World Gold Council (1998) and Barro (1979).[8] Research has shown inflation had subsided and remained stable in certain periods of historical times – in Britain (1596–1992), in the United States (1796–1997), in Germany (1873–1997), in Japan (1880–1997) and in France (1820–1997) – when money was pegged to gold and when there was no debasement of money value by governments lowering the pegged value to precious metal. Thus, the usury rate could only apply conveniently when money wealth has stability of value. Also, deductive reasoning suggests that the usury rate is contingent on a stable value of wealth. Hence, the issue of the usury rate is a debatable one even in modern times, and in religious literature as well. Perhaps it should be defined in real returns to be valid.

Islamic scholars have generally tended – there are many exceptions to this statement – to consider any return that is pre-fixed in a financial transaction, and is not based on profit-sharing, meaning the reward is earned before sharing the risk of the enterprise (as discussed in Note 1), as not ethical earning. No scholar has said all pre-fixed interest charges are usurious, at least in the serious literature. Some scholars have also suggested – as in Egypt, and also under Iranian laws in practice – that the bank deposit interest rate is considered not usurious, perhaps because bank interest rates are much smaller, and are mostly a shade higher than the inflation in countries, so it is risk-free, thus deposits are not to be considered risky lending. Indeed, bank rates charged to borrowers do have risk, but rates applied to deposits in banks can be shown to be just about equal to the inflation rate in the long run. Certainly, depositors' earnings are not big enough to constitute a return that doubles and quadruples, a necessary condition to make a return usurious in Islamic finance. The debate on interest versus usury continues.

Nevertheless, the fact remains that the bank interest rate to borrowers is pre-agreed with borrowers, and such contracts have risk which makes the pre-fixed interest earned by banks come from not sharing in the risk of the venture to which the money is being lent. Demanding a return before it is earned, or a financial transaction based on interest on interest, which is common in defaulted loan and personal credit-card-based loans, have the potential to extract twofold to fourfold returns from the borrowers. Such cases would become unethical usurious practices, considered by most scholars as not permitted under Islamic moral and ethical principles. Interest on interest is not permitted, while debt forgiveness or principal repayment reschedule is permissible: see Chapra (1992, 2000) on sovereign debt repayments. Debt forgiveness has been practiced across the world for 4,000 years, in Babylonia, China, India and Greece (Goetzmann and Rouwenhorst, 2005). In Chapra's article, the ethical principle of no interest on interest (quadrupling is the source of this gain) in lending by Islamic banks is singled out as a fair deal. He argues that this would promote less agony for poor countries – say the 23 indebted nations in the Paris Club – borrowing from giant conventional banks, which charge interest on interest, while also gaining a good deal of profits from the currency depreciation of these countries.

4. Now we discuss the fourth ethical principle in another banking activity, namely mortgage finance. In addition to purely making available an amount of savings to fund economic activities in mostly debt contracts, banks also buy and sell 'things' such as cars, houses, ships, airplanes. These transactions are not purely wealth-producing economic activities, although capital gains may accrue as increases over what was paid in the purchase value of an asset. These are activities to enable purchase of costly items, be they cars, motorcycles, aircraft, houses, commercial properties, or even a cow in micro-finance and so forth. This creates a financial transaction where the bank is the provider of the money as an agent to enable purchase (loan for entrepreneurship does not involve merely buying chattels). It is a buy-and-sell or buy-and-rent arrangement. Here too, the Islamic principle of

honest brokerage comes in to ensure ethical dealing. After a mortgage purchase is done, the lender is required to build equity ownership in the asset bought right from the start, as the mortgage is being paid off. Modern banks collect initial payments entirely as interest charges, with insufficient equity being built for the owner of the asset in the early period of loan.[9]

Modern banks can start deducting the interest portion of the deal much faster. The principle of ownership protection and proportional or equal equity from day one of purchase is an equitable financial principle, though it is not at all widely promoted even by Islamic banks because they have opted to use the exact amortization tables of the modern banks without serious consideration of the details of this principle.[10] This may be termed the fourth ethical principle applied strictly to Islamic mortgage transactions in buy–resale contracts. This is the private property ownership preservation principle ensuring the lender is not reneging on ownership of the borrower solely because a lender has the exploitative power in an unequal transaction.

5. Turning to investment companies[11] to discuss how ethically acceptable returns should be earned on invested capital, we find a fifth sound ethical financial principle developed in historical times. The money invested in the financial transactions in the hands of the investing entity is not used to produce socially-incompatible products such as intoxicants for non-medicinal purposes, production of non-religion-sanctioned, unlawful (*haram*) goods or services such as gambling, prostitution and terrorism. Hence, a mutual fund manager screens the nature of the economic activities of the company in which the investment is made before investing in a mutual fund, or selecting an object for mutual funds to invest in. That means investors must not earn unethical earnings by investing money wealth in debt instruments with pre-fixed interest or common stocks of firms (there are about 150,000 common stocks traded in 91 markets) engaging in anti-society activities. There are some 110 Islamic mutual funds, many operated by the world's leading firms, which choose to invest only in permitted investments. There are analysts and institutions specializing in identifying which of the investments, for example, of the 2,800 listed firms on the New York Stock Exchange satisfy the ethical standards under this fifth principle. The Dow Jones Islamic Index is an example of this. There are some 54 such indices in the world (Iqbal, 2007), while more countries are identifying similar lists as for example in Australia by S&P in 2008.

The simple argument in this ethical dictum is that capital resources must be denied for unethical and immoral activities, as well as the production or consumption of forbidden anti-social goods. Such prohibitions are widely documented in other belief systems as applying to their followers as well, namely Christianity, Islam and Jewish. In all the three scriptures, there are prohibitions of certain consumables that include pork, intoxicants, and also usury and exploitation based on money power.[12] By enacting new laws in the last decade, modern societies have plugged the sources that fund terrorist activities: these are the cases of the IRA or Mao's Shining Path or *Naxalites* in India or *al Qaeda*. The ethical issues of investment from a secular viewpoint are found in Lewis and Cullis (1990). About 100 green and ethical funds are operating in the US markets that specifically require that their funds are only investing in firms with good environmental policies, but also firms that avoid producing weapons, funding gambling and prostitution. These ethical mutual funds have been promoted since the 1970s apart from the Islamic funds.

6. We may now discuss a sixth principle in Islamic finance. A widely-accepted principle of equity and morality in human society dictates that self-interest, approaching greed, should not enter into the pricing of financial transactions.[13] Thus, modern Islamic mutual funds (and insurance to be discussed shortly) employ salaried managers/agents, who are not permitted to earn commission. They should not be charging a commission, since commissions are known to reduce income to members of the mutual funds, as is the case in mutual insurance for over 100 years because commission agents can enrich themselves (the principal–agent problem) by churning – a term meaning undue trading – at the expense of the principal. There is a burgeoning literature in mutual fund research that is pointing to the role of commissions as being detrimental to investors in mutual funds, resulting in driving down commission rates.

7. Turning now to Islamic insurance, all the principles we have stated above are all applicable. One new seventh ethical principle applies to insurance. It is agreed by the operators of Islamic insurance (*takaful*) that the length of time over which an insured person lives is determined by Divine power. Major catastrophes are also called Acts of God. Should a person other than the owner of that life as the insured person benefit from the profits made on a wager on the length of that life? Hence, the essential principle on which *takaful* differs from the modern conventional insurance is that the profits accruing to the insurance company from risk transfer contracts must be redistributed to the policyholders as excess profits after all costs are deducted.

    This principle was widely recognized in the 19th century movement against insurance companies in the US, resulting in the growth, particularly in the US, since then of mutual insurance such as the American Mutuals, Liberty Mutuals, etc. that came about exactly from this viewpoint. Lang and Gordon (1995) describe how partnership as a device can be used in this form of insurance as well. However, with the birth of unbridled capitalism since 1986 (the Reagan–Thatcher policy effect), many such mutual firms are now de-mutualizing themselves in the 2000s, with a view to putting their hands on large built reserves, which are the undistributed profits of the firms, thus securing rewards for the board of directors, the managers and the existing policy holders at the time of demutualization, a time-delayed theft. The future profits of a demutualized firm will no longer accrue to the future insured policyholders after the massive raid on the reserves by managers, and the previously insured, in recent years.

Takaful insurance is based on the co-operative principle, and it can also be practiced by a joint-stock company if willing to return profits, beyond a reasonable rate, to the policyholders. Also, the insurance agents, if employed on a commission basis, take a huge part of the premium equal to few years of premium contributions, so much so that the policyholder in modern insurance does not build equity (cash value) during several of the initial years. In a newspaper report in Malaysia in 2006, joint-stock conventional insurance companies made a petition to the government when a *takaful* insurance company returned profits to the policyholders. This practice of returning excess profits was making many joint-stock-based modern insurance companies lose their clients to the *takaful* firms, as the latter's insurance was substantially cheaper with returned profits. The customers of all religious beliefs flocked to the *takaful* insurance companies.

That signifies that incorporating sound ethical principles, established as pro-society financial practice, is beneficial to human societies, and promotes Pareto optimality, a widely used economic criterion for policy decisions. *Takaful* insurers have this potential to grow very fast provided they actually practice the mutuality principle, and also manage the firm efficiently, a matter on which there is little research. Shareholders of insurance companies bring a mere 5 per cent of their assets as equity but earn very high profits (even though in recent years with more frequent natural disasters, they are not earning as much)!

In addition to banking, mutual funds and insurance, there are few other Islamic finance entities. We name a few of them, as we elected not to cover the ethics applicable to such financial bodies: *zakat* fund in banks; charity organizations; pilgrim funds; co-operatives for mutual help that are found in rural areas as the microfinance units called *kuttu*, *havala*, etc. These are not likely to be very significant for the growth of Islamic finance, although they will continue to exist at micro-finance levels as informal transactions. Hence, in this chapter, Islamic finance is narrowly defined to include banking, finance, investment companies (mutual funds) and insurance, in order to limit the discussion. It is tempting to also include the direct financial markets – these markets trade some \$23 trillion of value a year; bond markets have some US\$80 trillion in value, and so on – but they are also not covered in this chapter, though these principles apply to their operations as well.

Table 2.1 provides a summary of our discussion. The seven principles have features that are compared with the modern banking principles in banking, investment and insurance.

In conclusion, then, one could provide this schema, as in the table, for differentiating the fundamental principles that are behind the 45-year-old Islamic finance as compared with modern finance. Seven ethical–moral practices appear to have evolved over several millennia as human wisdom; as the collective conscience of humanity. Modern banking also brought in new ethical principles that changed onerous practices prevalent before its advent. Islamic finance appears to increase the ethical behavior in debt, in investments, in insurance contracts to the extent that makes financial transaction more pro-society and more symmetric in contract terms. These principles prescribe the ways in which financial transactions may be conducted among the more enlightened, civilized, civil and moral societies today, as modern banking removed exploitation of the non-moneyed class at one time. Should these practices be able to survive? We discuss the spread of this experiment in the next section.

3.0 ASSESSMENT OF ISLAMIC FINANCE IN THE MIDDLE EAST AND BEYOND

3.1 Density of Islamic Financial Institutions

The worldwide penetration and progress of this new body of financial practices, based on profit-sharing as being more ethical than modern banking practices, is examined in this section. Modern banking started after a mellowing of the religious ban in 1751 on interest-based financial transactions, after the slow process, over a century of debate within Christianity, between Protestants and Catholics. Modern principles of financial practices can be traced to the development of banking based on pre-fixed, but non-usurious, interest in lending contracts, the demand for which was spurred by the establishment of large-scale commerce by the Western empires over the last five centuries, and by the need to mobilize

Table 2.1   Evolution of ethical–moral principles on financial transaction

No	Principles	Modern Finance	Islamic Finance
1	Profit-sharing in financial transactions	Equity: Required Debt: Not required, based on pre-fixed interest paid	Equity: Required Debt: Also required. Profit share declared after earned, but profit share ratio pre-agreed
2	Risk-sharing in financial transactions	Equity: Required Debt: Not required as interest payment pre-fixed	Equity: Required Debt: Also required since profit shared after earned
3	Return demanded is not excessive (usury)	Equity: Does not apply Debt: Applies. Usurious rate illegal for 4,000 years	Equity: Does not apply Debt: Two schools. Majority opinion all pre-fixed interest is usurious and so illegal
4	Ownership preserved in asset purchases financed by lenders	Yes, to some extent, but not fully	Yes, ownership is preserved, but each payment reduces principal at 50:50 basis
5	Capital not provided for production of anti-social outputs	No restriction of capital: intoxicants, prostitution and gambling. No money for terrorist activities	Any activity that is not pro-society not given capital: liquor, gambling, prostitution, also interest-based earnings
6	Risk of agents exploiting the principal of funds	Commission is heavily regulated, and restricted Rules and practices attempt to reduce adverse incentives	In insurance, commission is not permitted as it reduces the profits to policyholders Adverse incentive problem
7	Insurance profit must go to insured. No profits to accrue to other than insured	Mutual insurance: Yes, but lending based on interest. Joint-stock company: Organizer of insurance gets all the profits	*Takaful* insurance requires that only the insured gets the profits, and that insurance company does not lend on pre-fixed interest as returns

huge funds for an industrializing world over the last three centuries. Modern banks replaced informal lending, and monopolized debt.

There are some 500 financial institutions that are engaged in Islamic finance activities in banking, finance and insurance around the world.[14] Those 500 entities are engaged mostly in banking (about 300 of them), about 100 operate mutual fund companies and the remaining 100 are financial co-operatives or risk-managing insurance companies, or money-market firms trading in Islamic financial products. The majority of them are found operating within the 55 countries where most of the adherents to Islam live as majority Muslim communities. The number of these adherents is variously estimated as anywhere between 800 to 1,000 million in those countries. About 350 financial institutions are found in these Muslim-majority countries. Another 150 are found in the rest of the world with Muslim communities forming minorities as, for example, in the United Kingdom, with 2–3 million Muslims. This minority world adds up to some 150 countries: about 400–500 million Muslims live as minorities in most of these countries.[15]

The total assets of the Islamic banks in 2007 is about US$3–4 trillion (depending on whose writing one reads) and the capital base of the banks alone is estimated to be US$400 billion as the most optimistic estimate. The capital base represents about 11–14 per cent of bank assets, which ratio is a shade higher than the average capitalization rate of modern banks.[16] Most writers agree that Islamic institutions are found in some 73 countries.

Another way of presenting the rough indicator of the spread of Islamic finance is to estimate the entities per million people as a measure of banking density. The 500 Islamic financial institutions represent 0.33 entity per 1 million Muslims, that is, one bank per 3 million people. If we only take the banks, numbering about 350, the banking density is about 0.25 (that is, one bank per 4 million population) or six banks on average in one Muslim majority country. Muslim minorities living in the 150-odd non-Muslim-majority countries have much smaller penetration of Islamic financial institutions: one entity per country although they have access to more modern banks of the conventional kind.

We compare this with the 255-year-old modern banking institutions, disregarding the finance and insurance entities. The world's 6.5 billion people (including the Muslims) have access to 12 banks per country and there are on average four modern banks per million population. That suggests that the density of Islamic finance (which is broadly defined to include finance and insurance companies as well, thus this number is an overestimate) is as follows. In majority Muslim countries, it is one-twelfth the size of the modern banking industry; in minority Muslim countries, it is even worse. Finally, the total assets of all the Islamic banks are estimated at US$3–4 trillion. Restricting our analysis to only the 40 countries reporting statistics to the BIS (Basle), thus not including all the 200-odd countries in the world, the total assets of BIS reporting banks amount to US$35 trillion. That indicates that the Islamic banks account for just one-tenth of the assets of BIS reporting banks. By including all banks in all countries, the number would be about one twentieth of all banks. Finally, the size of the Islamic banks, when compared to the size of the largest banks in the world, would suggest that the total assets of the 350 Islamic banks is just about equal to the total assets of the third largest bank in the US, and also the world.

Given that the profit-sharing–risk-sharing Islamic banks (presumably based on a fairer financial contract than the pre-fixed, non-risk-sharing interest rate) started merely 45 years ago, this may be the reason for the much less-favorable banking density compared with the 255-year-old modern banks. These are based on no risk-sharing and on pre-fixed interest charges for loan contracts (all equity contracts are profit-shared in Islamic as well as modern finance), for returns in pure debt financial transactions.[17] One additional feature of modern banking, in general, is that it relies clearly on compliance with the economic imperatives moderated by the laws applied by each legal domain on banking (exactly what the laws of the country has enacted). There are sound ethical principles in laws governing banking, but these do not cover the sharing of risk, nor the earning of returns after the use of funds (as is the case with equity financing in modern finance) that human societies over time appear to have promoted as being a fair contract in debt and equity finance.

Can this new idea, based on lofty principles of more ethical fair dealing in financial transactions, sustain itself by increasing its banking density around the world, in particular in the Muslim-majority countries? Once the banking density improves in the Muslim-majority countries, there will be growth impetus from this to other minority Muslim countries, where the presence of demand for services will ensure more banks will establish positions.[18]

Table 2.2 provides a summary of the Islamic financial institutions in the Organisation of Islamic Countries (OIC). There are 201 Islamic banks located in the 55 OIC countries. The total number of Islamic banks in one of the most recent sources is given as 311 (out of some 500 Islamic financial institutions): one source (Iqbal, 2007) provides a smaller estimate than the one we use. Of the 55 OIC countries, 25 of them are reportedly without Islamic banks, and the numbers in some countries do not agree, hence there is some degree of inaccuracy, as there always is in counting the numbers without an official database. Thus, the banking density from our sources is about five banks per country found in 55 countries that have

Table 2.2   Financial institutions located in OIC countries as at 2006

OIC Countries	Number	OIC Countries	Number
1 Afghanistan		29 Libya	
2 Albania	1	30 Malaysia	54
3 Algeria	1	31 Maldives	
4 Azerbaijan		32 Mali	
5 Bahrain	27	33 Mauritania	1
6 Benin		34 Morocco	4
7 Bangladesh	3	35 Mozambique	
8 Brunei-Darussalam	3	36 Niger	1
9 Burkina-Faso		37 Nigeria	2
10 Cote D'Ivoire		36 Oman	3
11 Cameroon		39 Pakistan	6
12 Chad		40 Palestine	5
13 Comoros	1	41 Qatar	3
14 Djibouti	8	42 Saudi Arabia	10
15 Egypt		43 Somalia	
16 Gabon		44 Sudan	9
17 Gambia	1	45 Suriname	
18 Guinea	2	46 Syrian Arab Republic	
19 Guinea-Bissau		47 Tajikistan	
20 Guyana		48 Togo	
21 Indonesia	4	49 Tunisia	2
22 Iran	8	50 Turkey	7
23 Iraq	1	51 Turkmenistan	
24 Jordan	2	52 Uganda	
25 Kazakhstan		53 United Arab Emirates	10
26 Kuwait	5	54 Uzbekistan	5
27 Kyrgyz Republic	3	55 Yemen	
28 Lebanon			

at least one Islamic bank. For the OIC group as whole, this ratio is 3.5 banks per country, a number to compare with the 12 conventional banks per country.

Casual observations across the world would suggest that this banking density is insufficient to cater to the banking needs of some 800 to 1,000 million living in those countries. There are also conventional banks in those countries, at a penetration rate many times this ratio, to cater to the overall demand for banking. Suffice it to say that the banking density of one bank per 5 million people, compared with the statistics for modern banks quoted earlier as four banks per million, represents the early growth phase of Islamic banking. That is, the density of Islamic banks in OIC

Table 2.3   Incidence of Islamic banks in non-OIC countries, 2006

Non-OIC group	Banks	Remarks
1 Australia	2	
2 Bahamas	6	
3 Canada	1	
4 Cayman Islands	2	
5 Denmark	1	
6 France	4	Societe General; BNP Paribas
7 Germany	3	Deutsche Bank
8 India	3	
9 Italy	1	
10 Luxembourg	4	
11 Russia	1	
12 South Africa	1	
13 Singapore	1	
14 Sri Lanka	2	
15 Switzerland	6	Union Bank of Switzerland
16 United Kingdom	23	Includes 5 top banks
17 United States	21	Citibank; HSBC
18 Others	29	

countries is one-twelfth of the modern banking density worldwide. In 45 years, the OIC has built a banking capacity amounting to 5 per cent of the capacity of the world average. This is substantial at the early phase of growth, yet it indicates the need for aggressive growth promotion to properly cater to the demands, since there is demand, for Islamic finance in the OIC countries.

How about the minority Muslim communities living in some 115 countries that are documented? There are 110 Islamic banks outside the OIC group. That suggests a banking density of 0.22, which is about the same rate as in the OIC group, about 1 bank per 5 million people. These minority Muslim communities would of course have access to a lot more modern banking. A closer examination of the locations of these 110 banks reveals that they are found in a limited number of countries: see Table 2.3. These statistics reveal that the 100 banks are found in some 45 countries, and that a handful of Western countries alone have 74 (67 per cent) of all the 110 Islamic banks. It appears that the density of Islamic banks in the Western countries is 1.25 banks per million people.

That is, there are six times more Islamic banks available to the population in the Western countries than in the OIC countries. This indicates two aspects. If this six-fold higher growth in Western countries is in fact based on demand – that must be the case, as no governments in these countries actively promote the advent of Islamic finance – then it suggests that Islamic finance, though driven by potentially higher growth within the OIC and the Middle Eastern countries, is growing faster in Western countries. But there is a missing factor. The missing factor could be any one, or combinations of many factors. The environment is not conducive to the growth of this new niche banking beyond the density we have computed (Egypt and Turkey are two such cases). It could be lack of confidence in the environment for effective banking (Pakistan and Sudan are such cases). It may also be the inability of the regions to attract the customers. Perhaps it is more difficult to build the infrastructure for Islamic banking in the OIC countries with some exceptions, such as Dubai and Malaysia. It is difficult to know what factor is behind the lack of speed in OIC countries compared to Western countries. This needs a careful study.

4.0 REGULATORY FRAMEWORK AND BANKING PERFORMANCE

In this section we discuss two topics: regulatory framework and banking performance. In a sense, all human institutions are constructs of some regulatory framework developed over time, and embody complex ethical and moral principles, though there may be room for improvement, such as the need today for environmental ethics given degradation of nature by unconstrained industrialization. Finance is not an exception to this historical truth as the framework for it developed over considerable time. Paper money developed in the 13th century out of need, when the Chinese emperors could not find enough bronze and silver sources. The regulation that made the paper money stick was the law that stipulated execution for counterfeiting. Whether or not some financial development is consistent with promoting societal welfare by controlling vested interests, and by protecting wealth of investors, is where ideas of ethics and morality of fair dealing must be brought to bear in financial transactions. That is exactly how modern fractional banking has to be judged against other forms of banking structures as an outcome of historical evolution. What, then, is the evolution of a common regulatory framework, and how does Islamic finance differ in this regard?

4.1 Money, Wealth and Modern Banking

The birth of modern banking took roots over a century or more after Martin Luther broke with the Catholic ban on interest as usury, and his followers questioned the Church's ban on lending for interest and also the dominance of lending by wealthy individuals. By the time Pope Benedict, in 1751, gave the Papal ruling (in 1950 Pope Pius XII confirmed the earlier ruling more explicitly), dissident bishops in the Germanic region had already given their tacit consent to lending activities to the Fuggers, based on interest. This blossomed later to become modern banking after a span of several centuries. The removal of the ban on interest was the regulatory framework that fostered the growth of modern banking! The basis of the lifting of the ban on interest was the reasoning by the Papacy that earnings made in the process of lending were described as honest earnings, as the people who do the banking are earning an honest reward for honest work. This was the context of the papal ruling that lifted the ban on interest.

Regulation of lending of wealth by the wealthy was largely conditioned by what interest was offered by the banks, although in Europe then, much of the lending was undertaken by ethnic groups (the Flemish merchants, the Jews, and in later years some traders in Germanic enclaves) who had obtained license from the rulers of a given place to trade in money. This settled the regulatory framework for modern banking as a legitimate activity long before fractional banking was in fact[19] officially accepted by law, restricting the moneyed class from exploiting the borrowers. The birth of modern banking with fractional money was perfected just about 250 years ago, with explicit licensing of fractional reserve regulations, and much later the supervisory framework – prudential rules – of lending activities.

We now explain what is money and wealth involved in lending, to understand how a regulatory framework requires stable money value. Money is the store of value, and money saved as wealth is what a person places at the service of the bank, or lends himself to another directly (buy a share or a bond) or places in a mutual fund. What is money? In 1694, some 315 years ago, the Bank of England issued paper money, which was convertible to a given value of a specified amount of precious metal (silver or gold). Paper money was used in China during the Sung Dynasty, but its continued use disappeared about 400 years ago. For over 600 years before the issue of paper money in England, coins were issued in England, each sterling pound value of that coin having a given value (see Hastings and Richardson, 1844b).

Thus, as was the practice in many countries then, a currency had a value pegged to the actual value of a precious item, usually silver or gold (in China it was bronze and silver). In England, as early as in the 10th century, one sterling pound coin equaled 240 silver pennies, and 240 silver pennies would weigh one pound in weight. One pound coin then (later one pound paper) could be exchanged for one pound of silver. Over time, the value of coinage as a token for the real value of a precious item has been devalued (defacement took place by greedy kings and inefficient governments). In the 20th century, for example, the US government devalued the dollar (in 1934) from 22 grains of pure gold to 13 grains, a 60 per cent devaluation; again, in August 1973, Nixon abandoned the dollar's tie to the value of gold. There are other examples of money devaluation in historical times in most countries.

The precursor to modern banking started when groups with a reputation of honesty undertook the custodial function of keeping money wealth. It was a long-established practice to take custody of money for safekeeping. For example, the Catholic Church acted as custodian of pilgrims' deposits as pilgrims hazarded the trip to Jerusalem; pawn shops kept valued items left by customers as did the Knights Templar, who became rich until the wealth of this group was taken over by Philip II of Spain, who killed the Templars' grandmaster. All these custodians of public wealth learned that if they could keep about one-fifth of the value in their custody, it would be sufficient to cater to reclaims by returning customers. Thus, four-fifths of other people's wealth can be lent without risk of all customers coming to claim their deposits at the same time (unless there is a run). This practice of lending custodial wealth as debt led to the birth of what is today the fractional banking.

Thus, the earliest regulation developed was aimed at protection of custodial assets, later came regulation about the reserve to ensure that there is some control on liquidity of assets for returning customers to get back the wealth. This led to the birth of a regulatory body (replacing the king's licensing freedom) with government establishment (for example, the Bank of England in 1604) to ensure that there was orderly licensing and management of wealth.

Thus, regulatory development was a snail-paced creeping effort to retain the value of wealth in place. Fractional banking as a licensed activity in modern finance, with the power of license in the hands of the government, began to emerge as a powerful force just over 250 years ago.[20] Fractional banking was opposed vehemently by many people, including key historical figures (such as Benjamin Franklin)[21] but the laws of Western countries accepted this idea: see Hastings and Richardson (1844b). Fractional banking spread throughout the world with the spread of Western banking ideas. Unlike the banks, the individuals wanting to lend their savings had to accumulate wealth, from which they could lend. But with fractional banking no one could lend, as the power to lend was regulated to be the sole privilege of banks.

In modern days the banks and governments have stopped individuals from lending by passing severe laws that permit only banks to lend! Modern banks slowly relegated the historical lenders to becoming depositors in the banking system. The interest banks pay to them is paltry, as it is about one-third of what the shareholders earn, although the bank shareholders' assets form a mere 8–14 per cent of the total assets. Most assets are from depositors. With modern banking, the profit-shared individual contracts of the rich (of the type that funded the East India Company or the Dutch East India Company) were dropped, and pre-fixed interest became the norm for depositors. With depositors accepting such low returns as 5–10 per cent on deposited wealth, and fractional banking providing free money creation to create debt contracts in the loan book of the banks, the stage was set for slowly forgetting the profit-shared–risk-shared basis of lending that prevailed for millennia.

Should individuals be participating in banking to preserve their wealth by a new form of depositing, namely profit-shared deposits? Islamic finance practice of profit share is reviving interest in this idea by reconnecting lending on this basis, but within the normal banking framework. Islamic banks accept deposits and pay a profit share based on banks' earning to the depositors. Unfortunately, studies show that this profit share is only a shade higher than the deposit rates of conventional banks, and is far lower than what the banks earn, as announced at the end of reporting period! But the idea of creating a market where borrowers of wealth could participate on profit shares has not yet been developed, except for the very wealthy individuals who place large sums directly in syndicated loans on a profit-shared basis. For example, in 2006, Euro 400 million was syndicated by banks for a German state infrastructure project using profit-share lending, so earning high returns. Regulation and infrastructure to practice this form of lending by banks has yet to be developed within the banking sector.

The world average rate of return to shareholders' equity in banks (which is equal to 8–14 cents in the asset base of banks) is about 15–30 per cent, according to BIS sources. In modern lending, regulation and competition limits deposit rates which tend towards a size slightly higher than the inflation rate prevalent to this group that provides up to 86 per cent of assets of banks. Individuals providing 86 or more cents in a dollar of assets are given a return equal to about a quarter to a third of the level of earnings going to the shareholders who provide 8–14 cents in a dollar. The provider of wafer-thin capital gets to gear his returns by monopolizing all lending activities, and earning three times more returns than the savers depositing the money in the bank. Regulation, and in some countries deposit insurance, ensures that the depositors' wealth value is protected in return for their acceptance of such low, but safe, returns. Thus, the banks began to dominate the debt market, and the regulations have tended to avoid any debate on this asymmetric reward to wealth providers, that is, the individuals versus the shareholders.

With the birth of fractional banking, most lending shifted from a wealthy class, potentially greedy and likely to exploit people, to banks run for the good of society. The banks could use four-fifths of the deposits of customers as well as more given by the money multiplier, and lend at a much higher rate than the deposit rates (as long as it is not a usurious rate) to make money for joint-stock shareowners of the bank. That yielded, over the last two decades, 15–30 per cent return on equity after paying to the savers a rate of return of about 5–10 per cent to the depositors of wealth.[22] Often, in developed countries, resident recipients of this 5–10 per cent return on deposits are required to pay income tax on it, while the recipients of dividends are also expected to pay tax on that income. With the birth of unbridled capitalism in 1986 and the politics of government moving closer to the capitalist class, the dividends of capitalists are being exempted from income tax in many jurisdictions, whereas the governments are consistently taxing the deposit incomes of the savers. That creates asymmetry in taxation. The public earning a third of the returns but providing upwards of 85 per cent of banking assets is taxed. The shareholders who earn three-fold more income as owners of banks – who provide just a sliver of their wealth as bank capital – are increasingly being exempted from tax. This is despite the fact that most income of the bank arises from the deposit base of savers via the money multiplier in the fractional banking system that has come to permeate the world as the dominant lender today!

4.2   Regulating Money and Lending: Historical Evolution

From the review of the meaning of money and the operation of modern fractional banking, it is clear that there are some very important regulatory developments. States issue licenses to firms formed by wealthy individuals to assume a dominant role in the private lending market, and outlaw lending by other wealthy individuals, the norm before the advent of the banks. Second, regulations permit the use of depositors' liquid assets, subject to reserve requirements, to enable creation of money and lending.

Third, the establishment of central banks, about 400 years ago, led to the development of a supervisory body for the banking system and later also for economic management of the economy. With the vast pool of money generated from fractional banking, and the flow of individual wealth to the banks as deposits at a low rate of pre-fixed return, the age-old problem of the usury rate became irrelevant, and lending activities with profit shares, as practiced for centuries, disappeared. The norm thus became lending by pre-fixed and non-risk-sharing debt contracts.[23]

To the extent that the Islamic banking is required also to operate within the banking laws, it is clear that these regulations of licensing, of

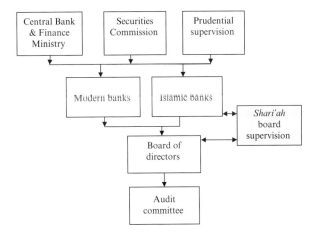

Figure 2.1   Broad structure of supervision of modern and Islamic banks

liquidity requirements, of prudential supervision by central banks, etc. are the same. However, the laws relating to Islamic finance require that these banks refrain from some of the practices of modern banks, so far as the seven ethical principles elaborated in this chapter are concerned.[24] Thus, interest-based contracts are replaced with profit–loss and fee-based contracts, and so on. In addition, Islamic banks have to establish a supervisory board of experts who would ensure that the operations of the banks in the design and trading of securities are in strict compliance with the seven ethical principles. Figure 2.1 is an example of the regulatory framework of modern and Islamic banks.

Islamic financial transactions are regulated by an extra supervisory body, shown as the *Shari'ah* board supervision, to ensure that the ethical principles are in practice built into the design of financial products and also in the institution's operations. This, according to commentators, introduces an element of conservatism, thus safety, into the way the management is over-sighted by this body, thus avoiding the risk of Islamic bankers engaging in high-risk financial activities that often lead to crisis in modern banking. For a view on regulatory frameworks, an important source is Archer and Karim (2002).

The operation of this extra supervisory body is the subject of severe criticism also. One is that the training of these people, mostly in religious doctrine, limits the quality of advice and deters Islamic finance from adopting some very good measures from modern finance. For Islamic finance to be truly consistent, it is not possible to take modern finance practices, and make cosmetic changes to these practices to enforce *Shari'ah* compliance.

The other criticism is that, given the innate conservative training of the present batch of board members, Islamic finance has tended to take some modern banking practices and make them kosher, rather than actually inventing new securities that are not merely *Shari'ah*-compliant with Islamic laws, but are in the true spirit of the dynamic that can be released in profit-share contract designs in debt securitization. One writer has called this a legal arbitrage, and urges Islamic finance to move away from this simplistic mode towards designing truly intrinsic contracts that could improve the interest–no-risk-based contracts as truly profit-share contracts (El Gamal, 2006). For a technical reading of how laws and rules in Islam are relevant as the basis of Islamic Finance, see Vogel and Hayes (1998).

4.3 Performance of Financial Institutions

During the last 5–7 years, a number of working papers have appeared that are discussed widely in conferences and seminars on the subject of how Islamic financial institutions are actually performing in terms of their management. This gives us second generation research outputs very much different from the first generation literature that was mostly laying the foundations of Islamic theory or doctrine about finance, and then describing the products and the regulatory issues as the dominant research issues addressed by researchers in the 1980s and 1990s. Much of the later generation papers[25] are still unpublished, but need to be referred to in order to get a feel on how, in reality, Islamic institutions are performing. An important source for this section is Iqbal and Molyneux (2005), although much of the assessment is based on papers presented at seminars and in conferences.

The main conclusions of the literature are strikingly simple. Islamic banks have performed just about the same as the conventional banks in terms of profitability, and in terms of other performance criteria. Returns on banks' total assets have ranged anywhere from 1.6 to 1.8 per cent per annum, which is about the same as the number for BIS banks. Return on equity is also similar, ranging anywhere from 11 to 23 percent per annum. Islamic bank's capitalization ratio, as mentioned in an earlier section, is a shade higher than the ratio of conventional banks: about 11–14 per cent against the 11 per cent for conventional banks. The slight difference is due to size difference.

On production efficiency of banks, as in conventional banks, there is room for improvement in cost efficiency, although Islamic banks appear to be more revenue efficient: see Brown and Skully (2005) and Bader, Ariff and Hassan (2007). Islamic banks are small to medium in size, and they are mostly found in the countries with majority Muslim populations. Two-thirds of the institutions are in such countries. With the introduction

Table 2.4   Number of Islamic banks in organization of Islamic countries, OIC, 2008

OIC Countries	Number	OIC Countries	Number		Number
1 Afghanistan		20 Guyana	4	39 Pakistan	6
2 Albania	1	21 Indonesia	8	40 Palestine	5
3 Algeria	1	22 Iran	1	41 Qatar	3
4 Azerbaijan		23 Iraq	2	42 Saudi Arabia	10
5 Bahrain	27	24 Jordan		43 Somalia	
6 Benin		25 Kazakhstan	5	44 Sudan	9
7 Bangladesh	3	26 Kuwait		45 Suriname	
8 Brunei-Darussalam	3	27 Kyrgyz Republic	3	46 Syrian Arab Republic	
9 Burkina-Faso		28 Lebanon		47 Tajikistan	
10 Cote D'Ivoire		29 Libya		48 Togo	
11 Cameroon		30 Malaysia	54	49 Tunisia	2
12 Chad		31 Maldives		50 Turkey	7
13 Comoros	1	32 Mali		51 Turkmenistan	
14 Djibouti	8	33 Mauritania	1	52 Uganda	
15 Egypt		34 Morocco	4	53 United Arab Emirates	10
16 Gabon	1	35 Mozambique			
17 Gambia	2	36 Niger	1	54 Uzbekistan	5
18 Guinea		37 Nigeria	2	55 Yemen	
19 Guinea-Bissau		38 Oman	3		

of Islamic contracts in international centers such as London, Zurich, etc., more and more dominant players such as HSBC, Citibank, etc. are already operating divisions to cater to the needs of those who want to participate in Islamic finance: see the *Euromoney* publications on this topic.

5.0   AN ASSESSMENT OF PROGRESSION

Ethics play an important and powerful role in human societies, bringing vast changes to the way humans conduct their affairs. While modern conventional banking was a response to the exploitation of the many by the few with large capital, the usury laws dented this exploitation to some extent for about 5,000 years. The birth of modern banking has been good for society, in that it not only increased the intermediation process, but it also introduced less exploitation. Profit-sharing, and then earning a reward as in Islamic finance in lending activities, may provide a fairer deal in financial transactions, since debt finance is dominant in most nations.

But the zeal of fractional banking, in collaboration with the political elites, ensured that banking based on interest began to dominate the debt markets. Depositors of wealth in banks have been weaned off taking risk, and they accept a very low rate of reward for their savings/wealth put at the disposal of banks. The banks give no more reward than to preserve the value of wealth against inflation, if debasement of money is absent!

Islamic finance is a contemporary challenge to modern finance. Interest on interest is opposed by this new experiment; equity in mortgage finance is promoted in proportion to the payment ratios; pre-fixed interest is replaced with after-risk-sharing reward, which makes possible a symmetric lending contract to earn risk–return beyond inflation; and mutual life assurance reduces the premium charged by the stockholder-held insurance. Should anti-societal production activities be starved of finance from banks? The answer appears to be a qualified yes, considering the costs borne in health care, and in crime fostered by gambling and alcohol in many societies. Private capital may still provide funding for these socially evil pursuits, but without the institutional finance, such activities will not grow as large as they have grown with public financing of these activities. These products will not be outlawed, will still be in markets, but will not be publicly promoted, and thus be less pervasive?

The penetration of ethical banking (be it Islamic finance or community banking) is likely to bring more benefits to human society in an era of ever-getting-bigger-and-powerful conventional banks, which appear to work for just the shareholder interest, often at the expense of the community which provides the deposit base for the money multiplier at local levels. Within 45 years, this new form of ethical banking appears to have achieved moderate success. What may develop in the future is, to some extent, already happening. With investors in the first decade of the 21st century looking for pro-society movements to alleviate environmental concerns, poverty, and lack of reasonable returns to savings, it is possible that movements with greater ethical content will survive. Conventional banking is adapting these ethical principles by operating parts of their institutions as Islamic divisions. This adaptation is likely to continue to grow, and thus create changes in the way modern banking is conducted in the coming decades.

NOTES

1. For example, the price of publicly-traded WorldCom bonds declined in value from over $1,000 to a low price of under $300 when news of fraud became public knowledge. The investors shared in the risk of investing and lost both the promised coupons and a big

part of principal. The coupon payments paid as quarterly interest is paid *after the firm has used the fund* for a quarter, not before it is used, as in bank loans collected as annuity is due, almost a universal practice of banks.

2. The first crude bank was formed in Genoa in 1406, but it took a long time to evolve as modern bank.

3. The author wishes to declare that a close reading of Islamic laws on financial transaction does not reveal that there are these explicit ethical principles in Islam. Far from it, closer understanding of financial rules reveal, at least by deductive reasoning, these simple principles underscore many complex rules, interpretations and debates in Islamic *fiqh* (jurisprudence) literature. By this process, the author's aim is not to give the impression that the complex rules can be so succinctly prescribed as just that many rules. For a recent authoritative writing on laws on this topic, see El-Gamal (2006).

4. That lending with no charges or profits shares is prevalent even today among the low-income households, which mobilizes large savings without entering the formal sector records: see Green et al. (2005); pp. 277-355.

5. The main commandment relating to prohibition of usury in Islam's Koran is: "O you who believe! Devour not usury, doubling and quadrupling (the sum lent). Observe your duty to God, that ye may be successful." (Chapter 3: Verse 130). Islamic jurists referred to this for a long time in historical writings as the *Riba-al-Jahiliya*, a practice of extracting excessive returns in debt contracts, at maturity, practised in the Middle Eastern and Mediterranean societies during the Christian era. This is the only definition found, whereas several references to usury in this scripture are about not to engage in *riba*. For an excellent treatment of usury, see Zaman (2008). For an argument why Islam has prohibited interest as *riba*, see Chapra (2000). Why has Islam prohibited interest? Rationale behind the prohibition of interest in Islam, *Review of Islamic Economics* 9: 5-20: See also Saeed (2007).

6. A fascinating book provides clear evidence of the longevity of human financial principles in Goetzmann and Rowenhorst (2005). Prohibition of interest is clearly spelled out in the Bible: Luke 6:34-35 (New King James Version) 34: "And if you lend to those from whom you hope to receive back, what credit is that to you? For even sinners lend to sinners to receive as much back.". 35 "But love your enemies, do good, and lend, hoping for nothing in return; and your reward will be great, and you will be sons of the Most High. For He is kind to the unthankful and evil.". See also Nelson (1969).

7. This was discussed in a Monash University conference in Kuala Lumpur in September 2005 during a presentation by a scholar on Hinduism.

8. The inflation in Zimbabwe in 2007 is reported to be about 2000%. In such a context, setting a percentage for usury rate of interest is meaningless unless usury rate is defined in real returns!

9. In the case of lease financing, the rent paid to the owner of the lease by the borrower of the 'leased asset' is unequivocally a payment for the services of the leased asset that belongs to the owner of the item. It is not interest, and the charges for debt contract for leasing often uses the prevailing interest rates.

10. It is interesting to note that mortgage financing practices vary across countries. Brazilians used to buy houses with cash savings until a few years ago! Some financiers of mortgage do not reveal the exact details of ownership in assets, and continue to deduct interest first and let owners build equity after several years, even in cases of part cash purchases!

11. For example, in 2004, there were 8,000 mutual funds managing a huge slice of wealth of US and foreign investors. In contemporary finance, it is an important financial contract, as the mutual fund industry has come to dominate investments in wealthier countries, since individuals cannot lend directly.

12. There are about 18 reference in the Old and New Testaments which expressly prohibits consumption of pork meat, alcohol, and gambling. Before Emperor Constantine unified the Church towards the end of the fourth century AD, the general practice

among the believers was to consider these items as non-permitted. With the crushing of the Unitarians by the emperor, these injunctions became less binding.

13. The New York Stock Exchange operates in such a way that the self-interest of the 20 specialists trading on the floor does not enter in their transactions: legal actions have been taken in cases. Brokerage commissions are also regulated to be very low, and frequent trading of shares by investment managers is regulated. These rules ensure that the security dealers do not reduce the earnings of investors.

14. The sources for the statistics are varied and often include the web-based sources. The estimate of the number of Islamic financial entities varies across sources. In this paper, we include banks, investment companies, co-operatives (including pilgrim fund companies) and insurance companies in the quoted number. The estimate quoted in this paper is in the mid-range of the numbers often found in unverifiable sources. In this paper, we rely heavily on one recent source (*Islamic Financial and Banking System Handbook*, 2007) for our statistics.

15. According to the United Nations statistics, there are 196 member countries. There are few non-members, thus the total number of countries in the world will be slightly above 200. We use 200 to compute the numbers in this paper.

16. Iqbal (2007), studying a selection of the banks, report the capital base to be anywhere from 9-11%. Our figure of 11-14% is based on a conference paper presented at the University of Melbourne in November, 2007, by Michael Skully from a study of Islamic banks listed in the BankScope database.

17. A distinction should be made about pure financial activities to separate those acts of buying-selling real assets: financial entities engage in both pure financial activities and buying-and-selling of real assets. A pure financial activity is one where parties engage in an agreement to deal with monetary resources, coins based on precious metals, and paper money in later history – mainly from savings of one party or savings entrusted to a third agent party such as a bank or an investment house – to put the monetary resources to work to produce some things as socially useful economic activity. For example, producing an aircraft, producing a liquor for medicine, or enabling a firm to pay its bills, etc. Banks and insurance companies may also enable two parties to buy a real asset: a house or a building or a ship. This is done as pseudo-financial transaction by arranging mortgage payments (while the property is owned by the buyer and the seller has been paid off by the bank or the insurance company) or by rental payments to the owner of the property by the user of the property. The ethical-moral principles considered by humans as proper for pure financial transactions have always been different and more stringent those for cases of goods exchange (in Islamic literature, referred to as fungible goods).

18. More countries are getting into this market. Hong Kong announced in May 2008 that it is going to issue Islamic Finance instruments: Indonesia in 2008 is issuing $10 billion *sukuk* bonds. One survey conducted in a small sample of Gulf countries cited in a conference speech in 2006 reported that, of the surveyed populations, only about a quarter of the respondents said that they would participate in the Islamic financial institutions. In countries, where Islamic banks have developed well within a dual-banking framework, Malaysia - the demand for Islamic financial products is wider than merely among Muslim community. We also know that high net worth individuals prefer profit sharing, as this obtains far more returns in lending contracts than placing savings in conventional transactions. Hence, it is difficult to say if demand for Islamic Finance is widespread beyond a segment of the population. Only if the products are superior to those offered in the alternative conventional finance entities would demand surge for these new products. This is a critical area of research, needing inquiry.

19. Prior to fractional banking became legalized, banks such as Bank of Amsterdam and Hamburg kept metallic or other values exactly equal to all the deposits of the clients. This is no more the case now.

20. There is a continuing debate as to whether fractional banking practised today is the only way to organise financial intermediation, with so much power given to banks

and to the central banks. There is active opposition in historical times to this form of banking. Thomas Jefferson opposed it: see Jefferson (1861). The first governor of Bank of England wrote: "The Bank hath benefit of interest on all moneys which it creates out of nothing" (see Paterson, 1694).

21. A reading of such oppositionists reveals similarity of arguments of some Islamic thinkers, who had argued, just as Aristotle did over 2000 years back, that money should not beget money. The added opposition to fractional banking was that banks create money out of nothing, in fact they create an illusion of money, it was alleged, which would in the long run enslave humans by its power to exact rent: see some of the historical sources in this paper: for example, Franklin's arguments.

22. Return to equity of banks is widely reported in the annual reports of banks: for a collection see BankScope database of some 2,000 banks across the world. It varies quite widely over time, and across countries as well as across the size of the banks. An average return of between 15-30 per cent is an estimate that will cover the actual rates over time and across countries. This rate is that of commercial banks, and not development banks, investment banks or exchange banks, which register much higher average returns because of their higher level of risk. One good source for periodic numbers is the Bank for International Settlement, which reports data from reporting banks in about 40 countries.

23. For keeping the discussion brief, this paper will not elaborate on how complex the regulatory framework has become, particularly since 1976. Such developments as the securities act, the trust act, governance acts, and prudential supervision acts are thus skipped.

24. If we extend our discussion to include other than banks, mutual funds and insurance, we could identify a few other principles, such as full disclosure principle, principle of reasonable risk (*gharar*), and so on. These other ethical principles relate to financial principles for safeguarding against undue risk-taking in financial contracts. Perhaps this can be attempted as a separate future effort.

25. There are several very recent sources in this paper. Of them three are acknowledged: El-Gamal (2005); Iqbal (2007); and Iqbal and Molyneux (2005).

REFERENCES

Archer, S. and R.A.A. Karim (2002), *Islamic Finance: The Regulatory Challenge*, John Wiley & Sons (Asia), Singapore.

Bader, M., M. Ariff and T. Hassan (2007), 'Efficiency of Islamic Banks: An International Comparison', Proceedings of Global Finance Conference, April 2007, Melbourne, Australia.

Barro, R. (1979), 'Money and the Price Level Under the Gold Standard', *The Economic Journal*, March.

Brown, Kym and Michael Skully (2005), 'Islamic banks: a cross-country study of cost efficiency performance', *Accounting, Commerce & Finance: the Islamic Perspective Journal*, 8 (1&2): 43–79.

Chapra, M.U. (1992), 'Islam and the International Debt Problem', *Journal of Islamic Studies* July: 214–232.

Chapra, M.U. (2000), 'Why has Islam Prohibited Interest? Rationale behind the Prohibition of Interest in Islam', *Review of Islamic Economics*, 9: 5–20.

Chown, J.F. (1994), *A History of Money*, Routledge, London.

El-Gamal, M.A. (2006), *Islamic Finance: Law, Economics and Practice*, Cambridge University Press, New York, New York, United States.

Goetzmann, W.N. and K.G. Rouwenhorst, (2005), *The Origin of Value*, Oxford University Press, Cambridge, MA, United States.

Hastings, Clarke S. and S. Richardson (1844a), *What is a Pound?*, Second edition, Macmillan, London, United Kingdom.

Hastings, Clarke S. and S. Richardson (1844b), *Creating New Money*, New Economics Foundation, London, United Kingdom.

Homer, Sidney and Richard Sylla (2005), *A History of Interest Rates*, Fourth Edition, Wiley Finance.

Iqbal, Munawar, (2007), *A Guide to Islamic Finance*, Edward Elgar, Cheltenham, UK and Northampton, MA, USA.

Iqbal, M. and P. Molyneux (2005), *Thirty Years of Islamic Banking: History, Performance and Prospects*, Palgrave Macmillan, New York.

Lang, K. and P.J. Gordon (1995), 'Partnership as an Insurance Device: Theory and Evidence', *RAND Journal of Economics*, 26: 614–629.

Lewis A. and T. Cullis (1990), 'Ethical Investments: Preferences and Morality', *Journal of Behavioural Economics*, 19(4): 395–441.

Nelson, B. (1969), *The Idea of Usury from Tribal Brotherhood to Universal Otherhood*, (Second Edition, Enlarged), The University of Chicago Press, Chicago.

Rusd, Ibn, (1198), *Bidayat Al-Mujtahid wa Al-Muwaqqi'in Al-Muqtasis, Dar Al-Marifah*, Archives in Beirut, Lebanon.

Vogel, F.E. and S.L Hayes (1998), *Islamic Law and Finance: Religion, Risk and Return*, Kluwer Law Foundation, The Hague, Netherlands.

World Gold Council (1998), *Gold as a Store of Value*, Research Study No. 22, November, 1998.

Zaman, R. (2008), 'Riba (Usury), and the Place of Interest in Islamic Banking and Finance', in *International Journal of Banking and Finance*, 6(1): 1–19.

3. Ethical principles in Islamic business and banking transactions

Mervyn K. Lewis

1.0 ISLAM AND JUSTICE

Islam means the 'tranquillity' and inner 'peace' (*salam*) that can be attained by submitting, surrendering, or giving oneself up to the Will of God as manifest in the revealed law. This word comes from the inquiry that lies at the core of the whole edifice of Islam: what kind of life ought one to live to attain bliss in the here and the hereafter (1:1–6; 7:96)?[1] The answer lies in reflecting on the purpose of life, i.e. why are we here? The revelation, the Holy Qur'an, the sacred book of Muslims, responds to such questions by taking the position that everything in the universe is part of a meticulous plan being executed by the First Cause – *Allah* – the Arabic word for God. *Allah* is One, Incomparable, Sovereign, Eternal, Omniscient and Omnipotent. His Will reigns supreme in the universe. He is the Creator of all, each with sustenance and purpose (11:6). He has created humankind not in vain but to serve as His viceroy on the earth (6:165; 35:39; 57:7). In this capacity, people are required to act as agents and trustees of God in managing the resources of the earth such that all benefit equitably and the original balance in creation is maintained (55:7–9).

To this end, trustees are bound by a covenant with God (7:172; 20:115), given limited free will (34:9; 35:15–16; 47:38), monitored on a continuous basis (6:59; 11:05; 50:17–18), and made accountable for all actions (50:16–35; 89:21–30). Personal responsibility is the cornerstone of such accountability. Thus 'no bearer of burdens can bear the burden of another' (17:15). This holistic approach to conduct does not differentiate temporal from the spiritual and requires people to surrender their limited free will voluntarily to the revealed will of God (51:56–7). Nothing in life thus remains 'profane'. Each and every act undertaken with the intention of fulfilling the covenant with God becomes an act of worship (51:56–7).

Embedded in the notion of trusteeship is a call for conduct based on a code of personal ethics and a blueprint of justice. Together these canons establish rights and obligations across a network of relationships

– familial, social, economic, political and environmental – and regulate community affairs. There are certain fundamental beliefs and actions to which Muslims individually must adhere. These are the fundamental articles and duties of the Islamic faith as contained in the Six Beliefs (in God, the angels, the prophets, the holy books, the day of judgement, and the decree of God) and the Five Duties (testimony/affirmation of God and Muhammad (*pbuh*), prayer, almsgiving, fasting and pilgrimage) which every Muslim must uphold or perform. At another level, Islam has permitted the retention of existing indigenous institutions and cultural and administrative practices in local communities, within the basic principles of Islam. There is no world body and no unified authority. Instead, emphasis is laid on facilitating peaceful interaction among a large number of communities, internally organized around their own sets of beliefs and ways of life different at least in some respects from one another.

Islam views justice as the precondition for preserving peace, equilibrium and harmony on earth, characteristics which are essential in their own right as well as to enable people to understand the demands of their position as the trustees of God on earth. Justice must be understood as a set of pairs of individual freedoms and limits, rights and obligations, and *masalih* and *mafasid* (social utilities and disutilities) elucidated by God (16:116) through His Prophets (7:157) so that human beings honour the rights of their fellow beings and do not exploit them. Justice also has to be complemented with benevolence so that in the words of Maududi (1994), the former removes conflict and bitterness from a society while the latter imparts grace and excellence to it by filling it with 'pleasant' harmony and 'sweet' accord.

In general, the Holy Qur'an brings three terms, *adl* (justice), *qist* (equity/fairness) and *meezan* (balance/scale) to signify justice and equity. Such is the centrality of justice that, on Normani and Rahnema's (1995) count, justice or synonymous terms appear more than a thousand times in the Holy Qur'an. Among the meanings of these words are: to straighten, setting in order, and fixing in the right place; to balance, counterbalance or establish equilibrium; to be equal or equivalent or to match; fairness, impartiality, absence of discrimination; and, honesty, straightforwardness, uprightness, righteousness and correctness. The antonym of *adl* is *zulm* which is used in the Holy Qur'an (2:124; 4:148) to mean indulgence in wrong, evil, iniquity, injustice, oppression and unfairness that eventuates in corruption (11:85) and disruption of peace, in fact sheer destruction (21:11). It also means darkness that beclouds and overshadows the truth (24:40; 57:9).

The Holy Qur'an (4:58, 105, 135; 5:8, 44–5, 48–50, 6:152; 7:29; 11:85; 16:90; 55:7–9; 57:25; 60:8) and *sunnah* elucidate all these different dimensions of *adl*, *qist* and *meezan* with reference to the Divine attributes, the standards of conduct required of individuals, and the characteristics of systems of governance put in place to rule a people. As al-Ghazali (translated by Bagley, 1964, p.55) illustrates, the paramount duty of government in Islam has been historically understood as to bring development and prosperity to the world through justice and equitable rule. The idea is to provide persons with the necessary security and patronage so that they can develop their full potential as free individuals and procure the needs and demands of their body and soul without violating the liberty of others.

2.0   ISLAM AND THE MARKET

Islam generally encourages trade and free markets, and an analysis of the behaviour of market participants to pecuniary incentives is also fully admitted. Where Islamic economics – the branch of knowledge that aims at analysing, interpreting and resolving economic problems with reference to the methodology of Islam – differs from conventional economics is with the issue of legitimising such behaviour over all spheres of human activity. Islam takes the institution of the market neither as a benchmark nor as a reference point for a reflection on organising other spheres of human interaction. Instead, market behaviour, considered as only one kind of interaction among many that constitute social organisation, finds its role and rules determined by reference to the Islamic theory of justice. It is this theory of justice that holds sway over all spheres of human interaction. In fact, so much is this so that the famous Muslim scholar Ibn Sina (Avicenna) once said that justice (*adl*) maintained by law is indispensable for sustaining the life of the human species on earth. In this larger context, the state enters the picture as a carrier, interpreter and implementer of justice through law. Consequently, an analysis of the state's economic role begins, as above, with an examination of the theories of justice rather than from a study of what markets can or cannot do, and feedback from the latter area illuminates how one part of the Islamic theory of justice knits with its other parts.

Islam's attitude to the market is shaped by the context in which the religion arose, in contrast with that of Christianity. Considering the different paths of evolution of the two civilisations, the Christianity that was absorbed into the remnants of the Roman empire some two centuries prior to the rise of Islam, faced the trappings of a feudal system that, albeit not of its own making, was legitimised by it through resources outside the teachings of Christ. In the feudal society, most exchange was in kind and, in line with Aristotelian ideas, which saw something degrading about trading and exchanging things rather than actually making them, Christianity retained for a considerable time an aversion to trading and market exchange.

In contrast, Islam had to deal with the problems associated with monetised free market exchange from its inception. The Arabia into which the Prophet Muhammad was born in 570 CE had no central authority akin to a state. The vacuum was filled to some extent by clans or tribes who prized their independence. A tribe was headed by a senior person known as *sheikh*, who would resolve intra-tribal matters through a mix of mutual consultation, custom and moral persuasion. He usually had no enforcement mechanisms *per se* at his disposal; the virtual subsistence level economy in the desert levelled all differences among people. In this sense, a desert Arab (*Bedouin*) was a born democrat (Hitti, 1970). However, the situation in commercial towns such as Makkah was different. Here markets operated freely and great differences in wealth left the poor, orphans, and women at the receiving end of exploitation and injustice (Esposito, 1995, pp.28–9).

The Holy Qur'an attributed this state of affairs to corruption of reason, lack of faith, moral ignorance, and pride in ancestry, strength and riches, a condition frequently present in the history of mankind (91:7–10; 17:49–51; 34:31–6; 48:26; 9:69). The remedy suggested involved the establishment of the rule of law in accordance with a blueprint of justice revealed through the Holy Qur'an and *sunnah* (5:49; 57:25). In this agenda, trading, as such, was not discountenanced but was extolled. What was needed was to elucidate which forms of exchange were unjust. On that account there is a detailed framework which prohibits usury, gambling and *gharar*, and even condemns unequal barter exchange encouraging instead monetised trade to avoid potential for uncertainty of value. A system of just exchange was thus mandated, in which a central feature is the Islamic position on property rights.

Islam preserves an individual's right to acquire and have property (4:29). However, the test lies in seeking property through means that are not unjust to fellow beings. To elaborate, Islam preserves the Judaeo-Christian ban on interest (or pre-determined returns) without distinction among any (2:275–9). Fixed interest is equated with *zulm* which, as mentioned above, is the converse of justice, that is oppression. In contrast, trade with mutual consent is made legitimate (2:275), writing and witnessing of trade contracts is encouraged (2:282) and the fulfilment of promises is mandatory (2:177). Nevertheless, transactions containing *gharar*, i.e. elements of uncertainty as regards the possession, quality, quantity, price or delivery date of the goods being transacted, are prohibited and so is outright gambling (5:90). Also, hoarding is disallowed; trading in pork and intoxicants is prohibited for Muslims (2:173, 219, 5:90); and deceit, bribery, pornography and prostitution (83:1–3; 17:32–9; 24:2) are considered as various manifestations of corruption that distort socio-economic equilibrium. Subject to these far-reaching reforms, the Islamic economic philosophy accepts the profit motive, protects lawfully gained private property, prohibits intervention in real supply- and demand-driven market prices, and admits the market economy in general.

Against this larger context, earning one's livelihood and engaging in economic activity is considered obligatory and next only to devotional worship. Work is thus equated with seeking the bounties of Allah (16:14). Through it, human beings can test their potentialities, suffice their earthly requirements and fulfil their obligations. Asceticism is discouraged and begging is frowned upon unless one is desperate (57:27). Income through one's own labour is considered a means to befriending God and trading within the Islamic ethical framework earns the Almighty's choicest blessings.

3.0   ECONOMIC AND BUSINESS PRINCIPLES

A large number of Islamic concepts and values define the extent and nature of business activity (Rahman, 1994). There are many positive values such as *iqtisad* (moderation), *adl* (justice), *ihsan* (kindness par excellence), *amanah* (honesty), *infaq* (spending to meet social obligations), *sabr* (patience) and *istislah* (public interest). Similarly there are a number of values which are negative, and thus to be avoided: *zulm* (tyranny), *bukhl* (miserliness), *hirs* (greed), *iktinaz* (hoarding of wealth) and *israf* (extravagance). Economic activity within the positive parameters is *halal* (allowed and praiseworthy) and within the negative parameters *haram* (prohibited and blameworthy) which has to be moderated. Production and distribution which are regulated by the *halal–haram* code must adhere to the notion of *adl* (justice). Collectively, these values and concepts, along with the main injunctions of the Holy Qur'an, provide a framework for a just business and commercial system (Lewis, 2007). A brief summary is provided here.

3.1   Trade and Commerce

Many verses in the Holy Qur'an condone trade and commerce, and the attitude of Islam is that there should be no impediment to honest and legitimate trade and business, so that people earn a living, support their families and give charity to those less fortunate. Nevertheless, Muslims should not allow their business activities to dominate so that making money becomes a first priority and they neglect religious duties; in particular, all trading must cease during the time of the Friday congregational prayer. Nor must the future be overlooked: upon death one is expected to leave behind a family and descendants who perpetuate the law of God, a permanent contribution which will benefit the community, and a source of income for the poor and the needy and/or to generate job opportunities for future generations.

3.2 Work and Production

Islam requires every individual to work and to produce. Prophet Muhammad teaches: 'Never be lazy and helpless' (Rahman, 1994, p.9). There is no good in an individual who does not want to produce and earn money. To Muslims, the unproductive hand is an unclean impure hand. According to Islam, work and investment are the only legitimate means of acquiring property rights (Askari and Taghavi, 2005). Thus, the route to economic achievement is hard work and assumption of risk. It is not through entitlement and inheritance. That is why Islamic law (by a detailed description in the Holy Qur'an) defines exactly how the estate is distributed after death. An individual's power of testamentary disposition is basically limited to one-third of the net estate (that is the assets remaining after the payment of funeral expenses and debts) and two thirds of the estate passes to the legal heirs of the deceased under the compulsory rules of inheritance, providing for every member of the family by allotting fixed shares not only to wives and children, but also to fathers and mothers.

Thus what Abbas Ali (2005, p.52) describes as the 'Islamic work ethic' implies that work is a virtue in light of a person's needs, and is a necessity for establishing equilibrium in one's individual and social life (Nasr, 1984). The centrality of work and deed in Islamic thinking is succinctly addressed in the Holy Qur'an:

> Is it they who would portion out the Mercy of thy Lord? It is We Who portion out between them their livelihood in the life of this world: and We raise some of them above others in ranks so that some may command work from others. But the Mercy of thy Lord is better than the (wealth) which they amass. (Az-Zukhruf, 43:32)

In this context, useful work is that which benefits others and society. Subsequently, those who work hard are acknowledged and are rewarded.

3.3 Poverty and Riches

Pursuing economic activities and achieving economic progress via work and investment must, however, be rooted in moral and legitimate foundations. Islam preaches moderation and a balanced pattern of consumption.

Luxury and overconsumption is condemned, as is poverty. Every being has a minimum requirement to be able to live in dignity. The system is balanced out through the act of *zakat* (almsgiving as an essential part of the system and faith). If this source is not enough, the Islamic government would apply a temporary tax on the rich and affluent to balance the budget as a religious duty (*fard kefaya*).

3.4 Communal Obligations

Individuals are expected to feel socially responsible for others in the community. One cannot enjoy life while others cannot. In general, the aim of the Islamic economic system is to allow people to earn their living in a fair and profitable way without exploitation of others, so that the whole society may benefit. Islam also emphasises the welfare of the community over individual rights. The focus in the Holy Qur'an is on the interests of the entirety of the Muslim society, rather than on the special interest of individual Muslims:

> And hold fast, all together, by the Rope which Allah (stretches out for you), and not be divided among yourselves. (Al-Imran, 3:103)

3.5 Stewardship of Resources

Mankind has been appointed God's vice-regent on earth and given the sacred duty of the stewardship of all natural and created resources. Ownership of property is therefore a trust (*amanah*) to be enjoyed conditionally so long as man follows the *shari'ah* and remains worthy of the trust. People have the right to use natural and other resources for the benefit of mankind. But earth is a trust from God and should be looked after by those who have charge of it and who will ultimately be accountable to God for their actions.

Rights to property in Islamic law may be divided into three categories – public property, state property and private property (Normani and Rahnema, 1995). Islam respects private property and the right of ownership is protected. Property may be acquired through inheritance, gift, purchase or by taking up common property and/or things on it.

3.6 Ethical Standards

Under Islam, the paramount rule in business is honesty and fair dealing (Hussain, 1999). A Muslim business person should therefore be a person of high moral values who would not set out to deceive or exploit others.

Monopolies and price fixing are prohibited. Generally the market should be free and not subject to manipulation. This is so that people will not be exploited by the more powerful in business transactions. Those engaging in trade and commerce should behave equitably. Vendors of goods should not hide any defects in them, nor lie about the weight or quality of the goods. Dealing in stolen goods is prohibited. Hoarding is forbidden when the intention is to force up the price in times of scarcity and so profit at the expense of others.

Products should be useful and not harmful as defined in the Holy Qur'an and Islamic law. Trading and investment can only be undertaken in activities which are not prohibited in Islam (prohibitions include gambling, alcohol, pornography and anything that is harmful to society). Agriculture and employment is encouraged as is dignity of labour, and the prompt payment of a fair wage.

3.7 Commercial Obligations

The general principle is contained in the Qur'anic verse: 'O you who believe! Fulfil (all) obligations' (S5.1). While generally cited as the basis of Islamic contract law, Yusuf Ali (1938) suggests that these obligations are multi-faceted covering divine obligations, mutual obligations of commercial contracts and social relationships, treaty-based obligations as members of civil communities, and general obligations and allegiances as a citizen of the state. In terms of commercial obligations, the definition of contract (*al-'aqd*) is similar to that in the common law, but is wider in that it includes dispositions which are gratuitous as well as endowments and trusts. A contract consists of an agreement made between two or more people. Islamic law provides freedom of contract, so long as the terms do not conflict with *shari'ah*. In particular, it permits any arrangement based on the consent of the parties involved, so long as the shares of each are contingent upon uncertain gain and are a function of productive transformation of resources. These conditions apply to the four root transactions of sales (*bay*), hire (*ijarah*), gift (*hiba*) and loan (*ariyah*), the first two of which feature prominently in Islamic financing.

4.0 USURY AND FINANCE

These principles apply also to Islamic finance, most notably the prohibition on *riba* (interest, usury), which falls under the requirement for justice in exchange and can be seen as part of the Prophet's agenda for social reform. Both the Holy Qur'an and the *sunna* treat interest as an act of exploitation and injustice and as such it is inconsistent with Islamic notions of fairness and property rights. A general principle of Islamic law, based on a number of passages in the Holy Qur'an, is that unjustified enrichment, or 'receiving a monetary advantage without giving a countervalue', is forbidden on ethical grounds. According to Schacht (1964), *riba* is simply a special case of unjustified enrichment or, in the terms of the Holy Qur'an, consuming (that is, appropriating for one's own use) the property of others for no good reason, which is prohibited.

In banning *riba*, Islam seeks to establish a society based upon fairness and justice (Holy Qur'an 2:239). A loan provides the lender with a fixed return irrespective of the outcome of the borrower's venture. It is much fairer to have a sharing of the profits and losses. Fairness in this context has two dimensions: the supplier of capital possesses a right to reward, but this reward should be commensurate with the risk and effort involved and thus be governed by the return on the individual project for which funds are supplied. Hence, what is forbidden in Islam is the predetermined return. The sharing of profit is legitimate and the acceptability of that practice has provided the foundation for the development and implementation of Islamic banking. In Islam, the owner of capital can legitimately share the profits made by the entrepreneur. What makes profit-sharing permissible in Islam, while interest is not, is that in the case of the former it is only the profit-sharing ratio, not the rate of return itself, that is predetermined.

In the interest-free system sought by adherents to Muslim principles, people are able to earn a return on their money only by subjecting themselves to the risk involved in profit-sharing. According to the Hanafi school, profit can be earned in three ways. The first is to use one's capital. The second is to employ one's labour. The third is to employ one's judgement which amounts to taking a risk. Al-Kasani, the Hanafi jurist, states: 'The rule, in our view, is that entitlement to profit is either due to wealth (*mal*) or work (*amal*) or by bearing a liability for loss (*daman*)' ([1910] 1968, vol. 7, p.3545).

With the use of interest rates in financial transactions excluded, Islamic banks are expected to undertake operations only on the basis of profit-and-loss-sharing (PLS) arrangements or other acceptable modes of financing. The compliance of Islamic banks with the letter and spirit of *shari'ah* has been subject to scrutiny by, amongst others, Kuran (1995, 1996, 1997) and Aggarwal and Yousef (2000). Their critique has two dimensions. One is that most instruments employed for Islamic finance – for example *murabahah*, *ijarah*, *istisnaa* and *salam* – while different in some respects from conventional fixed interest finance are still a far cry from the Islamic ideal of the genuine profit-and-loss-sharing arrangements, for example *mudarabah* and *musharakah* contracts. The other is that a major reason for quasi-fixed financing patterns lies in the prevailing low standards of honesty and trustworthiness that stand in stark contrast to the ethical principles outlined above and give rise to problems of adverse selection and moral hazard which can be avoided by sales-based and leasing-based instruments resembling conventional finance. Nevertheless, Chapra (2007) and El-Gamal (2007) argue that differences remain between the conventional and Islamic modes of finance. In particular, the link with commodities-based transactions in the Islamic system rules out short-selling and curbs excessive speculation, while ensuring as well that Islamic financing moves in line with the growth of the real economy.

5.0 CONCLUDING REMARKS

Muslims are expected to conduct their business and financial activities in accordance with the requirement of their religion to be fair, honest and just toward others. Business activity, in consequence, must be broadly inspired and guided by the concepts of *tawhid* (oneness and unity of God), *ihsan* (goodness) and *tawakkal* (trust in God) while regulated, within those boundaries, by a legal framework committed to values such as justice and the ban on *riba* (interest) and the prohibition of *ihtikaar* (hoarding) and other malpractices.

Of course, the desire to achieve justice in exchange or 'fair trade' is not confined to Muslims. However, there are some differences between the Islamic and some alternative visions. First, whereas the modern day welfare liberal might appeal to humanist principles or documents such as the Universal Declaration of Human Rights, the Islamic position is rooted in the metaphysical and the responsibilities of adherents as the trustees of God on earth. The nature of these responsibilities means that the challenge lies not in freeing oneself for what Aristotle calls as the pursuit of the highest good – contemplation of unchanging truths *per se* – but rather in using such soul-searching as a means to internalising universal moral truths so as to undermine inhibitions within people (e.g., pride, greed) that compel them to indulge in injustice and miserliness. The idea is that, with a reformed frame of mind, justice and benevolence flow naturally and so does socio-political action to universalise these attributes.

Second, while encouraging redistribution, there is considerable emphasis in Islam on preserving the social structure, in particular that of family. Justice and charity begin from home. Of course, no religion or ethic can claim a monopoly on such matters. Notably, 'charity begins at home', 'duties to parents, elders and ancestors' and 'duties to children and posterity' are among the principles of natural law that Lewis (1947) identified as held by people in a wide variety of cultures and civilizations. In the particular case of Islam, there are mutual rights and obligations among parents, children and near kin, and there is the obligatory distribution of inheritance among extended family. Also, through the concept of *'fard-e-kifaya'*, i.e. communal obligation, there are rights and obligations of individuals over community and vice versa. Furthermore, there are elaborate mechanisms to institutionalize philanthropy (Hasan, 2007). Together these provisions cultivate and reinforce social capital and create a large space for informal societal and communal modes of governance.

Finally, Islam calls for reforming those market exchanges – constituting the basis of entitlement to earnings – that it considers inherently oppressive, that is, usury, speculation and *gharar*. In this respect, there are parallels not only with other religions in the past (Judaism, Christianity, Hinduism), but also with the present day 'ethical investment' movement in the West that began with the application of Christian religious principles to investment and now embraces, under a decidedly secular banner, a variety of humanist, environmental and social responsibility concerns. So far, however, it is the case that the Islamic ethical rules are applied to a wider range of financial transactions (banking, insurance and investment funds) than is generally the situation in conventional markets.

NOTE

1. In references to the Holy Qur'an, the first number refers to the *sura* or chapter and the second to the *aya* or verse.

REFERENCES

Aggarwal, Rajesh K. and Tarik Yousef (2000), 'Islamic banks and investment financing', *Journal of Money, Credit, and Banking*, 32 (1), 93–120.

Ali, Abdullah Yusuf (1938), *The Holy Qur'an: Text, Translation and Commentary*, Beirut: Dar Al Arabia.

Ali, A.J. (2005), *Islamic Perspectives on Management and Organization*, Cheltenham, UK and Northampton, MA, USA: Edward Elgar.

Al-Kasani, Abu Bakr ibn Mas'ud ([1910]1968), (d.587/1191), *Bada'i' al-Sana'i fi Tartib al-Shara'i'*, 10 vols, Cairo: Al-Galia Press.

Askari, H. and Taghavi, R. (2005), 'The principle foundations of an Islamic economy', *Banca Nazionale del Lavoro Quarterly Review*, LVII (235), 187–205.

Bagley, E.R.C. (1964), *Counsel for Kings*, Al-Muluk, N. (trans), Oxford: Oxford University Press.

Chapra, M. Umer (2007), 'The case against interest: is it compelling?' *Thunderbird International Business Review*, 49 (2), 161–86.

El-Gamal, Mahmoud A. (2007), 'Mutuality as an antidote to rent-seeking shari'a-arbitrage in Islamic finance', *Thunderbird International Business Review*, 49 (2), 187–202.

Esposito, John L. (1995), *The Islamic Threat: Myth or Reality?* New York, Oxford: Oxford University Press.

Hasan, Samiul (2007), *Philanthropy and Social Justice in Islam: Principles, Prospects & Practices*, Kuala Lumpur: A.S. Noordeen.

Hitti, Philip K. (1970), *History of the Arabs*, 11th reprint 1986 edn, London: Macmillan Education Ltd., Macmillan International College Editions.

Hussain, Jamila (1999), *Islamic Law and Society. An Introduction*, Sydney: The Federation Press.

Kuran, Timur (1995), 'Islamic economics and the Islamic subeconomy', *Journal of Economic Perspectives*, 9 (4), 155–173.

Kuran, Timur (1996), 'The discontents of Islamic economic morality', *American Economic Review*, 86 (2), 438–442.

Kuran, Timur (1997), 'The genesis of Islamic economics; a chapter in the politics of Muslim identity', *Social Research*, 64 (1), 301–338.

Lewis, C.S. (1947), *The Abolition of Man*, New York: Macmillan.

Lewis, Mervyn K. (2007), 'It's a matter of principal', *Monash Business Review*, 3 (1), 20–21.

Maududi, S. Abul A'ala (1994), *Economic System of Islam*, translated in English by Riaz Husain, edited by K. Ahmad, 2nd edn, Lahore: Islamic Publications Ltd.

Nasr, S.H. (1984), 'Islamic work ethics', *Hamdard Islamicus*, 7 (4), 25–35.

Normani, F. and Rehnema, A. (1995), *Islamic Economic Systems*, Malaysia: S. Abdul Majeed and Co.

Rahman, Y.A. (1994), *Interest Free Islamic Banking*, Kuala Lumpur: Al-Hilal Publishing.

Schacht, J. (1964), *An Introduction to Islamic Law*, Oxford: Oxford University Press.

4. Adapting understanding of *riba* to Islamic banking: some developments

Abdullah Saeed

1.0 INTRODUCTION

Within Islamic economic literature today, there is a reasonable degree of consensus on certain principles. Many of these, in one form or another, are understood to be mentioned in the Qur'an and Sunnah, either directly or indirectly, and are often general enough to be applied to any community at any time or place. Among these principles are the prohibition of *riba*; freedom to engage in economic activities; private ownership of property; limited public ownership of certain resources; the community's collective responsibility towards its disadvantaged through the collection and distribution of *zakat* and *sadaqah*; and limited intervention by the State in the market to safeguard the interests of all parties concerned and freedom to engage in economic activities in the pursuit of profit. The economic and financial matters dealt with in classical *fiqh* have been given a high degree of importance by scholars and bankers alike, and newly developed contracts, instruments and tools have been developed to a certain extent on the basis of what classical jurists said. Thus the precedents of the past 1,400 years are a very important part of what the Islamic economic system is seen to be. However, because of the diversity of approaches, interpretations and understandings of these rulings and this historical experience, Muslims in the late 20th and early 21st centuries naturally differ on how a contemporary Islamic economic and financial system should be conceptualised. While some Muslims tend to be more closely bound by the actual practice of the past, others look to a more 'liberal' approach. Still others prefer a middle way, keeping an eye on the past while emphasising current needs and aspirations.

This chapter particularly explores some aspects of how Islamic bankers and their S*har'iah* advisers have developed a more pragmatic form of Islamic banking through a creative reinterpretation of the meaning of *riba*. The chapter is organised as follows: Section 2 provides a historical review of the concept of *riba* as understood over 1,450 years; Section 3 provides an assessment of how the concept has been adjusted over time, to the present position of strict interpretation; the conclusions are found in Section 4.

2.0   HOW *RIBA* HAS BEEN UNDERSTOOD

Of the principles of the Islamic banking movement largely agreed upon among Muslims today, the most important is the prohibition of *riba*. One of the most important emphases in the Qur'an is that the disadvantaged in the community should not be exploited through unjust practices. *Riba* was perceived to be unjust and exploitative (*zulm*),[1] therefore the Qur'an prohibited it in no uncertain terms. Given the deep-rooted nature of *riba* in pre-Islamic and early Muslim society, the Qur'an was insistent, declaring that those who transgressed should be prepared for 'war against God and the Prophet' (Q 2:279).[2] As *riba* occurred in Mecca and Medina in these times largely as a result of debt, God commanded creditors to give debtors in financial difficulty extra time for payment, without charging any 'increase' or interest (Q 2:280), and to forgive the debt if need be.

Although the term *riba* incorporates transactions involving loans (*qard*), debts (*dayn*) and sales (*bay'*), *riba* has been discussed primarily in the context of financial transactions in the modern period and is often equated with interest. As a result, Islamic financial institutions have been required to find ways of providing financial and investment services to the Muslim community on an interest-free basis. Therefore, all the operations of an Islamic financial institution, it is argued, must be free from interest.

While the equation of *riba* with interest has become commonplace among Muslims, there is still a large number who do not believe that *riba* can simply be equated with interest. One such scholar, Mohammad Omar Farooq, notes that there are a number of problems with the 'orthodox' understanding of *riba* as interest. He emphasises the following points: firstly, it is a misunderstanding that the prohibition on *riba* as interest is directly derived from the Qur'an.[3] There is no support from foundational texts (the Qur'an and hadith) that any conditions of an initial contract or agreement, including any stipulated excess over the principal, are covered by the Qur'anic prohibition of *riba*.[4] Nor is there *ijma'* or consensus that *riba* equals interest, even though this is the predominant view.[5] The prohibition on *riba* (specifically pre-Islamic riba (*riba al-jahiliya*) in Qur'an 2:275 is primary referring to loans.[6] Thus hadith concerning *riba* in the context of trade or credit sales (*riba al-fadl*) cannot legitimately be used to broaden the scope of the prohibition on pre-Islamic riba.[7] Classical *fiqh* only prohibited one form of *riba* – *riba al-jahiliya* – as did some of the

Companions of the Prophet.[8] Moreover, the discussion on *riba* and loans in the Qur'an occurs in connection to transactions or contracts characterised by *zulm* (injustice and exploitation), with the broader context of the verse discussing spending and charity (*sadaqah*).[9] Thus it is a certain type of *riba* – one that renders a debtor financially vulnerable to poverty or need – that is specifically prohibited.[10]

Farooq therefore argues that the prohibition on *riba* only applies when any increase or increment to the principal loan at the time of repayment is not stipulated as part of the initial contract, thereby making the borrower vulnerable to the dictates of the lender, is exorbitant – for example, in some cases even doubling or quadrupling the initial principal; or exploitative, causing the borrower to face severe financial hardship in the process of repaying the debt.[11] Thus interest charged on loans or debts that are mutually beneficial and mutually agreed upon, without any exploitative aspects and without any terms undisclosed, is not prohibited.[12] This view, however, is not widely accepted.

2.1 Interpretations of *'Riba'*

The view that *riba* and interest are not equivalent has given rise to scholarship that accommodates certain forms of interest. Muhammad Abduh and Rashid Rida, among the early thinkers of the modern period, addressed the question of interest on deposits. While uncomfortable with this they were willing to tolerate interest if a *mudaraba* (commenda) scheme could be devised to legitimise the interest.[13] The late Abd al-Razzaq Sanhuri, the Egyptian authority on Islamic law, saw compound interest as the primary focus of the prohibition of *riba* in the Qur'an. He was of the opinion that interest on capital could be justified on the basis of 'need' (*hajah*), but added that to prevent misuse and exploitation the state should limit interest rates and control methods of payment.[14] The Syrian thinker Doualibi argued that the Qur'an prohibited interest on 'consumption loans' not 'production loans', presumably because the Qur'an's treatment of *riba* was concerned with people who may have borrowed money just to meet their basic needs. Following this thinking others have argued that there is no *riba* when interest is given or taken by corporate bodies such as companies and governments. Others advocate that Islam prohibits 'usury' not 'interest'. Still others consider that *riba* should be equated with 'real', not 'nominal' interest.

A number of scholars of the mid to late twentieth century have also attempted to interpret *riba* from a 'moral' perspective, away from the literal reading that dominates much of the thinking concerning *riba*. Muhammad Asad, a modernist commentator on the Qur'an, maintained that *riba* involved 'an exploitation of the economically weak by the strong and resourceful'.[15] Fazlur Rahman, the Pakistani-American academic argued that the *raison d'être* for the prohibition of *riba* was injustice (*zulm*), as stated in the Qur'an. Rahman in particular bemoaned the fact that well-meaning Muslims with very virtuous consciences sincerely believe that the Qur'an has banned all bank interest for all times in woeful disregard of what *riba* (actually) was historically, and why the Qur'an denounced it as a gross and cruel form of exploitation and banned it.

Despite the appeal of these views, most attempts to 'justify' interest and reinterpret *riba* to accommodate 'interest' have not had wide-spread impact. Islamic bankers and economists have remained insistent that all forms of interest in practice today are indeed manifestations of *riba,* and therefore have no role in an Islamically acceptable financial system. Moreover, influential movements of the twentieth century like the Muslim Brotherhood of Egypt and Jama'at Islami of Pakistan and those influenced by their ideological frameworks have targeted interest-based banking and finance in Muslim societies as institutions that need trans-forming in line with what they consider to be Islamic norms and princi-ples.[16] Maududi, the founder of Jama'at Islami of Pakistan, for example, has asserted in his writings that there is no argument that *riba* is interest. In a similar vein, the Council of Islamic Ideology of Pakistan (CII), which developed a blueprint for the transformation of Pakistan's financial system in the 1980s, claimed, 'there is complete unanimity among all schools of thought in Islam that the term *riba* stands for interest in all its types and forms'.[17]

2.2 Principles of Islamic Banking

In addition to the prohibition of *riba*, Islamic banks must operate in accordance with other Islamic principles that apply to financial transactions and contracts. Banks must avoid transactions that involve exces-sive speculative risk (*gharar*), that is, contracts where a very significant element of uncertainty exists, or similar transactions such as gambling. They must also continue to follow the rulings provided by the Qur'an and Sunnah on prohibited contracts. The system created to administer Islamic banking and finance according to the injunctions of the Qur'an and Sunnah is referred to in the literature today as profit and loss sharing (PLS), where both the provider and user of the funds share in the outcome of the venture, be it positive or negative.[18] Instruments used in this system to mobilise and invest funds include *mudaraba* (commenda), *musharaka* (partnership), *ijara* (leasing), *istisna'* (manufacturing or 'made-to-order' contract) and *murabaha* (mark-up finance based on sale of goods).

3.0 HOW THE UNDERSTANDING OF *RIBA* HAS BEEN COMPROMISED THROUGH PRAGMATIC INTERPRETATIONS

When considering the principles of Islamic finance, it must be emphasised that the early idealistic vision of Islamic banking and finance, which occurred in the decades prior to the 1970s, has changed significantly in practice. The idealism of the early period of Islamic banking during the 1950s and 1960s saw models of Islamic banking and finance developed that adhered closely to conceptions developed by the classical jurists. However, the reality of operating in today's financial markets, in a context very different to that period, has meant that modern scholars have been challenged to reconsider these conceptions. Although the ideal models still exist, other more pragmatic approaches have been developed.

Overall, three approaches to Islamic banking have emerged that can be placed on a continuum: idealist, liberal and pragmatic. The idealist approach seeks to maintain the original vision of the Islamic banking literature of the 1950s and 1960s and to remain faithful to the contracts developed in *fiqh* during the classical period. At the opposite end of the continuum are Muslim scholars who argue that interest is not inherently evil and *riba* does not include modern bank interest. This 'liberal' approach even makes a case that there is no need for separate Islamic banks at all. Between these two extremes lies a more pragmatic approach, which is realistic enough to see that idealist models of Islamic banking have significant problems in terms of feasibility, but at the same time still maintains the interpretation of *riba* as interest.

The majority of Islamic bankers can be classified as pragmatists, prepared to balance practical realities with traditional Islamic principles. The result has been that these bankers and their *Shar'iah* advisers have opted for a more pragmatic form of Islamic banking, interpreting and reinterpreting relevant texts using an eclectic approach to the sources of Islamic law. Here the practical and feasible is given priority over the idealistic and impractical, even though this has led to a somewhat questionable outcome in terms of moving towards a so-called 'Islamic' system. In this chapter, we will look at only three dimensions of such pragmatism.

3.1 Pragmatic Understandings of *Riba*

In theory, Islamic bankers, economists and *Shari'ah* experts who support the idea of Islamic banking uphold the view that interest in all forms, nominal or real, fixed or variable, simple or compound, must be understood as *riba* and is thus prohibited.[19] This view was adopted at the expense of the views of more liberal thinkers such as Abdullah Yusuf Ali,[20] Fazlur Rahman,[21] Muhammad Asad[22] and Doualibi.[23] Almost all writers on Islamic banking from the 1950s onwards argued that *riba* should be interpreted as interest. For example Muhammad Umar Chapra, a theorist of Islamic banking, states that *riba* has the same meaning as interest.[24] The CII of Pakistan and another theorist, Mohammad Uzair, go further and claim that the matter is settled because there is consensus that *riba* is synonymous with interest.[25] The jurists (*fuqaha*) also accepted the legal maxim of classical Islamic law: 'Every loan which begets an advantage is *riba*.' This maxim therefore broadened the concept of *riba* to cover the prohibition of any loan or debt where an 'advantage' is assigned to a creditor, not necessarily in the form of a clearly spelt out 'increase' – i.e. interest – over and above the principal. This 'idealistic' interpretation of *riba* as interest in all forms, which attempts to remain faithful to the contracts developed in the *Shari'ah*, has been gradually weakened in practice.

This weakening has taken a number of forms. First, *riba* (interest) is increasingly seen by *Shari'ah* advisers to Islamic banks as primarily a legal concept, not an economic one. Since Islamic financing is based on being 'interest-free', it could be assumed that 'interest' is taken primarily in its economic sense. Though 'interest' has been understood by Muslim economists developing models of Islamic banking as an economic concept first and foremost, pragmatists among Islamic bankers have chosen a legal conception, which has affected their decisions in designing a large number of *halal* or permitted investment products. Pragmatic Islamic bankers have tended to interpret *riba* as occurring largely in the context of financial transactions; that is, as a contractual obligation by a borrower to pay an increase in a loan transaction. For them, Islamic law prohibits the giving of any positive return to the provider of capital in a purely financial transaction, like a positive return on bank funds. Interest is such a positive return and therefore should be prohibited, from their point of view. This understanding is governed by the requirements of the contract of loan (*qard*) in *fiqh*. If the contract changes, for instance, from a loan to a 'sale' (*bay'*), then the return, which in reality may appear not dissimilar to fixed interest in certain cases, would be perfectly acceptable. Such contracts include the mark-up in *murabaha* contracts, for example, which, from a legal point of view, are not purely financial transactions and positive returns are therefore considered permissible.

The view of *riba* as purely a *legal* concept has been objected to by many leading Islamic economists. The Pakistani experience of Islamic banking, for example, led many economists to question the practises on which this presumed model functioned. The main targets of criticism in relation to Pakistani experience were the mark-up and profit margin techniques in trade and rent that formed the backbone of Islamic banking. Many economists argued that there was no substantial difference between what was practised under the name of Islamic banking and the norm under the interest-based system – the difference existed only in name.[26] One critic, Ziauddin Ahmad, a prominent theoretician of the Islamic banking movement, argued that 'mark-up' was not a substantial alternative to interest given the philosophy behind the prohibition.[27] Thus for ideal-ists, a change from an interest-based system to a mark-up-based system was merely a change in name, leaving the substance intact. Considering the implications of the *murabaha* system, Nejatullah Siddiqi, one of the most prominent contributors to the development of Islamic banking, says '[f]or all practical purposes this [mark-up system] will be as good for the bank as lending on a fixed rate of interest'.[28] The CII of Pakistan, highly critical of mark-up, described it as merely a perpetuation of the old system.[29]

However, the views of these critics appear to have been too idealistic and out of step with the demands made on Islamic banks by the current financial and economic environment. As a result, their voices have been largely ignored in Islamic banking literature and practice.

The dilution of the interpretation of *riba* as interest continued with the acceptance by Islamic banks of the idea that an increase, called a 'fine', is permissible when a debtor does not pay a debt, as agreed, on time. In theory, Islamic finance literature holds that when a debtor misses or makes a late payment, the creditor cannot impose an increase on that person. Much of the practice of pre-Islamic *riba* appears to have been associ-ated with this. However, the practitioners of Islamic banking found that debtors who had concluded *murabaha* transactions, for example, were not paying on time as agreed. Since capital was seen to have an opportunity cost, any delay in repayment of the debt was considered a recoverable loss for the bank, at least in situations where the debtor simply opted not to pay the debt on time. Since under the interpretation of *riba* a creditor cannot impose an increase while giving time to the debtor to pay the debt, practitioners of Islamic finance argued for the imposition of a 'fine' as compensation for the loss suffered by the bank. In order to safeguard the integrity of the instrument, practitioners also argued that compensation should not be determined by the bank itself but by its *Shari'ah* supervisory board, or in consultation with a neutral third party. One Islamic bank in Egypt, for example, in its contract of *murabaha,* declares its right to demand compensation for any damages that have occurred because of a delay in payment on behalf of the client, the value of which will be decided by the Religious Supervisory Board (RSB).[30]

A third dilution of the conception of *riba* occurred in the discarding of the legal maxim according to which every loan that begets an advantage is *riba*. According to this principle, Islamic banks would not be able to make use of arrangements like the reciprocal placement of funds on an 'interest-free' basis with another bank on the understanding that the bank would in turn place funds with the Islamic bank on an 'interest-free' basis. The legal maxim, if followed, prevents the Islamic bank from making use of such a facility since these transactions lead to the accrual of an 'advantage' in kind. However such arrangements are now standard practice in Islamic banking.

A fourth departure from the strict interpretation of *riba* occurred when Islamic banks began to provide so-called 'rewards' to depositors, or received such rewards from bodies like a central bank. Strictly speaking, a bank depositor who is not placing funds in a PLS (or at-risk) account is not entitled to any return on these funds. In practice, however, many depositors do not want to risk their money by putting it into a PLS account; they instead prefer to keep their funds intact in the form of a savings deposit or a current account deposit. In some Islamic banks these funds constitute a significant portion of their deposits and are naturally utilised by the Islamic bank. In order to cater for these depositors' needs, a number of Islamic banks provide so-called 'rewards' to these account holders. The justification for this is that as long as there is no contractual obligation between the depositor and the bank to provide a specific reward or benefit to the depositor, the Islamic bank can provide such a reward at its own discretion. It is true that technically this argument can be supported by Islamic law, in that there are some hadith that suggest a borrower can repay more than the loan amount, if done voluntarily.

The practice of giving 'rewards' has now become institutionalised in a number of countries even though it is somewhat questionable from the perspective of the *Shari'ah*. In certain countries, for instance, depositors expect to receive these rewards, and not receiving them may lead customers to transfer to other banks. Islamic banks themselves, in some countries, also place large amounts of funds with other institutions on the understanding that such rewards will be given. This is clearly visible in certain instances, for example in Indonesia, where an Islamic bank places its surplus funds with the Central Bank on the expectation that it will give a certain percentage – say 3 per cent – as a 'reward'. This practice even extends to agreements between Islamic banks and governments and can involve millions of dollars. In some countries, such as Malaysia, rewards have become the basis of certain types of 'Islamic' bonds. Closer scrutiny of these practices, however, may reveal that what is happening is the application of interest in an economic sense, but not necessarily in a legal one.

3.2 Pragmatic Understandings of 'Profit'

In the literature on Islamic finance during the 1950s and 1960s, the concept of 'profit' was understood to be 'real' profit resulting from a real PLS venture, not interest by another name. In Islamic finance, however, some of what has come to be known as 'profit' is dangerously close to fixed interest. Although it has been challenged by a number of Islamic economists, this pragmatic approach has persisted. In Islamic law, as well as in the literature on Islamic banking, the concept of profit is closely associated with an uncertain positive return as a result of engaging in a PLS venture or a sale transaction. Instances of actual practice, however, show that what is called profit in some cases is far from this idealist understanding.

Murabaha transactions, for example, have replaced what in traditional banks amounted to loans on the basis of fixed interest for the purpose of acquiring consumer goods. In an Islamic bank, instead of asking for a loan, the client asks to 'purchase' the item concerned at a 'profit' for the bank. The bank and the client then enter into an agreement where the bank supplies the commodity, either through its own subsidiaries or another third party supplier, at an agreed price and with mark-up (profit). The client pays the agreed 'price' (the actual price plus mark-up) over an agreed period of time. In calculating this profit or mark-up, the bank takes into consideration the time it will take for the client to repay the amount, which has been determined in consultation with the client before the price of the sale by the bank is finalised; the shorter the time the less the mark-up and the converse. Once agreed on there cannot be any change in the sale price, which is an important difference between fixed interest and mark-up-based financing. One key point of contention among classical Muslim jurists here is whether mark-up can be related to the period of time. Some jurists vehemently argue that it cannot be, while others argue that charging extra for time is consistent with the 'practice of merchants'. The CII of Pakistan states that doubts may arise in relation to the increase the seller is receiving in the case of a deferred payment sale (that is, it is against the time given to the buyer for payment) and that the increase may resemble *riba*.[31] Mark-up in *murabaha*, therefore, comes dangerously close to the interest that it is presumably trying to replace. Islamic banks maintain that this is not the case, but in general their arguments are less than convincing to idealists.

A second area of pragmatic adjustment is the importance given to time when calculating profit for various Islamic banking contracts. Time enters into the calculation of profit/return not only in *murabaha* but also in a large number of other arrangements, including the profits on *murabaha*, *mudaraba* and *musharaka*; the profits on investment deposits; and in housing finance. Perhaps the position of those who reject the idea that mark-up/profit can be related to time, such as the CII of Pakistan is too idealistic for Islamic bankers, for whom such idealism simply cannot be put into practice. Such Islamic bankers would argue that 'mark-up' and time-based variation are legally valid, at least according to some jurists, and also extremely useful for the Islamic bank, without which much of their Islamic business could not be sustained. Therefore, in the interest of the continuation of Islamic banking, this position has been given priority over idealism.

A third practice that really dilutes the concept of profit is the consideration given to interest rates in calculating profit or mark-up in sale-based operations. These rates are often taken into account when determining mark-up on a bank's *murabaha* transactions.[32]

Another question currently being debated in the literature is whether profit can be pre-determined. This question has not been resolved but, at the moment, Islamic banks and fund managers at least appear to accept the view that a predetermined return is unacceptable. However, there are those who disagree. Muhammad Sayyid Tantawi, an Egyptian scholar of *Shari'ah*, argues that there is no legal reason or analogy (*qiyas*) that prohibits the determination of profits in advance, so long as the determination occurs between the two parties in the beginning. The most important consideration in the transaction is that it is free from prohibited aspects such as cheating, high risk, injustice, *riba* or other such characteristics.

3.3   Pragmatic Approach to Investment in Companies

Pragmatism has also manifested in the realm of investment, particularly where the stocks of leading companies are concerned.[33] Strict following of general *fiqh* rules on investment, partnership and shareholding precludes investment in companies whose business, in one way or another, involves a *haram* (prohibited) element, such as dealing in *riba* or the production, purchase or selling of prohibited goods or services. However, in the modern period investment in the stocks of publicly listed companies has become a major part of the investment strategies of interest-based banks and investment funds. Islamic banks and fund managers have also noticed this lucrative investment stream.

Efforts to find a solution to the problem posed by *fiqh* began earnestly when Islamic banks moved from the initial stages of institution building. Islamic banks' *Shari'ah* supervisory boards as well as the relevant committees of the Islamic Fiqh Academy based in Jeddah and the Islamic Development Bank have organised seminars and workshops to explore this important issue. The debate has centred on whether it is permissible to invest in companies whose business involves a prohibited element. Since most companies rely very heavily on interest-based finance for their activities and on interest-based investments to generate income from surplus funds, paying and receiving interest is part of the normal life of these companies. As interest is considered *riba* and therefore prohibited, there is a substantial problem in investing in these companies for concerned Muslim investors, even though the companies may be engaged in the production of *halal* goods or services. Scholars have been divided into two camps on this issue: one has declared that investment in the stocks of such companies is prohibited and unlawful, which is generally consistent with classical *fiqh* rules, while the other has declared that such investment is lawful provided that certain conditions are met, such as the proviso that the company is not involved in a prohibited activity. The second position appears to be pragmatic and holds that the prevalent nature of such companies throughout the world means that Muslim investors have to be involved in such companies. The important question for advocates is on what basis such involvement should take place.

Scholars have attempted to use *fiqh* to determine if and on what basis investment in such companies should occur. Since clear legal arguments have been difficult to find amongst classical *fiqh* sources, scholars have resorted to analogy (*qiyas*) and doctrines such as 'necessity', 'public interest' and 'general need' to find support for this position. However if interest is *riba*, the Qur'anic prohibition of *riba* is explicit and the Prophet's saying which 'curses' anyone involved in *riba* is also clear. This means that it has been a difficult task to justify any involvement in companies for whom dealing with interest (*riba*) is a day to day occurrence. Even so, concepts such as 'cleansing' profits of an investment from their prohibited elements (i.e. the component of interest) and setting a maximum limit for the involvement of the company in interest-based dealings have been devised to enable dealings with interest-based companies. Today, Islamic banks in general do not see any problem with considering the return on such investments *halal*.

Based on this, the Dow Jones has established its own Islamic arm, the Dow Jones Islamic Market Index, and Islamic banks have established their own funds to invest in such companies.[34] Companies that deal in products such as alcohol, pork or pork derivatives, entertainment, tobacco or arms; that have debt to asset ratios that are equal to or greater than 33 per cent or have accounts receivable to total asset ratios that equal to or are greater than 45 per cent are excluded. Similarly, the Shari'ah Supervisory Board has adopted a procedure designed to exclude companies with interest-based income from the Index Portfolio; that is, where the total amount of interest earned or paid is equivalent to a certain amount.

What we have here is one of the clearest cases of the dominance of pragmatism, justified on need and based on rather unfamiliar concepts in Islamic law, such as 'cleansing' of *haram* elements and quantifying *haram* elements from a mix of *halal* and *haram* packages.

4.0   CONCLUDING REMARKS

Pragmatism in Islamic banking is driven by a number of factors. Firstly, Islamic banks function in an environment where they are competing with an interest-based system. Therefore the feeling among many Islamic bankers is that they need to provide the same kinds of services and investment mechanisms to their clients. This perceived need is certainly at the forefront of the pragmatic nature of what is happening in Islamic banking and finance. Secondly, most Islamic bankers, financiers and economists are graduates of modern 'Western' economics, regardless of whether they studied at a Western university or locally, and are comfortable with looking at Islamic finance on the basis of their experience. This exposure leads them to believe that in order to survive, Islamic finance needs to follow Western practice to a certain extent. Thirdly, most Muslim government policies related to banking, finance and economic matters rely largely on Western approaches and view with suspicion any deviation from this. Fourthly, the rulings of the classical *fiqh* on many aspects of Islamic law are being reconsidered, and in some cases reinterpreted in light of contemporary circumstances. This is leading to both greater awareness and greater emphasis on the reasoning behind some Qur'anic injunctions and scholarship on how to apply these principles in the modern period. Finally, Islamic finance must function in a global environment, which means interacting with interest-based systems and their institutions, including banks, insurance companies, stock exchanges and foreign exchange.

To function within these constraints, Islamic bankers have had to be creative in their approach to the development of their operations. Although Islamic banking has its roots in the somewhat 'idealist' literature of the 1950s and 1960s, it has undergone a process of redefining what is acceptable, made possible by the flexibility available in interpreting *Shari'ah* texts, as well as by the need to keep pace with the present global environment. New approaches have facilitated the development of a viable Islamic banking sector. However unpalatable such adjustments may be to idealists, these approaches have provided Islamic banking practitioners with much needed flexibility to design *halal* investment products for their Muslim clientele, a practice that is only likely to continue in the future. Moreover, there is probably now great potential for these approaches to gain more appeal among non-Muslim clientele because of the global economic downturn. Although the broader banking and financial sector has been adversely affected by the worldwide financial crisis of 2009, many reports suggest that Islamic banking has remained at least in a number of contexts unaffected because, unlike other banking institutions, Islamic banks do not buy or sell debt or rely on stocks or bonds, and distance themselves from market speculation.[35] As economists ponder the factors that have led to the financial crisis and how to prevent such a situation happening again, it is likely that other models of banking and finance will be looked into, including Islamic banking. Although the outcomes of this process are unknown, it is likely that the Islamic banking and finance sector will remain strong and perhaps grow in importance in the future.

NOTES

1. Qur'an 2:279; Tabari, *Jami'*, III, 109.
2. The prohibition of *riba* is mentioned in four different contexts in the Qur'an. The first emphasizes that *riba* deprives wealth of Allah's blessing (Q 30:39). The second condemns *riba*, equating it with wrongful appropriation of property (Q 4:161). The third asks Muslims to avoid *riba* (Q 3:130). The fourth establishes a clear distinction between *riba* and trade, urging the believers to take only the principal sum and to forgo even this if the borrower is unable to repay (Q 2:275–80; Tabari, *Jami'*, III, 108–14).
3. Farooq, Mohammad Omar, *Toward Defining and Understanding Riba: An Outline Essay* (2007) <www.globalwebpost.com/farooqm/writings/islamic/intro_riba.doc> Accessed 25 May 2009, p. 7.
4. Ibid., p. 14.
5. Ibid., p. 9.
6. Ibid., p. 7.
7. Ibid., p. 8.
8. Ibid., p. 7.
9. Ibid., pp. 7–8.
10. Ibid., p. 15.
11. Ibid., pp. 14–15.
12. Ibid., p. 14.
13. Mallat, 'The Debate on Riba', p. 74 in Farooq, *Towards Defining and Understanding Riba.*
14. Sanhuri, *Masadir al-Haqq*, III, 241–4.
15. Asad, *The Message*, 633.
16. Saeed, Abdullah, *Islamic Banking and Interest*, Leiden: E.J. Brill, 1999, pp. 5–10.
17. Council of Islamic Ideology, *Consolidated Recommendations on the Islamic Economic System*, Islamabad: Council of Islamic Ideology, 1983, p. 7.
18. Saeed, *Islamic Banking and Interest*, pp. 51–75.
19. Mawdudi, Abu al-A'la, *Towards Understanding the Qur'an*, trans. Zafar Ishaq Ansari, Leicester: Islamic Foundation, 1988, I, p. 213.
20. Ali, A. Yusuf (trans.), *The Holy Qur'an*, Lahore: Sh.Muhammad Ashraf, 1975, p. 111.
21. Rahman, Fazlur, 'Islam: Challenges and Opportunities', in *Islam: Past Influence and Present Challenge*, Welch and Cachia (eds), Edinburgh University Press, 1979, p. 326.
22. Asad, Muhammad, *The Message of the Qur'an*, Gibraltar: Dar al-Andalus, 1984, p. 633.

23. Saleh, Nabil, *Unlawful Gain and Legitimate Profit in Islamic Law*, Cambridge: Cambridge University Press, 1986, p. 29.
24. Chapra, M. Umer, *Towards a Just Monetary System*, Leicester: Islamic Foundation, 1985, p. 57.
25. Council of Islamic Ideology, *Consolidated Recommendations on the Islamic Economic System*, Islamabad: Council of Islamic Ideology, 1983, p. 7 and Uzair, Mohammad, 'Impact of Interest Free Banking', *Journal of Islamic Banking and Finance*, Autumn 1984, p. 40.
26. Zaidi, Nawazish Ali, 'Islamic Banking in Pakistan', *Journal of Islamic Banking and Finance* (Karachi), Summer 1988, p. 29. One of the differences is that in sale-based transactions such as *murabaha*, if the debtor does not pay on time, the creditor, the bank, cannot impose any extra charge on the actual amount of the original sale transaction.
27. Ahmad, Ziauddin, 'The Present State of Islamic Finance Movement', *Journal of Islamic Banking and Finance* (Karachi), Autumn 1985, pp. 23–4.
28. Siddiqi, Muhammad Nejatullah, *Issues in Islamic Banking: Selected Papers*, The Islamic Foundation, 1983, p. 139.
29. CII, *Consolidated Recommendations*, pp. 97, 121.
30. FIBE, *æAqd Bayæ al-Murabaha.*
31. CII, *Consolidated Recommendations*, p. 36.
32. Quasim, Quasim M., 'Islamic Banking: New Opportunities for Cooperation between Western and Islamic Financial Institutions', in *Islamic Banking and Finance* (London: Butterworths, 1986), p. 25.
33. Nizam Yaquby, 'Participation and Trading in Equities of Companies which [sic] Main Business is Primarily Lawful but Fraught with some Prohibited Transactions', Paper presented at Fourth Harvard Islamic Finance Forum, Harvard University, 30 September–1 October 2000.
34. See, for example, Albaraka Dow Jones Islamic Index Fund http://www.altawfeekcom/abdjiffunddetails.htm.
35. http://www.asharq-e.com/news.asp?section=6&id=14245.

REFERENCES

Alsadek H. Gait and Andrew C. Worthington, *A Primer on Islamic Finance: Definitions, Sources, Principles and Methods* (2007) <http://ro.uow.edu.au/cgi/viewcontent.cgi? article=1359&context=commpapers> Accessed 26 May 2009

Abdul Gafoor, *Riba-free Commercial Banking* (2001) <http://www.islamicbanking.nl/article3.html> Accessed 26 May 2009.

Justice Muhammad Taqi Usmani, *The Text of the Historic Judgment on Interest Given by the Supreme Court of Pakistan* (undated) <http://www.albalagh.net/Islamic_economics/riba_judgement.shtml> Accessed 26 May 2009.

Mohammad Omar Farooq, *The Riba-Interest Equivalence: Is there an Ijma (consensus)?* (2006) <http://globalwebpost.com/farooqm/writings/islamic/r-i-consensus.html > Accessed 26 May 2009

PART II

Islamic banking principles, regulations and governance

5. Development, history and prospects of Islamic banking

Munawar Iqbal

1.0 INTRODUCTION

Banks are the most important financial institutions in a modern economy. They perform some very important functions for the society and in this process significantly influence the level of economic activity, the distribution of income and the level of prices in a country. Although over time they have come to provide a number of services such as safe custody of valuables, transfers of money, issuing letters of credit and guarantees, collection of utility bills, etc., their basic function remains financial intermediation which involves mobilizing savings and transferring them to entrepreneurs.

In any economy, there is a need to transfer funds from savers to investors because people who save are frequently not the same people who have the ability to exploit the profitable investment opportunities, i.e., they are not entrepreneurs. This function is performed through the process of financial intermediation in the financial markets. The most important operators in the financial markets are commercial banks. Financial intermediation enhances the efficiency of the saving/investment process by eliminating the mismatches inherent in the needs of surplus and deficit units of an economy. The surplus units are often small households who save relatively small amounts and the deficit units are the firms who often need relatively large amounts of cash. Financial intermediaries remove this size mismatch by collecting the small savings and packaging these to make them suitable to the needs of the users. In addition, users of funds in general need funds for relatively long-term deployment, which cannot be met by individual suppliers of funds. This creates the mismatch in the maturity and liquidity preferences of individual savers and users of funds. The intermediaries resolve the conflict again by pooling the small funds. Moreover, the risk preferences of small suppliers and large users of funds are also different. It is often considered that small savers are risk averse and prefer safer placements whereas the fund users deploy the funds in risky projects. Therefore, the funds cannot be directly supplied. The role of the intermediary again becomes crucial. They can substantially reduce this risk through portfolio diversification. Furthermore, small savers cannot efficiently gather information about investment opportunities. Financial intermediaries are in a much better position to collect such information, which is crucial for making the investment successful.

2.0   ISLAMIC BANKING THEORY

The role of banks as financial intermediaries is highly useful and socially desirable, but interest, which is prohibited in Islam, plays a central role on both the assets and the liabilities side. Since banking services are needed, whether the society is Islamic or secular, Islamic scholars have come up with an alternative financial intermediation model which endeavours to perform the basic function of transferring funds from surplus units in the society (investors) to deficit units who can gainfully employ them (entrepreneurs) through a number of financial instruments that do not involve interest. Simply speaking Islamic banking is just another way of financial intermediation without interest. Like other banks, they are profit-seeking businesses. However, they follow a different model of financial intermediation. They have developed several alternative modes through which savings are mobilized and passed on to entrepreneurs. None of these involves interest. They take the form of either risk-and-reward sharing or trading in commodities/assets.

These instruments include:

On the liabilities side:
1.   *Mudarabah* (passive partnership)
2.   *Wakalah* (agentship)
3.   *Qard* (loan)

On the assets side:
1.   *Mudarabah* (passive partnership)
2.   *Musharakah* (active partnership)
3.   Diminishing *musharakah* (diminishing partnership)
4.   *Bay al-Murabahah* (sales contract at a profit mark-up)
5.   *Ijarah* (leasing)
6.   A lease ending in the purchase of the leased asset
7.   *Salam* (deferred contracts)
8.   *Al-Istisna* (contract of manufacture as working capital)

9. *Sukuk* (asset-based borrowing contracts)
10. *Tawarruq* (substitute asset backing a loan)

A brief description of these instruments is given below:

Mudarabah (Passive Partnership)

This is a contract between two parties: a capital owner (*rabb al-mal*) and an investment manager (*mudarib*). Profit is distributed between the two parties in accordance with the ratio that they agree upon at the time of the contract. Financial loss is borne by the capital owner; the loss to the manager being the opportunity cost of his own labour, which failed to generate any income for him. Except in the case of a violation of the agreement or default, the investment manager does not guarantee either the capital extended to him or any profit generation.

As a mode of finance applied by Islamic banks, on the liabilities side, the depositors serve as *rabb-al-māl* and the bank as the *mudarib*. *Mudarabah* deposits can be either general, which enter into a common pool, or restricted to a certain project or line of business. On the assets side, the bank serves as the *rabb-al-māl* and the businessman as the *mudarib* (manager). However the manager is often allowed to mix the *mudarabah* capital with his own funds. In this case profit may be distributed in accordance with any ratio agreed upon between the two parties, but the loss must be borne in proportion to the capital provided by each of them.

Musharakah (Active Partnership)

A *musharakah* contract is similar to *mudarabah,* with the difference that in the case of *musharakah* both partners participate in the management and provision of capital and also share in the profit and loss. Profits are distributed between partners in accordance with agreed ratios, but the loss must be distributed in proportion to the share of each in the total capital.

Diminishing Musharakah (Diminishing Partnership)

This is a contract between a financier (the bank) and a beneficiary in which the two agree to enter into a partnership to own an asset, as described above, but on the condition that the financier will gradually sell his share to the beneficiary at an agreed price and in accordance with an agreed schedule.

Bay al-Murabahah (Sales Contract at a Profit Mark-up)

Under this contract, the client orders an Islamic bank to purchase for him a certain commodity at a specific cash price, promising to purchase such a commodity from the bank once it has been bought, but at a deferred price, which includes an agreed upon profit margin called mark-up in favour of the bank.

The transaction consists of an order accompanied by a promise to purchase and two sales contracts. The first contract is concluded between the Islamic bank and the supplier of the commodity. The second is concluded between the bank and the client who placed the order, after the bank has possessed the commodity, but at a deferred price, that includes a mark-up. The deferred price may be paid as a lump sum or in instalments. In the contract between the Islamic bank and the supplier, the bank often appoints the person placing the order (the ultimate purchaser) as its agent to receive the goods purchased by the bank.

Ijarah (Leasing)

In the simple lease contract the usufruct generated over time by an asset, such as machinery, airplanes, ships or trains is sold to the lessee at a predetermined price. This is called an operating lease, as against a finance lease. The operating lease has a number of features that distinguish it from other forms of leasing. Firstly, the lessor is himself the real owner of the leased asset and, therefore, bears all the risks and responsibilities of ownership. All defects, which prevent the use of the equipment by the lessee, are his responsibility, even though it is possible to make the lessee responsible for the day-to-day maintenance and normal repairs of the leased asset. Secondly, the lease is not for the entire useful life of the leased asset but rather for a specified short-term period (for a month, a quarter, or a year) unless renewed by mutual consent of both the parties.

A Lease Ending in the Purchase of the Leased Asset

Since the entire risk is borne by the lessor in the operating lease, there is a danger of misuse of the leased asset by the lessee. The financial lease helps take care of this problem by making the lease period long enough (usually the entire useful life of the leased asset), to enable the lessor to amortize the cost of the asset with profit. At the end of the lease period the lessee has the option to purchase the asset from the lessor at its market value at that time. The lease is not cancellable before the expiry of the lease period without the consent of both the parties. There is, therefore, little danger of misuse of the asset.

Salam (Deferred Contract)

Salam is a sales contract in which the price is paid in advance at the time of contracting, against delivery of the purchased goods/services at a specified future date. Not every commodity is suitable for a *salam* contract. It is usually applied only to fungible commodities.

Al-Istisna (Contract of Manufacture as Working Capital)

Al-Istisna is a contract in which a party orders another to manufacture and provide a commodity, the description of which, delivery date, price and payment date are all set in the contract. This type of contract is of a binding nature, and the payment of price could be deferred.

Wakalah (Agentship)

Under this contract, an Islamic bank serves as an investment manager for some clients. Usually the Bank establishes a Mutual Fund in which clients buy units. The fund promoter (bank) is the *wakeel* (agent) of the unit holders and charges a fixed fee for its services. It can in turn appoint a fund manager on a fixed salary (*ageer*) or on profit-sharing basis (*mudarib*). The profit or loss is passed on to the fund providers after deducting the bank's fees. The funds have to be invested in ways that do not involve interest. In addition, certain activities/industries that deal in commodities or activities considered unethical by Islam cannot be financed.

Tawarruq (Substitute ASSET Backing a Loan)

Tawarruq literally means obtaining cash against something. In the classic *fiqh* literature there is an instrument called *tawarruq* for obtaining cash in case of difficulties facing an individual. It works like this. Suppose A asks B for a loan. B says that I do not have any cash but I can lend you a hundred grams of gold. A takes that loan in kind, sells it in the market and gets the cash that he needed. At the time of repayment, A goes to the market, buys a hundred grams of gold of the same quality and returns it to B.

Tawarruq as a financial instrument is being used by some banks, both conventional and Islamic, as follows. Say, A goes to the bank for obtaining cash on loan. The bank buys, at a credit price, on his behalf some commodities on paper. In order to do that A signs a *wakalah* contract appointing the bank as his agent for this purchase. The bank certifies that it has done so at, say a credit price of $1.0 million due after one year. A undertakes to make this payment to the bank. A becomes the owner of these commodities. He now signs another *wakalah* contract, this time appointing the bank as his agent to sell those commodities on cash. The bank certifies that it has done so at a cash price of $900,000 and pays this amount to A. All of these transactions are only on paper. The client walks away from the bank with $900,000. It can easily be seen that it is money obtained now ($900,000) for more money to be paid later ($1.0 million). The real asset involved in the process is no more than a dummy. A single piece of real asset can form the basis of innumerable successive *tawarruq* deals. The instrument has become very popular and is being widely used by both Islamic and conventional banks. But it is extremely suspicious from the point of *Shari'ah*-compliance. My own opinion is that it is not.

Sukuk (ASSET-based Borrowing Contracts)

Sakk (singular of *sukuk*) literally means cheque or promissory note for receivable. Technically *sukuk* refer to financial instruments meant to mobilize resources from the market based on the strength of one's balance sheet, credentials, track record, goodwill and prospects of the proposed project. They are meant to provide an Islamic alternative to conventional bonds. Because the traditional Western interest paying bond structure is not permissible, the issuer of a *sukuk* sells an investor group the certificate, who then rents it back to the issuer for a predetermined rental fee. The issuer also makes a contractual promise to buy back the bonds at a future date at par value.

Sukuk can play a positive role in mobilization of savings on a vast scale. They benefit investors as well as those who have projects to finance that bear the promise of eventually generating sufficient revenue to meet the costs yet leave a surplus. Their proliferation increases the efficiency of the financial system. Also, they are capable of meeting the credit needs of government and businesses in a manner that keeps credit supply linked with real assets.

Financial engineers have come up with fancy, often confusing, names for various types where 'engineering' is more in names than in substance. The basic ideas are quite simple. *Sukuk* are basically, certificates based on ownership of certain assets. Generally, these certificates are negotiable in secondary markets. They represent 'ownership' in the assets underlying the issue. Those with variable returns are based on *mudarabah* or *musharakah*. More useful are those with pre-determined, fixed incomes. The most popular of these is the one based on *ijarah* (lease). There are *sukuk* based on *salam* or *istisna* contracts. Also there are hybrid issues whose underlying asscts are mixtures of these. *Murabahah* receivables being debt obligations are not considered fit for *sukuk* issue. But they have been accepted in such a mixture as long as they are in a minority. Due to this last point, while *sukuk* offer a usefully potential mechanism for secondary market resource mobilization, they also open the way for sale of debt receivables (as minority share in a general *sukuk* issue). Since, as mentioned before, the sale of debt except at its face value is not generally acceptable by Islamic jurists, the buy-back arrangement in *sukuk* offerings where debt receivables are a noticeable proportion, remain suspect from a *Shari'ah* point of view. Recently (November 2007), the chairman of the *Shari'ah* Board of AAOIFI gave a public statement that in his view 85 per cent of the *sukuk* structures are non-*Shari'ah*-compliant. The issue at stake was that most Gulf Islamic bonds have been sold with a repurchase undertaking – a promise that the borrower will pay back their face value at maturity, or in the event of default, mirroring the structure of a conventional bond. A promise to pay back capital violates the principle of risk- and profit-sharing on which such bonds should be based, Usmani said. That jolted the market all around the globe. Markets were seized up, money flows were frozen, and confidence evaporated. The land of Islam, where lies the world's fastest-growing debt market, was worst affected. Mohamad Nedal Alchaar, secretary-general of the AAOFI told a conference in Dubai that only $14 billion worth of *sukuk* had been issued in 2008, as compared with $40–50 billion in 2007.

3.0 HISTORICAL ACCOUNT OF ISLAMIC BANKING AND FINANCE

Islamic banking emerged some 50 years ago. At that time, it was considered wishful thinking since interest was deeply entrenched in almost all financial dealings. However, serious research work over the next two decades proved that Islamic banking is not only feasible and viable, but also an efficient and productive way of financial intermediation. In response, several Islamic financial institutions (IFIs) emerged under heterogeneous social and economic milieu. What started as a small rural banking experiment in the remote villages of Egypt in the early 1960s has now reached a level where many international banks are offering Islamic banking products.

The practice of Islamic banking received a huge boost in the 1970s due to the oil boom during that period which created a huge surplus of petro-dollars. The successful operation of IFIs in competition with conventional banks in the private corporate sector and the country experiences in Iran, Sudan, Malaysia and Bahrain during the 1980s gave confidence to the practitioners of Islamic banking that the new model offers a viable alternative to conventional banking. Commercial interests and the fascinating features of the Islamic banking model attracted worldwide attention. Many conventional banks, including some major multinational Western banks started offering Islamic products. The practice of Islamic banking has now spread from East to West all of the way from Indonesia and Malaysia towards Europe and the Americas. The industry has been growing at double-digit rates during the last 35 years (see Box 5.1).

3.1 (1940–60): Development of Theoretical Models of Islamic Banking

Financial intermediation is important for any economy. In any economy, there is a need to transfer funds from savers to investors because people who save are frequently not the same people who have the ability to exploit the profitable investment opportunities, i.e., they are not entrepreneurs. This function is performed through the process of financial intermediation in the financial markets. The most important operators in the financial markets are commercial banks. Financial intermediation enhances the efficiency of the saving/investment process by eliminating the mismatches inherent in the needs of surplus and deficit units of an economy. The surplus units are often small households who save relatively small amounts and the deficit units are the firms who often need relatively large amounts of cash. Financial intermediaries remove this size mismatch by collecting the small savings and packaging these to make them suitable to the needs of the users. In addition, users of funds in general need funds for relatively long-term deployment, which cannot be met by individual suppliers of funds. This creates the mismatch in the maturity and liquidity preferences of individual savers and users of funds. The intermediaries resolve the conflict again by pooling the small funds. Moreover, the risk preferences of small suppliers and large users of funds are also different. It is often considered that small savers are risk averse and prefer safer placements whereas the fund users deploy the funds in risky projects. Therefore, the funds cannot be directly supplied. The role of the intermediary again becomes crucial. They can substantially reduce this risk through portfolio diversification. Furthermore, small savers cannot efficiently gather information about investment opportunities. Financial intermediaries are in a much better position to collect such information, which is crucial for making the investment successful.

BOX 5.1 TIME LINE OF THE DEVELOPMENT OF THE ISLAMIC FINANCIAL INDUSTRY

1940–
1950–60
- Critique of interest from Islamic perspective
- Muslim economists offer ideas of interest-free banking possibilities.
- Non-bank applications of interest-free finance start.

1960–70
- Profit-sharing models of interest-free banking defined
- Tabung Haji Malaysia, whose main function was to collect and accumulate small savings for intending pilgrims, started investing the collected money in Islamic modes and crediting the profits earned from that activity to deposit holders proportionately. In this way, Tabung Haji Malaysia (1963) can be considered to be the first IFI.
- Experiments of bank-like institutions start (the Mit Ghamr experience in Egypt).
- Trade-based modes of Islamic finance developed.

1970–80
- First Islamic commercial bank (Dubai Islamic Bank) established (1974).
- First Islamic international multilateral development finance institution (IDB) established in Jeddah (1975).
- Pakistan declares its resolve to Islamize entire financial system (1979).
- New modes of Islamic finance are developed. Prominent among them is *istasna*.

1980–90
- Islamic banking industry witnesses very rapid growth; passes $100 billion mark.
- Two more countries (Iran (1983) and Sudan (1984)) declare Islamizing entire financial systems.
- Islamic investment funds start.
- Conventional banks including major international banks start Islamic products/windows.

1980–90	• Development of new modes of Islamic finance continue. The most prominent among them are products that go under the generic name of *sukuk*.
	• Academic institutions around the world start Islamic finance teaching. Prominent among them are International Institute of Islamic Economics, International Islamic University, Islamabad, Pakistan; Kulliyah of Economics, International Islamic University, Kuala Lumpur, Malaysia; Loughborough University Markfield Institute of Higher Education, Leicester, UK, and Durham University, Durham, UK among others.
	• IMF, World Bank get involved.
1990–2000	• Islamic investment funds show phenomenal growth.
	• Dow Jones announces Islamic indices (1999).
	• Islamic insurance (*takaful*) institutions start and grow.
	• Existing Islamic banks grow and new ones established.
	• Harvard University launches 'The Islamic Finance Project (IFP)' as a continuation of the Harvard Islamic Finance Information Program (HIFIP), established in 1995. In 1997, it started an annual Harvard University Forum on Islamic Finance. Prominent Harvard Professors started writing on Islamic finance.
	• Asset-based Islamic financial products attract attention.
	• Islamic secondary markets start.
	• Several support institutions established.
	• Accounting standards for Islamic banks start.

2000–	● Islamic Financial Sector (IFS) crosses $900 billion mark while *sukuk*, the fastest growing sub-sector, reaches $40 billion.
	● IFS shows tremendous growth (37 per cent in 2007)
	● Shariah-compliance debates cause a jolt to *sukuk* market in particular, and IFS in general. But despite that phenomenal growth continues due to new oil boom.
	● Shariah standards for Islamic banks start.
	● Development of Islamic financial architecture continues.
	● Accounting, regulatory and control issues gather steam.
	● Islamic Financial Services Board (IFSB) established (2003).
	● Preparation of regulatory standards begins.
	● First Islamic Rating Agency established (2005).
	● Islamic Arbitration Centre established.
	● Public sector resource mobilization through Islamic modes gains momentum.

3.2 (1950–60): Need for Islamic Banking Felt

The role and functions of banks outlined above are indeed highly useful and socially desirable, but unfortunately, interest plays a central role in each of these functions. Islamic financial intermediation endeavours to replace interest by partnership between owners of capital and human resources (entrepreneurs) on the basis of profit sharing as a basic form of co-operation between capital and entrepreneur. The functions that the banks perform are important whether the economy concerned is secular or Islamic. People *need* banking services. However, conventional banks perform their borrowing and lending activities and most other functions on the basis of fixed interest. In an Islamic economy, both giving and taking of interest is prohibited. Now, since the banking services are needed but interest is prohibited, Islamic economies have to find alternative ways of performing various banking functions. This challenge provides the rationale of Islamic banking. Islamic scholars have provided a number of alternative ways of performing necessary banking activities.

Islamic banking models developed

The functions of Islamic banks and other financial intermediaries are similar to their conventional counterparts. Muslim economists have shown that there are alternative Islamic modes and models through which these functions can be performed. In fact, they have shown that Islamic models can perform these functions in a better way. These models are briefly described below.

Two-tier *mudarabah*

Under this model, a bank is organized as a joint stock company with the shareholders supplying the initial capital. It is managed by the shareholders through their representatives on the board of directors. Its main business is to obtain funds from the public on the basis of *mudarabah* and to supply funds to businessmen on the same basis. Its gross income comprises the share in the actual profits of the fund users, in accordance with an agreed ratio of profit-sharing. That income, after deducting the expenses incurred in managing the funds, is distributed pro rata on share capital as well as deposits. The bank retains, in favour of its shareholders, a part of profits accruing to deposits in accordance with the predetermined profit-sharing ratio.

In addition to the general investment deposits mentioned above, there could also be specific investment accounts in which deposits are made for investments in particular projects. It is also possible to conceive special investment accounts in which deposits are made on the condition that they be invested in particular business activities, for example, trade financing on a *murabahah* (mark-up) basis, or leasing, and so on. Then, there could be current accounts in which deposits are made to be withdrawn at any time. These are checking accounts on which banks pay no profit but they are allowed to use these deposits profitably at their own risk. Demand deposits are in the nature of loans to banks whose repayment is guaranteed. In sum, bank funds could comprise share capital, demand deposits and various types of investment deposits.

The main feature of the model described above is that it replaces interest by profit-sharing on both the liabilities and the assets side of the bank. This change brings about a number of positive effects for the efficiency, equity and stability of the banking system.

One-tier *mudarabah* combined with multiple investment tools

When the academic works on Islamic banking as an alternative to interest-based banking were initiated, the discussion was essentially based on the traditional forms of Islamic modes of finance such as *mudarabah* and *musharakah*. Subsequent writings also on the practices of Islamic banking have made important contributions, on the one hand to the evolution of new forms of Islamic business enterprises and on the other to conceptual development of Islamic modes and financial instruments. Substantial developments also took place in developing new variants of the traditional modes of finance. The traditional modes of finance were based on either partnerships or the principle of deferred trading of goods and services. The practice of Islamic financial institutions has led to the evolution of different types of permanent, temporary as well as declining partnerships based on the principles of *musharakah* and *mudarabah*, with easily adaptable arrangements with respect to managerial responsibilities. Islamic banks have also developed various forms of price and object deferred sales such as: short-term *murabahah* (declared cost- plus profit-based financing), instalment sale (long- and medium-term *murabahah*); pre-paid or price-deferred manufacturing orders (*istisna*) and pre-paid or rent-deferred leasing (*ijara*).

These developments have led to the emergence of a different model of Islamic banking. Under this model, the relationship between savers and the bank is organised on the basis of *mudarabah*. However, in its relationship with the entrepreneurs, the bank uses a number of other financial instruments permissible from the *Shari'ah* point of view, none of which involves interest. A wide variety of Islamic modes of financing is possible. A number of these financing techniques are being used in practice. The principal among these are: *murabahah*, leasing, PLS, *salam*, *istisna* and loans on the basis of a service charge (i.e. recovering only the actual administrative expenses incurred on mobilizing funds).

Islamic bank working as an agent (*wakeel*)
It is also possible that Islamic banking is arranged on a basis of agency principle. An Islamic bank will manage funds on behalf of its clients on the basis of a fixed commission. The terms and conditions of the Wakalah contract are to be determined by mutual agreement between the bank and the clients.

Distinguishing features and benefits of Islamic banking

A. Distinguishing features of the Islamic banking model

1. *Risk-sharing:* The most important feature of Islamic banking is that it promotes risk-sharing between the provider of funds (investor) and the user of funds (entrepreneur). By contrast, under conventional

banking, the investor is assured a predetermined rate of interest. Since the nature of this world is uncertain, the results of any project are not known with certainty *ex ante*. Therefore, there is always some risk involved. In conventional banking, all this risk is borne by the entrepreneur. Whether the project succeeds and produces a profit or fails and produces a loss, the owner of capital gets away with a predetermined return. In Islam, this kind of unjust distribution is not allowed. In Islamic banking both the investor and the entrepreneur share the results of the project in an equitable way. In the case of profit, both share this in pre-agreed proportions. In the case of loss, all financial loss is borne by the capitalist and the entrepreneur loses his labour.

2. *Emphasis on productivity as compared to creditworthiness:* Under conventional banking, almost all that matters to a bank is that its loan and the interest thereupon are paid on time. Therefore, in granting loans, the dominant consideration is the creditworthiness of the borrower. Under profit- and loss-sharing (PLS) banking, the bank will receive a return only if the project succeeds and produces a profit. Therefore, an Islamic bank will be more concerned with the soundness of the project and the business acumen and managerial competence of the entrepreneur. This feature has important implications for the distribution of credit as well as the stability of the system.

3. *Moral dimension:* Conventional banking is secular in its orientation. In contrast, in the Islamic system all economic agents have to work within the moral value system of Islam. Islamic banks are no exception. As such, they cannot finance any project which conflicts with the moral value system of Islam. For example, they will not finance a wine factory, a casino, a night club or any other activity which is prohibited by Islam or is known to be harmful to society. In this respect Islamic banks are somewhat similar to 'Ethical Funds' now becoming popular in the Western world.

4. *Wider set of products:* An important point to be noted in the way Islamic banking works is that it offers a wider choice of products. In addition to some fixed-return modes that can serve necessarily the same functions that interest serves in conventional banking, Islamic banks can use a variety of innovative profit-sharing financing techniques. The addition of various profit-sharing modes to the available menu of available financial products renders several advantages.

5. *Closer link between monetary and real sectors:* Another important feature of Islamic banking is that even in case of fixed return modes that create debt, like interest-based financing, there is a crucial difference. Debt creation in Islamic finance is generally not possible without the backing of goods and services and the resultant debt instruments are

not tradable except against goods and services. Monetary flows through Islamic financial modes are tied directly to the flow of goods and services. Therefore, there is little room for a sudden and mass movement of such funds as compared to the flow of interest-based short-term funds. Hence destabilizing speculation is expected to be significantly curtailed.

B. Benefits of Islamic model of financial intermediation   Several potential benefits can arise from the emergence of Islamic banking. These include:

1. The range of contracts available to savers and entrepreneurs is widened. The menu ranges from low risk trade-linked products to high risk-sharing contracts.
2. The financial system is enriched by the establishment of financial institutions with different *modus operandi*. This diversity enhances the stability of the financial system because the behavioural characteristics of different types of banks are likely to vary.
3. Competition among alternative banking models is expected to increase the efficiency of the financial system.
4. The financial needs of Muslims can be met in accordance with their faith. Since the public's acceptance of the services provided by the industry play a vital role in creating stable and efficient markets, plurality and inclusiveness are important for the development of financial markets.
5. The allocation of financial resources on the basis of profit- and loss-sharing (PLS) gives maximum weight to the profitability of investment as compared with creditworthiness in the conventional system. Such allocation of resources is expected to be more efficient than that on the basis of interest.
6. As a result of PLS contracts, the liabilities side of the balance sheet tends to become symmetrical with the assets side. This helps making Islamic banks less vulnerable to external shocks and insolvency.
7. The liability to share bank losses by investment depositors motivates them to be more vigilant about the operations of their banks and to demand greater transparency and more effective audit. Banks are also under pressure to evaluate their clients' projects more carefully and to monitor the risks more effectively.
8. Since in the case of both profit-sharing and sale-based contracts, bank assets are created in response to investment opportunities in the real sector of the economy, and all financing is linked to commodities or assets, the real factors related to the production of goods and services (rather than speculative manoeuvres) become the prime determinants of the rates of return.

9.   Debt creation in Islamic finance is generally not possible without the backing of goods and services. Monetary expansion would thus tend to take place in step with the growth of the real economy. This is expected to control inflationary pressures. Destabilizing speculation would also be significantly curtailed as would the erratic and mass movement of short-term funds.

10. Like 'Ethical Funds', Islamic banks do not provide finance to projects considered socially undesirable. That introduces greater social responsibility.

3.3   (1960–75): Early Experiments in Islamic Banking

When commercial banking emerged after the industrial revolution, a very large majority of Muslim scholars expressed their serious reservations with this model of financial intermediation due to its reliance on interest rate and called for the development of alternative mechanisms to perform the financial intermediation function in Muslim societies. Muslim masses to a very significant extent refrained from dealing with commercial banks. However, the growing needs of traders, industrialists and other entrepreneurs in rapidly monetizing economies were pressing. The Muslim economists and banks took up the challenge of developing alternative models of financial intermediation. Valuable theoretical work was done in early 19th century. At that time most of the Muslim world was under colonial rule. When Muslim countries gained their independence after World War II, practical experiments in interest-free financing started at a modest scale and gradually expanded in scope.

While credit societies and cooperatives working on an interest-free basis existed in several Muslim countries even during the colonial period, the semblance of banking institutions started emerging in the early 1960s. A pioneering experiment of putting the Islamic principles governing financial dealings into practice was conducted in Mit-Ghamr, Egypt, from 1963 to 1967. Deriving inspiration from the idea of German saving banks, the Mit-Gamar initiative mobilized small savings from the rural sector largely through savings accounts. No interest was paid to the account holders. However, as an incentive they were eligible for small short-term interest-free loans for productive purposes. They were allowed to withdraw their deposits on demand. In addition investment accounts on the basis of profit sharing were also introduced. The funds so mobilized were invested on the basis of profit-sharing with entrepreneurs.

The first interest-free institution with 'bank' in its name, Nasser Social Bank, was also established in Egypt in 1971. This was the first time that a government in a Muslim country showed an interest in incorporating an interest-free institution. Even though the objectives of the Nasser Social Bank were mainly social, such as providing interest-free loans to the poor and needy, scholarships to students and micro-credits to small projects on a profit-sharing basis, the involvement of a public authority in interest-free banking sent important signals to Muslim businessmen having surplus funds.

3.4   (1975–90): Islamic Banking Gathers Steam

The period between 1975 and 1990 was the most important period in the history of development of Islamic financial industry. Some very important developments took place in this period. These include:

1. Establishment of the first Islamic bank (Dubai Islamic Bank) in the private corporate sector.
2. Establishment of the Islamic Development Bank as a multilateral Islamic development finance institution.
3. Start of countrywide Islamization experiments in Pakistan, Iran and Sudan.
4. Establishment of a large number of Islamic banks.
5. Establishment of Islamic Widows in Multinational conventional Banks.
6. Islamic financial institutions other than banks start coming on the scene in increasing numbers. These included insurance companies and investment funds.

3.5   (1990–2000): Islamic Financial Industry Matures

During 1990–2000 Islamic banking matured into a viable alternative model of financial intermediation. It won respect and credibility in terms of both theoretical developments and practical experiences. On the one hand, several financial products compatible with *Shari'ah* were developed and on the other hand, Islamic banks showed good results in practice while using these products. While the growth of the banking industry continued, though at a slower rate, more attention was given to non-bank financial institutions.

Initiatives for the establishment of some of the infrastructure institutions supporting the Islamic financial industry also started in the 1990s. In the beginning, Islamic banking institutions had to work within the institutional framework that supports conventional banking. They were at a comparative disadvantage because that framework was not specifically geared to their needs. A beginning has been made towards constructing a network of supporting institutions for the Islamic financial industry. The following infrastructure institutions have now been established:

1. Accounting and Auditing Organization for Islamic Financial Institutions (AAOIFI).
2. Islamic Financial Services Board (IFSB).
3. International Islamic Financial Market (IIFM).
4. International Islamic Rating Agency (IIRA).
5. International Islamic Centre for Reconciliation and Commercial Arbitration.
6. General Council of Islamic Banks and Financial Institutions (GCIBFI).

3.6   (2000 and Beyond): Despite Success Many Challenges Remain

As has been noted, Islamic banking and finance has been one of the fastest growing industries consistently over the last 40 years. Such a long growth track record is unprecedented.

Crucial growth factors
The practice of Islamic banking received a big boost in the 1970s due to the oil boom during that period which had created a huge surplus of petro-dollars. The successful operation of IFIs in competition with conventional banks in the private corporate sector and the country-level experiences in Iran, Sudan, Malaysia and Bahrain during the 1980s gave confidence to the practitioners of Islamic banking that the new model offers a practicable alternative to conventional banking. Due to commercial interests it attracted worldwide attention with many mega international banks coming in which lent credibility to the new model. According to various estimates the industry now commands between $500–900 billions in assets and is still one of the fastest-growing industries in a number of countries.

Yet, the Islamic banking system, like any other system, has to be seen as an evolving reality. This experience needs to be evaluated objectively and the problems ought to be carefully identified and addressed. Despite showing tremendous success in various areas, Islamic banking still remains a nascent industry. It started in a hostile environment and has struggled for more than a quarter of a century. It has scored a number of successes but it still faces several challenges. Some of these are:

- Ability to face increased competition
- Need to increase the size of Islamic banks and building strategic alliances

- Changing technology
- Adjusting to the emerging shape of financial firms
- Establishment of secondary markets and inter-bank market
- Need for transparency, regulation and supervision
- Better corporate governance
- Need for diversification in the use of Islamic modes of finance
- Financial engineering
- Research, training and development
- Unresolved *Shari'ah* issues (e.g. delinquent borrower, indexation, sale of debt, *tawarruq*, etc.

4.0 FUTURE PROSPECTS

The future prospects of the Islamic financial industry are very bright. It is a known fact that the birth of the Islamic financial industry in the early 1970s owes a lot to the oil boom during that period which had unleashed a large sum of petro-dollars. Like the first oil boom, a huge amount of petro-dollars is again afloat due to the post Iraq war increase in oil prices. There are trillions of petro-dollars looking for an appropriate parking place.

According to Merrill Lynch and Cap Gemini, in the Middle East alone, high networth individuals (HNWI) control assets worth over $1.1 trillion (World Wealth Report 2006): the experience of the oil boom of the 1970s, and the tremendous interest shown by major international financial players, point towards the Islamic banking industry as their preferred abode.

The number of HNWI individuals in the Middle East has been growing at a rate of 9.5 per cent over the past few years and is projected to continue through 2009. These levels represent the fastest rate of growth in the world. This is why many mega international banks including Chase Manhattan, Citibank, Hong Kong and Shanghai Banking Corporation (HSBC), Islamic Bank of England, Union Bank of Switzerland, Deutsche Bank of Germany, National Bank of Kuwait, the Saudi British Bank, National Commercial Bank of Saudi Arabia and many other banks have opened Islamic windows.

5.0 CONCLUSION

It was some 40 years ago that Islamic banking emerged on the banking horizon. It envisaged providing modern banking services without dealing in interest. At that time, it was considered wishful thinking since interest was deeply entrenched in almost all financial dealings. However, serious research work over the next one-and-a-half decades proved that Islamic banking is not only feasible and viable, it is also an efficient and productive way of financial intermediation.

In response, several Islamic financial institutions (IFIs) emerged under heterogeneous social and economic milieu. What started as a small rural banking experiment in the remote villages of Egypt in the early 1960s has now reached a level where many mega international banks are offering Islamic banking products. In brief, Islamic banking should contribute to greater allocative efficiency, market discipline, financial stability and social responsibility. In a world beset with financial crises, these strengths inherent in Islamic banking should offer a new ray of hope for achieving the cherished goal of systemic stability.

The experience of the last 47 years has shown that Islamic banking is a viable, dependable and well-supervised activity. It is just another way of performing the financial intermediation function. Islamic banks are subject to the same regulatory standards and fall under the purview of the same supervisory authorities as conventional banks. In addition they have to comply with the Islamic rules which means that their overall legal and supervisory environment is more stringent. In brief, Islamic banking adds a healthy dimension to the international financial system.

6. Development of legal issues of corporate governance for Islamic banking

Ishaq Bhatti and Maria Bhatti

1.0 INTRODUCTION

Although there is currently no unified understanding of 'corporate governance' under Islamic financial law, a model of Islamic corporate governance (ICG) may be proposed by reconciling *Shari'ah* law objectives with the 'stakeholder model of corporate governance'. This is viable due to the emphasis *Shari'ah* law places on property and Islamic financial contractual rights. Furthermore, such a model is also analogous to the proposed OECD principles emphasizing the mechanism of business ethics, decision making, bookkeeping and final accounts and adequate disclosure and transparency. This chapter discusses the concept, framework and structure of ICG and then considers whether such a model is viable in today's multi-faith and multicultural society of 21st century and the challenges it might face.

The rest of this chapter is organised as follows. The next section begins with explaining in brief the concept of ICG and its implication in the Islamic financial industry. The fundamentals of the business ethics of ICG are given in section 3 which explains the two main unique features of ICG. Section 4 describes the general framework and decision-making processes and elaborates on the fundamental institution of *Hisbah* on which the process of ICG is really built. It elaborates on disclosure processes, professional and honest bookkeeping and the process of complete transparency for all parties involved in contracts. The structure of the ICG model is given in section 5 with a question as to whether this model is applicable in the high-tech environment and financial sophistication of the 21st century. Section 6 discusses the need for an excellent ICG in the Islamic world as a role model for the global financial system to bring human harmony on a global level. The final section contains some concluding remarks.

2.0   THE CONCEPT OF ISLAMIC CORPORATE GOVERNANCE

Despite the rapid growth of Islamic finance and corporations since the mid-1970s, little is written on corporate governance from an Islamic perspective or 'Islamic corporate governance' (ICG) (Zulkifli 2008, p. 1). After World War II, the economic organization and commercial practices were inherited from Western colonial powers and therefore, the Islamic 'legal' system lost its intellectual legacy and scholarship, instead it was left to the masses to interpret according to their own whims (Lewis 2006, p. 5). Although there has been some interest in corporate governance by organizations including the Islamic Development Bank and the AAOIFI[1], there is no unified expression in Arabic of 'corporate governance' (ibid.). This is a major issue, especially considering the fact that in the midst of the recent financial crisis in the Western world, the small but rapidly growing Islamic financial industry has 'weathered the storm' (Yeates 2008). While share markets in London and New York have faced loss, the Dow Jones Islamic financial index has risen 4.75 per cent in the recent September quarter and lost a modest 7 per cent in 2007 (ibid.). Therefore, further research and improvement in this rising industry is vital.

Timur Kuran, a leading academic on Islamic economics, states that classical Islamic law did not recognize the concept of 'corporation' (Kuran 2005, p. 787). Early Muslims were motivated to develop an organization with indefinite existence due to the huge start-up costs of providing social services and the need for having an organization that allowed one to spread the costs over an extensive time frame (ibid.). Therefore, they came up with the concept of *waqf* or an unincorporated trust. Ibn Battuta, a famous Muslim traveller, describes the significance of the *waqf* in his accounts, such as the ones that provided drinking water, paving of streets, assistance to travellers, financing of pilgrimages and wedding outfits to impoverished brides (ibid., p. 792). According to Marshall Hodgson, the *waqf* served as a 'vehicle for financing Islam as a society' (ibid.). A *waqf* was different from a corporation because the founder of a *waqf* was an individual, it was forever controlled by its founder through directions in the founding deed, and in terms of self-governance, a *waqf*'s rules of operation were predetermined. The instructions were enforced through judges or local custom if the deed was silent on certain issues (ibid.).

The lack of recognition of a 'corporation' in Islam creates several problems; including the fact that the vital difference between a corporation and a partnership is that the former is given a distinct legal personality by law. The fundamental difference between a legal structure that is incorporated and one that is not, is the fact that the corporation is given contractual rights, just like an individual under law. It is capable of owning property, entering contracts, suing and being sued and thus is separated from its shareholders (Lewis 2005, p. 6). Therefore, while a developed and complex system of Islamic jurisprudence exists covering a *waqf*, limited partnership (*shirkah al-inan*) and trustee financing (*mudarabah*), there are doubts as to how far the rules can be carried over to the modern corporate entity (ibid.).

An attempt towards creating a form of Islamic corporate governance has been made by various scholars, who argue that while Islam did not officially recognize the concept of corporation governance, the Holy Qur'an (Islamic foundational text) and the Sunnah (the way and manners of the prophet) provide principles and guidelines about how decision-making should take place in an Islamic context (ibid.). According to Wolfensohn, the former president of the World Bank, 'Corporate governance is about promoting corporate fairness, transparency and accountability' (Abu-Tapanjeh 2008, p. 3). Furthermore, the OECD states that, 'Corporate governance . . . can be defined narrowly as the relationship of a company to its shareholders or, more broadly, as its relationship to society' (ibid.). The concept of Islamic corporate governance is no different, except that it uses the 'premise of Islamic socio-scientific epistemology premised on the divine oneness of God' (Hasan 2008, p. 3).

3.0　BUSINESS ETHICS

The two unique features of Islamic corporate governance are firstly, that it is governed by Islamic law or *Shari'ah* (which literally means 'road' or 'path') and governs all aspects of an individual's life. This concept is hard for many Westerners to understand since Christ did not promulgate law like the prophets of the Old Testament but came to break the law in the name of the spirit (Nasr 2005, p. 115). Therefore, there came to be a divergence in the West between the sacred and the secular, which does not exist in the Islamic world. In Islam, every act of a Muslim must conform to the *Shari'ah* and they must observe the ethical standards as set by Islam (Lewis 2005, p. 14). These ethical standards include what is fair and just, nature of corporate responsibilities and standards of governance.

Secondly, one needs to consider the effect that *Shari'ah* law and certain Islamic economic and financial principles have on corporate practices and policies (Abu-Tapanjeh 2008). For example, there are the institution of *zakah* (the alms tax), ban on *riba* (usury) and prohibitions on speculation, and the development of an economic system based on profit- and loss-sharing (Lewis 2005, p. 15). Therefore, in the context of corporate governance, decision making extends beyond the conventional approach to include obligations that extend beyond shareholders, financiers and management to suppliers, customers, competitors and employees (Lewis 2006). The spiritual as well as the worldly needs of the Islamic community are met (ibid.). This means that, unlike other forms of corporate governance, the ultimate goal of Islamic corporate governance is *Maqasid Shari'ah*, which was a term coined by a famous Muslim scholar, called Al-Ghazali, and it refers to the protection of the welfare of people, including their faith, life, intellect, posterity and wealth (Hasan 2008, p. 3).

Muslims distinguish Islamic governance by stating that the concept of ethics in Anglo-Saxon models of corporate governance is based on 'secular humanist' values rather than religious authority and, therefore, Islam ensures stronger accountability assuming that the participants in the corporation are God-fearing. They also argue that Western corporate culture is based on 'self-interest' and there is not enough focus on the wider needs of society (Lewis 2005, p. 14). Finally, they distinguish themselves by arguing that ICG is based on the 'stewardship' theory as opposed to the 'agency theory'. Under ICG, the major actors are viewed as stewards who are motivated to act in the spirit of partnership. On the other hand, proponents of ICG argue that the Anglo-Saxon model is based on an 'agency theory' where 'self-interested opportunistic agents' have to be watched and controlled (ibid.).

4.0   FRAMEWORK OF ISLAMIC CORPORATE GOVERNANCE

The question then becomes what the framework of Islamic corporate governance is. The question about governance is essentially about decision making, this can be answered by asking the following questions: *by whom*, *for whom* and with what resources (Lewis 2005, p. 6).

4.1   Decision Making ('By Whom' and 'For Whom')

In the Islamic framework, decision making occurs through *shura* or a 'consultative council' and this council used to be comprised of tribal elders during the pre-Islamic and Islamic era. It was a process through which a decision was arrived at after a problem was discussed and members of the council expressed their personal opinions until a consensus was reached (ibid.). It is based on the following two verses of the Qur'an:

> And consult them on affairs (of moment). Then, when thou has taken a decision, put thy trust in Allah. (Al-Imran 3:159)

Those who respond to their Lord, and establish regular prayer; who (conduct) their affairs by mutual consultation; Who spend out of what We bestow on them for sustenance. (Al-Shura, 42:38)

In Islam the 'Shuratic decision-making process' is seen as an essential trust provided from God and, therefore, those engaged in it are expected to engender truthfulness, justice and the 'spirit of consensus-seeking' when engaging in the process (Lewis 2005, p. 16). Furthermore, everyone is expected to contribute their knowledge and the procedures apply to all who are affected (shareholders, suppliers, customers, workers and community) (ibid.). The starting point and ultimate end of all business, economics and human activity is God. Thus, everything is done 'for God' and the means that are used to achieve good governance can not deviate from the *Shari'ah*.

4.2 Institution of Hisbah

Historically, under the Abbasids (750CE), an institution was established called the *hisbah*, or the 'inspector of the market' that was responsible for ensuring that all community affairs and market behaviour was conducted according to *Shari'ah* law, ensuring that Islamic ethical standards were maintained. The office holder of the *hisbah* was called the *muhtasib*, whose job it was to 'correct weights and measures, fair trading rules, checking business frauds, auditing illegal contracts, keeping the market free, and preventing hoarding of necessities' (Lewis 2005, p. 17). Traditionally, *hisbah* represented a core element of Islamic corporate governance in that society (Abu-Tapanjeh 2008). The institution's role became significant as businesses and commercial activity in the Islamic society expanded. It is the right of Muslims that they may get an enforcer, regardless of the presence or absence of a *muhtasib*, so that they may enforce Islamic corporate governance (Lewis 2005, p. 17). The issue, however, is whether and to what extent such a system can be revived in its traditional form (ibid.).

4.3 Disclosure and Transparency

In the Qur'an, the word *hesab* or 'account' is repeated more than eight times and refers to 'account' in a generic sense, which is that human beings have an obligation to 'account' to God on all matters (Lewis 2006, p. 2). Accountability is an essential goal in Islam because the belief is that resources are provided to an individual from God in the form of a trust (Abu-Tapanjeh 2008, p. 8). Therefore, since accountability is ultimately towards God, it is vital that disclosure of financial facts and accurate information be available to users so that they can make sound financial decisions (ibid.). The rationale behind this is that since individuals are accountable to God and God has provided them with resources, God expects them to conduct the economic system in a fair and just way. Accountability in this context means accountability to the community (*umma*) or society. If the purpose behind accounting is to serve public interest, it also follows that the *umma* also has the right to know about the operations and transactions of the organization (Lewis 2006, p. 9). The rationale behind adequate disclosure is also that the Qur'an promotes truth as a vital element of the Islamic ethic and therefore, 'disclosure of all necessary for accomplishment of the faithful obligations and the making of economic and business decisions consistent with that ethos is the most important tenet of an Islamic accounting system' (ibid.). Therefore, it is argued that an ethical Islamic accounting system promotes proper disclosure and transparency in business dealings (Abu-Tapanjeh 2008, p. 8).

4.4 Bookkeeping and Final Account ('With What Resources')

Several verses of the Qur'an indicate that transactions in business dealings should be written down in an account to ensure financial transactions are determined according to balanced sheets and any unlawful possession of assets is prohibited (Abu-Tapanjeh 2008, p. 8). *Maqasid Shari'ah*[2] prohibits acquiring wealth in unlawful means, which leads to social inequality and social waste (ibid.).

> Oh you who believe! When you deal with each other in transactions involving future obligations in fixed period of time, reduce them to writing and let a scribe write down faithfully as between the parties. (2:282)
>   And if you are travelling and cannot find a scribe, then there be a mortgage taken. . .And do not conceal any evidence for the whoever hides it, surely his heart is sinful. (2:283)

Islam is very clear in terms of the principles regarding how one should undertake financial reporting and accounting practices and emphasizes that it should be based upon the spirit and teachings of Islam. The Islamic belief is that doubt and uncertainty should not exist and that is why all the parties' rights and obligations should be fully documented for verification (Lewis 2006, p. 10).

4.5 Religious Audit

The third plank of Islamic corporate governance system is the process of religious supervision guaranteeing conformity to the Islamic moral code. A religious audit is essential because it assures that insiders and outsiders are abiding by Islamic law in business dealings (Lewis 2005, p. 17). The functions of the religious auditors include:

1. Providing the board and management advice about the religious acceptability of the firm's agreements and developments.
2. Providing an independent report to inform shareholders about whether management is complying with Islamic principles and whether the business is run Islamically.
3. An audit regarding *zakah* or the special alms levy – to establish that the fund is properly administered and distributed.

There is also a system inside the organization itself, ensuring that the operations of the firm are in line with the reports given by requirements of external auditors and the state-mandated regulatory system (ibid., p. 18).

5.0   STRUCTURE OF ISLAMIC CORPORATE GOVERNANCE

According to Zamir Iqbal[3] and Abbas Mirakhor,[4] the structure of Islamic corporate governance closely resembles the stakeholder model of corporate governance (Iqbal and Mirakhor 2004). Other academics such as Zulkifli Hasan (2008, p. 11) and Chapra and Ahmed (2002) also emphasize the notion of equality in protecting the rights of stakeholders regardless of whether they hold equity.

The objective of firms in the stakeholder model of corporate governance is to maximize the welfare of all stakeholders and this is consistent with *Shari'ah*'s emphasis on principles of property rights, the contractual framework and its goal of achieving a just social order (Iqbal and Mirakhor 2004, p. 976). According to the shareholder model of corporate governance:

1. Shareholders should have control.
2. The managers have a fiduciary duty to serve the shareholder interests alone.
3. The objective of the firm is the maximization of shareholders' wealth (Boatright 2006, p. 109).

Comparatively, stakeholder theorists reject these propositions and argue that:

1. All stakeholders should have the right to participate in corporate decisions that affect them.

2. Managers have a fiduciary duty to serve the interests of all stakeholder groups.
3. The objective of the firm is the promotion of all interests (not just those of shareholders) (Iqbal and Mirakhor 2004, p. 964).

Supporters of the 'stakeholder theory' argue that shareholders are just one of the numerous groups of stakeholders and, therefore, it is important to consider other stakeholders such as the customers, suppliers, employees and local communities (Heath and Norman 2004, p. 247). They state that 'In the same way that a business owes special and particular duties to its investors . . . it also has different duties to the various stakeholder groups' (Gibson 2000, p. 247).

There are two reasons why ICG closely resembles the stakeholder model. Firstly, the emphasis on 'property rights' in Islam justifies why stakeholders should be included in decision-making and accountability and this inclusion is based on the following principles of Property law in Islam (Iqbal and Mirakhor 2004, p. 970).

1. The concept of 'collectivity', meaning that the community, society and state have a right to share the property acquired by individuals or firms.
2. The property of others (including shareholders) can not be harmed or damaged.
3. The rights of others are considered property and subject to the Islamic rules governing the violation of any of those property rights.
4. Rights are considered property (*al-mal*), therefore, if property is acquired through unlawful means, the property will lose its legitimacy and associated rights (ibid., p. 971).

The rights and responsibilities associated with property rights mean that one can not waste, destroy, squander or use the property for purposes that are not permitted by *Shari'ah*. Furthermore, wasting and squandering (*israf* and *tabdhir*) are specifically mentioned in Islam and this implies that the firm is expected to preserve the property rights of the wider society as well as those who have participated in the transaction processes of the firm (ibid.).

Secondly, the emphasis that the *Shari'ah* law places on the 'contractual framework' means that every individual, society, corporation and state is bound by the contract which defines the rights and obligations of the parties (Hasan 2008, p. 12). This is based on the following Qur'anic verse: 'O ye who believe, fulfil contracts' (Chapter 5: Verse 1).[5] Abiding by contracts is vital for a Muslim because the concept of justice and faithfulness ('*amanah*') exists under Islamic law, which requires that individuals adhere to their contractual obligations in order to prevent betrayal, faithlessness and treachery ('*khiyanah*').

The implication of this in corporate governance is that every stakeholder has a duty to perform contractual obligations according to the terms stipulated in a contract. Under *Shari'ah* law, the implicit as well as the explicit obligations under a contract are recognized, which includes a wide spectrum of obligations including the recognition and protection of the property rights of stakeholders, community, society and the state (Iqbal and Mirakhor 2004, p. 973). Broadly speaking, any group or individuals with whom the firm has explicit/implicit contractual obligations may qualify as a stakeholder (ibid.). This is based on the saying of the Prophet Muhammad, in which he says 'So give to everyone who possesses a right his right' (ibid., p. 977). In Arabic, the term 'right' is known as *haq* and it refers to something that can be claimed justly, and rights are also seen as 'property' because they have their beneficial uses and can be possessed. Therefore, it is important under *Shari'ah* law to be conscious of the rights of all stakeholders involved (ibid., p. 977).

The duty of shareholders to provide business capital, management to run business, and employees to perform their duties, all arise through a contractual framework (Hasan 2008, p. 12). Hasan (2008, p. 13) explains the structure of Islamic corporate governance as based on the 'stakeholder model' of corporate governance as shown in Figure 6.1.

This model of ICG proposes that it is: (1) based on the principle of property rights and contractual framework, (2) governed by Islamic law or *Shari'ah*; and (3) all stakeholders are included – the management, shareholders, employees, suppliers, depositors and the community (ibid.).

According to this model of Islamic corporate governance, the *Shari'ah* board advises and supervises the corporation to make sure it abides by *Shari'ah* law. The board of directors act on behalf of the shareholders with the duty to monitor and oversee the overall business activities (ibid.). Also, the managers have the fiduciary duty to manage the firm as a trust for the stakeholders (not the shareholders alone) (ibid.).

5.1 Is this Model of ICG a Viable One?

According to scholars such as Abu-Tapanjeh (2008), the ICG model achieves the objectives proposed by the global report on corporate governance by the Organization of Economic Co-operation and Development (OECD). The OECD principles were first proposed in May 1999 due to growing awareness of the need for good corporate governance in order to strengthen investor confidence and national economic performance

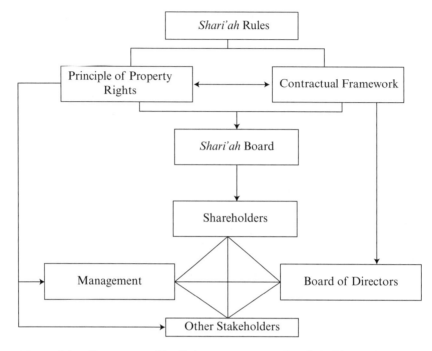

Figure 6.1   Governance, Shari'ah *governance and stakeholders*

(OECD 2008). The OECD principles were also the basis for the report conducted by the World Bank Group about corporate governance (ibid.). The principles provide specific guidance for policymakers, regulators and market participants to improve the legal, institutional and regulatory framework underpinning corporate governance. Since being issued in 1999, they have become the international benchmark for corporate governance and form the basis for reform initiatives taken by the government and the private sector (ibid.). The aim of these principles is to ensure the basis for an effective corporate governance framework including: the rights of shareholders, equitable treatment of shareholders, role of stakeholders in corporate governance, disclosure and transparency and the responsibilities of the board (ibid.). These principles are based upon four concepts: mechanism of business ethics, mechanism of decision making, adequate disclosure and transparency, and the mechanism of bookkeeping and final accounts (Abu-Tapanjeh 2008, p. 10). As shown above, each of these four concepts can be found in the ICG model.

It is also argued that the ICG framework is consistent with the six OECD principles. The first OECD principle is 'Ensuring the basis for an effective corporate governance framework' (OECD 2008). According to the annotation, this means promoting a transparent and efficient market with rule of law and division of responsibilities. As shown above, under the heading 'Disclosure and Transparency', this principle is similar to the ICG model; however, the difference is that the rule of law in ICG must be *Shari'ah*, which includes the ban on *riba* (interest) and *ihtikar* (hoarding).

The second principle states that, 'The corporate governance framework should protect and facilitate the exercise of shareholders' rights'. According to ICG, all rights of stakeholders (including shareholders) should be protected due to the emphasis on property rights as described above (Abu-Tapanjeh 2008, p. 10). However, the difference in ICG is that accountability is to God, not only the shareholders.

The third principle states, 'The corporate governance framework should ensure the equitable treatment of all shareholders, including minority and foreign shareholders. All shareholders should have the opportunity to obtain effective redress for violation of their rights' (OECD 2008). According to the Islamic concepts of *zakat* ('special alms levy'), the *Shari'ah* board is expected to oversee the collection of *zakat* and its distribution to the relevant parties (Lewis 2005, p. 18). This ensures equitable distribution of wealth to all stakeholders and disadvantaged members (Abu-Tapanjeh 2008, p. 10).

The fourth principle is that the role of stakeholders in corporate governance is to be recognized by creating wealth, jobs and sustainability of financially sound enterprises (ibid.). This is consistent with the following Islamic concepts: *infaq* (spending to meet social obligations), *istislah* (public interest), and the fact that distribution must be regulated by the *halal* (allowed and praiseworthy)–*haram* (prohibited and blameworthy) code (Lewis 2005, p. 20). Furthermore, equality is also promoted due to the encouragement in Islam to avoid the following negative values: *bukhl* (miserliness), *hirs* (greed), *iktinaz* (hoarding of wealth) and *israf* (extravagance) (ibid.).

The fifth principle, 'Disclosure and transparency', has already been discussed above as *Shari'ah* law stipulates that the firm should be accountable to all its stakeholders.

Finally, the last principle states 'The corporate governance framework should ensure the strategic guidance of the company, the effective monitoring of management by the board, and the board's accountability to the company and the shareholders (Abu-Tapanjeh 2008, p. 10) Again, the difference here is that the board in ICG is not accountable just to the company but to God, and therefore must ensure that there is effective compliance with *Shari'ah* law. However, due to the concept of *shura* or a 'consultative council' as discussed above under 'decision-making', it is essential under ICG that the board consults and is accountable to the company and its shareholders.

Following the discussions above, it makes it clear that the model of ICG is consistent with many of the principles proposed by the OECD. However, one crucial difference mentioned by Tapanjeh is that corporate governance in OECD entitles the power of decision making and participation of business dealings to limited people holding a higher designation, such as BOD and senior management (ibid.). On the other hand, the ICG model provides all related stakeholder models with full rights and responsibility to participate in corporate governance (ibid.).

The issue then becomes whether the ICG model is a viable one. According to academics such as Mervyn Lewis and Timur Kuran, there are various challenges for this model. Kuran argues that the first challenge is the fact that until the 19th century, the concept of a 'corporation' was never recognized under Islamic law and that until quite late, Middle Eastern producers, merchants and investors saw no need for standardized bookkeeping, professional management, or free transferability of shares (Kuran 2005, p. 23). Therefore, Islamic corporate governance has developed at a slow pace, and one questions to what extent and how effectively *Shari'ah* law and ethics are able to carry over to the 'modern corporate entity' (Lewis 2005, p. 21).

Many also criticize the abovementioned model of ICG by arguing that those that propose it seem to think that ICG is a distinct model of corporate governance. Proponents of ICG distinguish it from Anglo-Saxon models of corporate governance by arguing that the latter has a 'shareholder-value-centred' view of corporate governance, and since it does not extend to a wide circle of stakeholders, it fails to incorporate their claims, rights and obligations (Iqbal and Mirakhor 2004, p. 963). The proponents of ICG also have a tendency to deem Anglo-Saxon models as extreme 'self interested' models of corporate governance operating in a 'ruthless economy' where competition and market disciplines force players into line so that 'shareholder values' prevail (Lewis 2005, p. 23).

On the other hand, they believe that the ICG is based on principles of ethics, morals and social welfare due to the *Maqasid Shari'ah*.[6] Mervyn argues, however, that such accounts fail to consider other theories of corporate governance such as the work of corporate reformers such as Margaret Blair and Nell Minow and other diverse approaches to corporate governance at the global level (Lewis 2005, p. 23). For example, Peter Ducker is a reformer who argues that 'shareholder value' is preoccupied with short-term results and proposes a balance between long-range prosperity and the survival of the enterprise (ibid., p. 13). Another management guru, Charles Handy, encourages the 'citizen company', which operates in an environment where businesses are seen as communities and not property (Handy 1999).

The 'essentialist critique' is not just aimed at proponents of the ICG model; it also extends to the supporters of the stakeholder theory. Heath and Norman (2004, p. 248) use the example of Enron to argue in their article that stakeholder theorists undermine the significance of shareholders interests and control in furthering the interests of other stakeholders. They also argue that while stakeholder theorists are all against the classical conception of managerial obligation where, as Milton Friedman quotes, the only 'social responsibility of business is to maximize profits', many academics refuse to recognize that the stakeholder theory itself is broken down into several theories relating to corporate social responsibility (CSR) (ibid., p. 249). However, this article will not discuss the debate about whether there exists a unified stakeholder theory or whether it consists of several theories. In the end, the main criticism of the ICG model is that while it is consistent with the classic stakeholder theory that promotes corporate social responsibility and also conforms to OECD principles, there is still room for more research in terms of how such a model, based upon classical Islamic thought, can be practically viable in the modern world.

It is important not to separate corporate governance from broader governance issues. Many proponents of ICG seem to claim a moral high ground by arguing that the ICG model is morally certain and ethical, in comparison to the governance structure that has led to the downfall of companies such as Enron or Arthur Anderson (Lewis 2005, p. 24). However, to draw such a stark contrast can often ignore the corruption that currently exists in various Muslim countries. Many OIC countries, such as Kuwait, Malaysia and Qatar, fall into the highest quartile on the corruption index (ibid.). Thus, despite the fact that proponents of the ICG discuss how the model of ICG and *Shari'ah* law's emphasis on justice and ethics may theoretically condemn corruption, many of these academics fail to discuss how such a model of ICG could be implemented in Muslim communities where corruption is already widespread in the business community (ibid.).

6.0   THE NEED FOR GOOD CORPORATE GOVERNANCE IN THE MUSLIM WORLD

In order for the Islamic market to successfully develop, good corporate governance is necessary and also in accordance with *Shari'ah* law principles and the true spirit of Islam. It is important in the Islamic financial sector as well as the corporate sector. The recent rise and growth in Islamic investment and establishment of Islamic corporations has far outpaced the ability of regulators to establish or agree upon the finalized form of Islamic corporate governance. They need to come up with Islamic corporate governance that is attractive to and consistent with international standards as well as being compliant with *Shari'ah* law (Bank of New York Mellon 2008).

Effective Islamic corporate governance is consistent with Islamic principles, such as preventing *gharar* (risk, uncertainty) and unjust business transactions (ibid.). Good corporate governance encourages 'capital formation, creates incentives to engage in value-maximizing behavior, lowers the cost of capital, and fosters strong markets'(ibid.), but more than that at the heart of it are structures and processes, which require individuals to exercise their responsibilities with integrity, judgment and transparency, which are all principles central to *Shari'ah* law. However, Islamic institutions face various challenges in establishing an effective corporate governance system as it must strictly abide by *Shari'ah* law. Nevertheless, a *Shari'ah* Supervisory Board is significant for two reasons; firstly, the majority of investors and clients of an Islamic corporation would lose confidence if the management of the bank continued to violate *Shari'ah* law. Secondly, the huge emphasis that the *Shari'ah* system places on ethics is believed to prevent Muslims from behaving unethically (ibid.).

7.0   CONCLUDING REMARKS

Governance is the relationship that a government has with its constituents. On the other hand, corporate governance refers to the relationship between the corporation and its constituents. The ICG model proposes that the constituents are wider due to the emphasis that *Shari'ah* law places on property and contractual rights. This means that while the conventional conception of corporate governance is 'shareholder-centric', the focus in ICG is wider and extends to suppliers, customers, competitors and employers. Thus, it is more in line with the 'stakeholder theory' of corporate governance. Furthermore, the strong focus of *Shari'ah* law on ethics, accountability and transparency allows ICG to be consistent with the OECD principles on corporate governance. The Islamic economic system is ultimately based upon maintaining a just and harmonious social order in which the rights of the whole community are protected through the *Shari'ah* board, which ensures that the institution adheres to the rules of *Shari'ah* law. Theoretically, the concept of ICG is quite stable and in line with various theorists that emphasize corporate social responsibility. A good corporate governance structure is also necessary due to the rise of Islamic institutions. However, one questions whether such a model can be practically implemented in Muslim countries, when most of them are developing or are third world countries that are often ranked high on the corruption index.

NOTES

1. Accounting, Auditing and Governance Standards for Islamic Financial Institutions.
2. 'The protection of the welfare of people, including their faith, life, intellect, posterity and wealth'.
3. Senior Information Officer at the World Bank.
4. Executive Director of the International Monetary Fund.
5. The Holy Qur'an, <http://www.usc.edu/dept/MSA/quran/> at 23 October, 2008.
6. Ultimate objectives of Islamic law, which is the protection of the welfare of people, including their faith, life, intellect, posterity and wealth.

REFERENCES

Abu-Tapanjeh, Abdussalam Mahmoud (2008), 'Corporate Governance from the Islamic Perspective: A Comparative Analysis with OECD Principles', *Critical Perspectives on Accounting*.

Bank of New York Mellon (2008), 'Improving Corporate Governance in Islamic Finance', www.bankofny.com/CpTrust/data/tl_islamic_finance.pdf at 23 October 2008.

Boatright, John R. (2006), 'What's Wrong – and What's Right – with Stakeholder Management', XXI (2) *Journal of Private Enterprise*.

Chapra, M.U. and H. Ahmed (2002), 'Corporate Governance in Islamic Financial Institutions', Financial Institutions Division, Department of Finance Discussion Paper.

Gibson, Kevin (2000), 'The Moral Basis of Stakeholder Theory', 26 *Journal of Business Ethics*, 245–257.

Hasan, Zulkifli (2008), 'Corporate Governance from Western and Islamic Perspectives', Conference Paper presented at the Annual London Conference on Money, Economy and Management, 3–4 July 2008, Imperial College, South Kensington, United Kingdom.

Heath, Joseph and Wayne Norman (2004), 'Stakeholder Theory, Corporate Governance and Public Management', 53 *Journal of Business Ethics*, 247–265.

Iqbal, Zamir and Abbas Mirakhor (2004), 'Stakeholders Model of Governance in Islamic Economic System', 11(2) *Islamic Economics Studies*.

Kuran, Timur (2005), 'The Absence of the Corporation in Islamic Law: Origins and Persistence', 53 *American Journal of Comparative Law*, 785–834.

Lewis, Mervyn K. (2005), 'Islamic Corporate Governance', 9 (1) *Review of Islamic Economics*, 5–29.

Lewis, Mervyn (2006), 'Accountability and Islam', Conference Paper presented at Fourth International Conference on Accounting and Finance in Transition, Adelaide, 10–12 April, 2006.

Organization for Economic Cooperation and Development (2008), www.oecd.org/daf/corporate/principles at 23 October 2008.

Yeates, Clancy (2008), 'Islamic Finance Rides the Storm', http://business.smh.com.au/business/islamic-finance-rides-the-storm-20081010-4yft.html at 27 October 2008.

7. Corporate governance and Islamic banks

Michael T. Skully

1.0 INTRODUCTION

Corporate governance has been a buzzword of the decade with governments worldwide seeking to strengthen their rules and regulations on how the management and directors of publicly listed companies behave toward their shareholders. While much recent academic research has been directed at the impact of these changes – particularly the Sarbanes Oxley Act of 2002 – the governance of banks has received less academic attention. This is odd given that most researchers realise that banks are different and so exclude them from their samples.

These differences are many and include such factors as the opaqueness and lack of transparency in bank operations and reporting, their excessively high leverage (two-centuries-old capital adequacy problem) compared to normal corporations, the presence of other stakeholders particularly depositors, their special regulatory treatment (special laws and regulators), any moral hazard issues related to deposit insurance and 'too-big-to-fail' policies, and all the important externalities associated with bank failure. If commercial banks are different, then Islamic banks are probably even more so. True, they have all of the characteristics of a commercial bank but some important differences too.

This chapter examines Islamic bank governance in respect to its goals and objectives, *Shari'ah* supervisory boards, investment account holders, internal governance structure and external governance matters.

2.0 GOALS AND OBJECTIVES

If Islamic banks are different from conventional commercial banks, then it is probably a result of the function of their goals and objectives. As Akhtar (2006, p. 2) explains, their uniqueness 'stems from two principle elements: (i) faith-based approach that mandates conduct of business in accordance with Shariah principles; and (ii) profit motive that recognises business and investment transactions and maximization of shareholders' wealth'. So religious compliance is certainly a key difference but it is not the only one. The Islamic Financial Services Board (ISFB) provides some further insights as its own definition of corporate governance is (ISFB, 2006, p. 27) 'a defined set of relationships between a company's management, its board of directors, its shareholders and other stakeholders' that sets the framework on which the company is run. This appears effectively the same definition as for a conventional governance study, but it is with 'stakeholders' where one finds a difference. As the ISFB (2006, p. 27) explains, an Islamic bank's 'stakeholders' includes not only employees, customers, suppliers and government regulators but also the community, 'particularly the Muslim ummah [community]'.

This relationship with the Muslim community needs further explanation as Islamic bank customers must be certain that their bank complies with all aspects of Islamic law. This 'religious risk' factor cannot be understated, for while conventional bank customers might lose their savings, non-*Shari'ah* compliance has a much higher, indeed eternal, opportunity cost for a Muslim customer. So a key aspect of Islamic bank governance, as Grais and Pellegrini (2006b, p. 2) observe, is the 'need to reassure stakeholders' that their bank's activities 'fully comply with the precepts of Islamic jurisprudence'. The *Shari'ah* Supervisory Board (SSB) of an Islamic bank plays a key role in this reassurance process and so is fundamental to Islamic bank governance.

Returning to the Islamic Financial Services Board's (IFSB) corporate governance definition, the word 'depositors', which might be found in a similar commercial bank statement, is not specifically mentioned. This is because while Islamic banks do take deposits, the bulk of their funding comes from products that look similar to a commercial bank deposit but are in fact quite different, the most obvious being the funds raised from investment account holders (IAHs). These quasi equity providers, and how they are treated, also make Islamic bank governance different.

These differences, however, should not be viewed as any disadvantage to good governance within Islamic banking. To the contrary, as Suleiman (2005) notes, 'Islamic religious ideology acts as its own incentive mechanism to reduce the inefficiency that arises from asymmetric information and moral hazard' found in conventional banking. In fact, as Gooden (2001, p. 2) commented, as Islamic banking's 'very existence is based on a religious faith and a desire to comply with the laws and values of that faith, one would expect Islamic banks starting from a moral and ethical base to be eager to embrace the highest standard of corporate governance'.

3.0 *SHARI'AH* SUPERVISORY BOARDS

The concept of the SSB, on the surface at least, seems quite straight-forward. It is a group of respected scholars with Islamic law expertise appointed by the bank's board of directors to provide them with guidance on new bank products and services as well as ensuring all current opera-tions are conducted along appropriate religious lines. While the manage-ment is responsible for complying with Islamic law, their activities are nevertheless audited and confirmed by the SSB. The SSB's formal compli-ance statement ensures that the bank's clients know that their religious interests are protected. From a governance standpoint, however, the SSB's position is more complex and so requires discussion. This section exam-ines whether the banks disclose they have an SSB, the size of the SSBs, the treatment and content of the SSB report, the SSB members' qualifications, independence, professional involvement and finally some suggestions for SSB disclosure.

At the most basic level, customers would like to know that their bank has an SSB and who its members are. Given the SSB's importance in reli-gious compliance, some details about their experience and qualifications might be expected, too. So this information would logically be readily available in both the bank's annual report and website. Surprisingly, not all Islamic banks seem to agree. As shown in Table 7.1, from a sample of 84 Islamic banks across 25 countries covered by Bankscope, only 55 of them reported that they have an SSB. Or, alternatively, a third of them obviously felt that this information was not required. On a country basis, Malaysia performed best with all eight of its sample banks disclosing details regarding their SSBs. Turkey similarly had all four banks report-ing. Kuwait and Saudi Arabia also had full disclosure but had only two banks each in the sample. Countries with only one bank in the sample but that had full disclosure included: the Cayman Islands, Indonesia, Lebanon, Palestine and the UK.

While there is no literature suggesting the specific number of members an SSB should have, the sample numbers, as shown in Table 7.2, ranged from one to 14 members with an average of four. There was not much dif-ference between countries with Bangladesh with an average of 11 members being the major exception. Kuwait also had a higher average with six and Brunei and the Cayman Islands averaged five each. Bangladesh also had the largest single SSB with 14 members. In contrast, one bank in Pakistan reported a one member board, but this would seem more correctly counted as an advisor.

The actual SSB report, or at least its opinion, would have seemed a must for the website, if not the annual report, but Maali et al. (2006, p. 284)

Table 7.1   Disclosure of Shari'ah *supervisory boards*

Country	No of Islamic banks examined	Number that disclosed SSB
Bahrain	15	12
Bangladesh	3	2
Brunei	2	1
Cayman Islands	1	1
Denmark	1	0
Egypt	3	1
Gambia	1	0
Indonesia	1	1
Iran	7	2
Iraq	1	0
Jordan	2	1
Kuwait	2	2
Lebanon	1	1
Malaysia	8	8
Mauritania	1	0
Pakistan	6	5
Palestine Territory	1	1
Qatar	4	3
Saudi Arabia	4	1
Sudan	5	3
Tunisia	1	0
Turkey	4	4
United Arab Emirates	5	2
United Kingdom	1	1
Yemen	4	3
Total	84	55

found that of the 29 Islamic banks studied, only 21 disclosed their SSB's *Shari'ah* opinion, and these reports ranged from a minimum of 11 sentences to a maximum of 20. Most reports indicate that the bank conducted its operations in accordance with Islamic law, that any non-*Shari'ah*-compliant earnings and the *zakat* (calculated appropriately) were given to charity, but some specific comment on the IAHs' treatment would seem appropriate. This sample found a similarly mixed practice of SSB report disclosure. Twenty of the 27 banks with websites included the SSB report in their annual report. Table 7.3 in this case shows Malaysia as the country without full compliance.

Although this lack of an actual SSB report might seem surprising, Maali et al. (2006, p. 286) were less concerned. They felt that as many banks

Table 7.2 Shari'ah *supervisory board size*

Country	Mean	Minimum	Maximum	Banks
Bahrain	3.67	2	7	12
Bangladesh	11	8	14	2
Brunei	5	5	5	1
Cayman Islands	5	5	5	1
Egypt	4	4	4	1
Indonesia	3	3	3	1
Jordan	4	4	4	1
Kuwait	6	6	6	2
Lebanon	5	5	5	1
Malaysia	4.43	3	6	7
Pakistan	3	1	4	3
Palestine Territory	5	5	5	1
Qatar	3.67	3	4	3
Saudi Arabia	5	5	5	1
Sudan	2.67	2	3	3
Turkey	3	3	3	1
United Arab Emirates	3	3	3	2
United Kingdom	3	3	3	1
Yemen	3.67	3	5	3
Total	4.00	1	14	47

Table 7.3 *Disclosure of SSB statement in annual report*

Country	Number of banks with AR	SSB statement in AR	Per cent
Bahrain	6	6	100.0
Cayman Islands	1	1	100.0
Iran	2	0	–
Kuwait	2	2	100.0
Malaysia	7	5	71.4
Pakistan	2	2	100.0
Palestinian Territory	1	1	100.0
Saudi Arabia	1	0	–
Turkey	2	0	–
UAE	1	1	100.0
United Kingdom	1	1	100.0
Yemen	1	1	100.0
Total	27	20	74.1

provide their SSB report separately to customers, there was no 'need for detailed disclosure in the annual reports'. Another view might be that it is not the report so much, as Nienhaus (2007, p. 139) suggests, but rather 'the reputation and public recognition of the members'. Perhaps as a result, some banks disclose the names, background and qualifications, and the roles and duties of their SSB (see the Dubai Islamic Bank as one example). Sadly such practice is not as common for, as Grais and Pellegrini (2006c) found, of most Islamic banks who reported on the SSB's existence and composition, less than half made any further details readily available. Similarly, many provided no information of the SSB's professional background.

Besides their names and background, it would also be useful to know how the SSB members were appointed. According to the Accounting and Auditing Organization for Islamic Financial Institutions (AAOIFI) (2003) Governance Standard 1, the SSB is an 'independent body of specialised jurists in Islamic commercial prudence'.

It requires that three SSB members be elected by the shareholders upon the recommendation of the board of directors. Some disclosure on this election process as well as the term of office would be appropriate. Grais and Pellegrini (2006a, p. 18) found that several countries at least formally set the SSB's terms of reference as well as to a lesser extent, their composition, appointment and dismissal of members and criteria for appointment. The formal disclosure of the SSB's terms of reference would seem an appropriate requirement for other countries to consider. Nienhaus (2007, p. 137) recommends even more disclosure such as 'the relevance and the relative weighting of their Islamic and secular qualifications, their scholarly reputation and general popularity, their doctrinal strictness or intellectual flexibility, their main occupation and source of income, the duration of their SSB membership and criteria for appointment and so on as well as the quantitative and qualitative dimensions for their financial and non-financial rewards'.

The latter details provide some insights into the degree of SSB members' independence from the management. Some distance would seem desirable to ensure objectivity and so should be disclosed. As Nienhaus (2007, p. 137) observes, 'it is plausible to assume that top executives will have a strong influence on the composition of the SSB and on the financial and non-financial rewards for SSB members'. It should be remembered that unlike an external auditor, the SSB is a direct part, though perhaps thought separate, of the bank itself. In practice, this does not appear so much of an issue. Grais and Pellegrini (2006c, p. 8) found in a study of some 6000 fatwas involving over 100 *Shari'ah* scholars worldwide, 90 per cent were found to be consistent across banks suggesting 'an overall consistency in the interpretation of the sources'.

Within this section, it is also important to highlight that the SSB function is not entirely religious. Grais and Pellegrini (2006a, p. 17), for example, argue that SSB has five main roles: certification, verification, 'calculation of payment of zakat, disposal of non-Shariah compliant earnings, and advice on the distribution of income or expenses among the bank's shareholders and investment account holders'. In this latter role, then, the SSB has some direct operational input. It is a powerful one, too. The AAOIFI guidelines state that the SSB can decide if any IAH losses are due to 'misconduct or negligence' and if so, these should 'be deducted from the Islamic bank's share in the profits of the jointly financed investment'. Such decisions require something more than just a religious background. As Asri and Fahmi (2004) note, the AAOIFI regulations therefore allow the SSB to include 'other experts in the field of accounting, economics, lawyers and bankers' to assist its deliberations.

This concept of professional as well as religious expertise should perhaps be given some further attention. As Governor Akhtar (2006, p. 6) noted, the SSB ruling must be 'not only 100% Shariah compliant but these are also compatible with the legal and financial infrastructure available to Islamic banks'. No doubt for this reason, the State Bank of Pakistan requires besides the normal 'fit and proper' aspects of integrity, honesty and scholarship, potential SSB members must also demonstrate 'experience in understanding the Islamic financial transactions'.

Most banks disclosed the names of the SSB members, but not always their educational or religious background. Fewer still provided information as to their past experience and hardly any discussion was offered as to their independence. So there seems much room for improvement, at least for some banks, and so the following checklist is provided in Box 7.1. Further on SSBs, the research for this chapter also discovered that at least one Islamic bank had two SSBs. This was the Kuwait-based International Investment Company which utilised an International Advisory *Shari'ah* Committee (from 1999 to 2002) to gain an international perspective to its religious compliance. This is not to be confused with a more secular International Advisory Board as used by the Bahrain-based Bank Arcapta.

Besides an SSB, some Islamic banks also had a special *Shari'ah* Advisor to assist them. The role of this person, however, is not well disclosed. In some cases, they seem also to be a SSB member (Meezen Bank) but not so in others (Tadamon Islamic Bank).

Before finishing this SSB discussion, it should be remembered that Islamic banks should also have an internal *Shari'ah* review unit. This operates independently but typically as part of the internal audit department. The AAFOIFI certainly recommends each Islamic bank have one but the disclosure of its existence is not common. Indeed, the research for

---

BOX 7.1   SUGGESTED DISCLOSURE ON *SHARI'AH* SUPERVISORY BOARDS

- Names of all SSB board members
- Educational qualifications
- Years and types of professional experience (religious and financial)
- Election procedure and term of office
- Number of meetings members attended
- Statement of independence (at least not full-time bank employees)
- SSB's obligations and powers
- Any shareholdings of members
- Current and past SSB reports

---

this chapter found little specific mention of these units. The Dubai-based Dubai Islamic Bank, however, not only provides such details but also discusses the role of a special Shariah Supervisor who seems quite separate from the SSB.

4.0   INVESTMENT ACCOUNT HOLDERS

As mentioned previously, Islamic banks differ from their commercial bank counterparts in that other than current account deposits, their external funding is mainly from investment account holders (IAHs). It might be tempting to call these IAHs depositors, too, but this would be incorrect. In theory at least, the funds placed in investment accounts operate more like a mutual fund. The money is placed in the fund and then invested in partnership with the bank into funding the bank's clients. The success or failure of these activities determines the profits returned to these IAHs. They can operate as either restricted or unrestricted IAH, but the ISFB (2006, p. 20) found that more Islamic banks operated unrestricted ones. With the former, the bank acts as an external fund manager and so these funds, according to Grais and Pellegrini (2006b, p. 3), should be kept off the bank's direct balance sheet. Similarly, a bank should not 'mix its own funds with those of investors without their prior permission'.

Unrestricted IAH funds can be commingled with the bank's own capital for mutual benefit, but this is where governance becomes of some concern. It should be just a matter of splitting the risks and rewards in line with the

IAH contract, but this exercise is often more complicated. If the bank does not offer competitive returns, then IAH investors will move their money to other institutions. Alternatively, if the IAH receives too good a return, the shareholders may not be pleased, and the board and management will suffer accordingly. As El-Gamal (2005) notes, 'this complex set of competing incentives has made the issue of corporate governance of Islamic banks one of the most difficult'.

There is also the issue of IAHs having much the same risks as the shareholders but without a direct opportunity to influence the bank's decision making. El-Gamal (2005) expresses this more strongly, saying that IAHs 'lack internal corporate protection through representation on the board of directors, and lack legal and regulatory protection as creditors and first claimants to the bank's assets'. Lewis (2005, p. 22) argues further that 'a governance structure is needed that gives investment account depositors in banks a number of rights, including the capacity to influence the bank's investment decisions, to access investment performance and be supplied with a continuous flow of information'. Indeed some have suggested that IAHs might even be given the ability to vote for all directors together with normal shareholders or have the right to elect a certain portion of the board.

The practicality of IAH voting, however, seems somewhat doubtful. Firstly, as Gooden (2001, p. 5) notes, the IAHs and shareholders face a different set of risks in that the latter 'will be required to bear any losses suffered in relation to the funds of current account holders'. Secondly, there is always the question as to whether this entitlement would be valued. Again to quote Gooden (2001, p. 4), 'the practical reality is that most small investors do not want, and have not the time to devote to, active participation in the companies' in which they invest. Finally, as Grais and Pellegrini (2006a, p. 27) warn, such elections 'would bring with it additional agency problems and the risk of multiplying rather diffusing the asymmetries of information'.

So what might make sense instead, would be a regime that ensures a regular supply quality reporting to IAHs. Gooden (2001, p. 6) recommends that these IAHs' reports should be 'along similar lines to those produced by investment managers of unit trusts'. This same approach is reflected in IFSB (2006, p. 6) recommendations that IAHs should have the 'right to access all relevant information in relation to their investment accounts' but that this 'should not be misconstrued as a right to intervene in the management of the investments'. So in terms of a formal corporate governance role, it seems that IAHs' investors should definitely be silent partners. This does not mean that they should be uninformed partners, and so the following suggested checklist of IAH disclosure is provided in Box 7.2.

BOX 7.2   SUGGESTED DISCLOSURE TO INVESTMENT ACCOUNT HOLDERS

- Performance achieved
- Profit-sharing arrangements
- Expenses charged
- Composition of underlying portfolio
- Level of risk undertaken
- Degree of co-mingling with other funds
- Operation and amount of any performance reserves
- Verification by SSB

Before leaving this section, some mention should be made of performance reserves and their use with IAHs. As mentioned, most banks are very concerned about their IAHs' returns. Given that all years are unlikely to be profitable, many banks use a special reserve account where part of the surplus from the very good years is set aside to offset the poor returns of any bad years. While the IAH customers with money invested in the bad years will appreciate these past 'savings', the good year IAH customers may be surprised by their own generosity. So the bank must make it very clear whether its IAHs are subject to any smoothing of returns operations and under what circumstances money would be deducted or added to IAH earnings. The fairness of these decisions should also be a matter addressed by the SSB and its report.

5.0   INTERNAL GOVERNANCE STRUCTURE

While much of the Islamic bank governance literature concentrates on SSB and IAH matters, there is much more to corporate governance. The standard academic literature is also concerned with the specific structure of the board of the directors itself as well as its interaction with the management. These governance variables that should be addressed in Islamic bank annual reports and websites include the actual number of directors on the board (board size), whether these directors are full-time employees (insiders) or not (outsiders), whether these outside directors are independent from the management or major shareholders, and the committee structure through which the board conducts its business.

In their reports or websites, banks provide information directly in response to an email, letter or fax. They claim that it is counted as having

Table 7.4 Islamic bank disclosure of director information

Country	Number of Islamic banks examined	Number that disclosed BOD size	Number that disclosed external directors	Number that disclosed independent directors
Bahrain	15	11	11	6
Bangladesh	3	3	2	2
Brunei	2	1	1	0
Cayman Islands	1	1	1	0
Denmark	1	0	0	0
Egypt	3	2	1	0
Gambia	1	0	0	0
Indonesia	1	1	1	1
Iran	7	6	6	2
Iraq	1	0	0	0
Jordan	2	1	1	0
Kuwait	2	2	2	2
Lebanon	1	1	1	1
Malaysia	8	8	8	8
Mauritania	1	0	0	0
Pakistan	6	5	5	5
Palestine Territory	1	1	1	1
Qatar	4	4	1	1
Saudi Arabia	4	3	3	2
Sudan	5	4	2	2
Tunisia	1	0	0	0
Turkey	4	4	4	4
United Arab Emirates	5	4	3	3
United Kingdom	1	1	1	0
Yemen	4	3	2	2
Total	84	66	57	42

Note: These figures actually overstate the position as banks that did not disclose this information.

disclosed information. This may be a reasonable expectation but, as shown in Table 7.4, it is not realised in practice with some 22 per cent not bothering to disclose even the number of directors. The position worsens for more detail with more than a third not reporting on the position of external directors and only reporting on independent directors. The actual number of directors on a board has long been a matter of academic interest, but there is no specific view as to the optimal number of directors a firm should have. Some countries, however, require that a certain number of independent directors sit on a listed company's audit committee. In Australia, for example, this means that a board must have at least three directors but most firms have more. In terms of Australian banking, five is the regulatory minimum but, given the complexity of modern banking, a larger board is probably appropriate. In fact, some US research suggest that larger, more complex banks actual require larger boards (Adams and Mehran, 2003).

There is some limit to effective board size. So while adding one director might improve performance, too many directors could actually make things worse. The position on what number of directors is too small or too large will vary with each firm due to their own unique business and governance characteristics. In terms of Islamic banks, Chapra and Ahmed (2002) found that the director numbers in 1997 varied from a low of 4 to a high of 27 directors with an average of 12.2.

In contrast, this sample (using 2006/2007 data but unfortunately not the same banks) found a lower average of 7.95 with a median of 8 and a range from a low of 3 directors to a high of 15. Based on the academic corporate literature, 8 directors would seem a suitable average. As shown in Table 7.5, there were differences between countries. Bangladesh had the largest average board size of almost 13, but one bank from Egypt had the largest board with 15 directors.

It is not just the number of directors that should be important but also their quality. Sufficient disclosure is required, so like SSB members, shareholders can evaluate it. Box 7.3 provides some specific recommendations as to the details that should be provided.

The position of internal versus external directors is also significant in the academic literature. Outside directors are thought to be more objective in evaluating proposals from the management while inside directors, those that are already full-time employees of the bank, are better placed to make more informed decisions. On the balance, the preference is to have more external than internal and perhaps limit full-time employee directors to the managing director (CEO). Chapra and Ahmed (2002, p. 99) found that of the 14 Islamic banks surveyed, executive directors (insiders) averaged only 2.3 or 29.1 per cent with a low of 0 full-time directors to a high of 7. This chapter found even less with an average of 1.2 internal directors with a median of 1 and a range of 0 to 5. Table 7.6 provides the specific country details. These numbers, however, may be unrepresentatively low given others' comments. Rebeiz (2006, p. 16), for example, noted that for Islamic banks in the Middle East North Africa (MENA) region, 'the boards of directors are composed predominately of inside directors who are executives of the bank while the outside directors are not completely independent since they have some personal relationship with the management team either as siblings, friends or business partners'.

Table 7.5 Islamic bank board size by country

Country	Average number of directors	Minimum number of directors	Maximum number of directors	Number of Islamic banks
Bahrain	7.36	5	10	11
Bangladesh	12.67	12	13	3
Brunei	6	6	6	1
Cayman Islands	8	8	8	1
Egypt	9	3	15	2
Indonesia	3	3	3	1
Iran	5	4	6	6
Jordan	9	9	9	1
Kuwait	9.5	9	10	2
Lebanon	7	7	7	1
Malaysia	7.5	5	10	8
Pakistan	8.2	7	10	5
Palestine Territory	9	9	9	1
Qatar	7.75	6	9	4
Saudi Arabia	9.67	8	11	3
Sudan	8.50	7	11	4
Turkey	8.75	7	10	4
United Arab Emirates	8	7	9	4
United Kingdom	7	7	7	1
Yemen	9.33	6	11	3
Total	7.95	3	15	66

BOX 7.3   SUGGESTED DISCLOSURE ON DIRECTORS

- Names of all board members
- Educational qualifications
- Years and types of professional experience
- Any current other board appointments and employment
- Any business involvement with the bank
- Election procedure and term of office
- Age and years served as a director at the bank
- Membership (chairing) of board committees
- Attendance at board and committee meetings
- Remuneration paid by the bank
- Any bank shareholdings

Table 7.6   Islamic bank external director percentages by country

Country	Average percentage of external directors	Minimum number of external directors (%)	Maximum number of external directors (%)	Number of Islamic banks
Bahrain	75	0	100	11
Bangladesh	4	0	8	2
Brunei	83	83	83	1
Cayman Islands	88	88	88	1
Egypt	67	67	67	1
Indonesia	67	67	67	1
Iran	36	0	83	6
Jordan	89	89	89	1
Kuwait	94	89	100	2
Lebanon	29	29	29	1
Malaysia	89	71	100	8
Pakistan	80	57	90	5
Palestine Territory	89	89	89	1
Qatar	100	100	100	1
Saudi Arabia	88	64	100	3
Sudan	36	0	71	2
Turkey	88	86	90	4
United Arab Emirates	33	0	100	3
United Kingdom	86	86	86	1
Yemen	59	36	82	2
Total	74	0	100	57

The appointment of independent directors is one way to avoid the problem of outside directors with close ties to the management or major shareholders. An independent director's only relationship with the bank and its shareholders should be his/her employment as a director: no client, past employment or other business relationship. The corporate governance literature finds such directors often have a very positive impact on the board's ability to the monitor its management and so improve firm performance. Islamic banks no doubt appoint independent directors just for that reason. This chapter, as shown in Table 7.7, found banks with independent directors had an average of 4.19 of them on the board with a median of 3.5 and a range from 2 to 8.

This compares to an average of 6.74 external directors. The difference is for good reason as it is not always easy to detect which external directors are independent and which are not. Some externals may be independent, but this is not clear in their banks' report. As this should not be the case,

Table 7.7 Islamic bank independent director percentages by country

Country	Average percentage of independent directors	Minimum percentage of independent directors	Maximum percentage of independent directors	Number of Islamic banks
Bahrain	33	0	90	6
Bangladesh	4	0	8	2
Indonesia	33	33	33	1
Iran	0	0	0	2
Kuwait	44	0	89	2
Lebanon	0	0	0	1
Malaysia	43	29	57	8
Pakistan	24	0	90	5
Palestine Territory	33	33	33	1
Qatar	100	100	100	1
Saudi Arabia	0	0	0	2
Sudan	0	0	0	2
Turkey	10	0	29	4
UAE	19	0	57	3
Yemen	18	0	36	2
Total	35	0	100	42

BOX 7.4   SUGGESTED DISCLOSURE OF INDEPENDENT DIRECTORS

Each independent director should be so specified in the bank annual report and websites such as Mr John Smith, independent director

---

it leads to the recommendation contained in Box 7.4. In addition, there is also merit in ensuring that independent directors are in a majority on the board and that the board chair is similarly independent.

Board committees are another part of corporate governance. They are created by the board of directors to address the monitoring and policy setting of certain aspects of the bank's operations. They do not replace the board's direct responsibilities, but rather allow the operational details to be examined carefully first at the committee level. The committees then recommend an appropriate policy or course of action for the board as a whole to decide. The committee names and roles vary from country

Table 7.8   Islamic bank board committees by country

Country	Number of banks	Audit committee	Nomination committee	Remuneration committee	Risk management committee	Executive committee
Bahrain	12	4	2	2		4
Bangladesh	2					
Brunei	1					
Cayman Islands	1					
Egypt	2					
Indonesia	1				1	
Iran	6					
Jordan	1					
Kuwait	2					
Lebanon	1					1
Malaysia	8	4	5	5	5	
Pakistan	5	2				2
Palestine Territory	1					
Qatar	3	2				2
Saudi Arabia	2	1				1
Sudan	5	1				1
Turkey	4	2				
UAE	4					
UK	1					
Yemen	3					
Total	65	16	7	7	6	11

to country, but typically include an audit committee, nominations committee, remuneration committee and risk management committee. This research, as reported in Table 7.8, found that while not all banks reported on these committees, most also had an executive committee but not, as expected, a governance committee.

The audit committee is probably the most prominent in that it is responsible for the board's interaction with the independent external auditor as well as the internal audit unit. IFSB (2006) recognises its importance by recommending that the audit committee includes at least three non-executive directors members elected from the board. Its purpose is to review and monitor the accounting process and systems and report to the board on its findings. The Shamil Bank of Bahrain's (2006, p. 11) annual report provides a more comprehensive explanation. This is 'to review the bank's financial reporting process, international controls, risk management systems, and process for monitoring compliance with policies, procedures, laws, and regulations and the bank's own code of conduct'. So this committee definitely has a compliance monitoring role. This approach is also perhaps reflected in the use of the title, 'audit and examinations committee', among Malaysia's Islamic banks.

The nomination committee reviews the board's performance and that of individual directors as well as seeking the best mix of education and experience among the directors. Its work is supplemented to some extent by that of the remuneration committee and these two committees are actually combined in some banks into a 'nomination and remuneration committee'.

The remuneration committee members have the somewhat thankless job of setting the amount paid (and its packaging) to the senior executives of the bank as well as to their fellow directors. Their work often goes unappreciated as the executives and directors will no doubt feel underpaid but the shareholders will complain about their generosity. This committee may have a broader role in some banks as reflected in the 'human resources and compensation committee' used by BankIslami Pakistan Ltd.

The risk management committee is also common within the banking industry and is particularly important in Islamic banks when the profit- and loss-sharing aspect on both the asset and liability side of their balance sheet is considered. Other committees not expected but discovered in this research included a 'board loan review and recovery committee' (Affin Islamic Bank), a 'board financing review committee' (Bank Islam Malaysia) and an 'insider trading committee' (Shamil Bank of Bahrain).

A governance committee was expected to be a common feature among Islamic banks. As the IFSB (2006, p. 3) explains, it is intended to 'oversee and monitor the implementation of the governance framework together with the management, the audit committee and the SSB' as well as pay particular attention to the 'unique fiduciary duties' associated with IAHs (ISFB, 2006, p. 18). As with other board committees, the governance committee is normally chaired by an independent director supplemented as the IFSB (2006, p. 4) recommends by at least a member from the audit committee, a *Shari'ah* scholar from the SSB and a non-executive director with other legal or business expertise. In practice, most Islamic banks may perform largely this same function through the use of an 'executive committee'. The actual role of this latter body and whether it is the same as a management committee (where the CEO meets regularly with the senior bank staff) is a matter of further research. Chapra and Ahmed (2002, p. 100) similarly found the executive committee to be the most common at 10 of their 14 banks. In contrast, only two banks had a governance committee.

Another area for further research is the actual interaction between these various board committees with the bank staff and departments within the

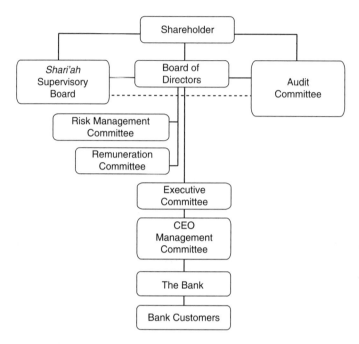

Figure 7.1   Islamic bank organisational chart

bank as well as the SSB, shareholders and external auditors. At least an indication of this is provided in Figure 7.1 where a potential organisational chart is provided.

While something similar to the above discussion on the composition and roles of the various board committees would seem useful to bank shareholders, surprisingly few banks provide any indication as to their committees' specific terms of reference.

6.0   EXTERNAL GOVERNANCE MATTERS

Besides the governance matters discussed so far, Islamic banks – like other banks – have their governance closely observed by bodies external to the bank itself. The most obvious of these is its home country's prudential bank regulator. As with normal banks, the board's attention to good risk management and regulatory compliance is a major concern. Furthermore, the Basel Committee on Banking Supervision's (BCBS) Basel 2's Pillar Two (BCBS, 2006b) requires that the regulator examine these matters and take action should they appear substandard. In response, most countries' prudential regulation policies have been expanded to cover a range of governance matters concerning their commercial banks. These have been driven by the work of the BCBS and its early governance suggestions in 1999 and more recently in 2006 (BCBS, 2006a). There is no reason for Islamic banks to be excluded from these policies.

Prudential regulators should also be very concerned that their Islamic banks be not only managed well but also run in accordance with Islamic law. So to assist them, most have established national *Shari'ah* advisory boards or councils for that purpose. They help ensure that SSBs at the individual bank level perform appropriately. Some countries have introduced credit rating agencies, which besides normal financial matters, may also report on *Shari'ah* compliance.

Finally, another external prudential concern is the degree to which others control banks. From an academic viewpoint, a highly concentrated ownership has the advantage of removing any potential agency conflicts between the owners and the managers as the two groups are then often comprised of the same people. Rebeiz (2006, p. 16) noted that agency cost was seemingly not much of a problem for Islamic banks in the Middle East North Africa region due to the importance of '100% family controlled firms'. In contrast, regulators may feel more confident with a diverse ownership basis. This would typically produce a more diverse, and usually independent, board of directors and such boards are believed to reduce risk. Conversely, the Asia crisis provided many examples of the risks of lending (crony loans and tunnelling) to group-affiliated firms and their customers. Chapra and Ahmed (2002, p. 99) found that the largest shareholders among their sample banks controlled 25.2 per cent of the shares ranging from a low of 3.7 to a high of 60 per cent. In comparison, the top five largest shareholders on average held a 51.7 per cent share with a range from 14.7 to 91.7 per cent; and the top ten shareholders held 62.5 and 25.8 to 99 per cent.

7.0 CONCLUSION

This chapter attempted to examine certain aspects of the corporate governance of Islamic banks. These included why Islamic bank governance might be different from that of conventional banks, the role of the *Shari'ah* supervisory boards and the degree of disclosure as to the board members and their reports, the investment account holders and their impact on governance matters. The remainder of the chapter looked more closely at the Islamic bank board structure to include board size, independence and committee structure as well as discussing some external governance matters. In the process, the chapter notes that there are significant differences in the quality and depth of disclosure practised by Islamic banks as well as in the approaches taken or at least in respect to what is available in their English annual reports and internet websites (an important limitation to be addressed). The conclusion is that while some Islamic banks afford good governance disclosure, most could improve their performance. The chapter has sought to assist this process by offering a number of suggestions as well as several checklists. It is hoped that these may prove of value to the industry and that future disclosure will be improved accordingly.

REFERENCES

AAOIFI (2003), *Accounting, Auditing & Governance Standards for Islamic Financial Institutions*, Bahrain: Accounting and Auditing Organization for Islamic Financial Institutions.

Adams, R. and Mehran, H. (2003), 'Is corporate governance different from bank holding companies?' *FRBNY Economic Policy Review*, 9: 123–42.

Akhtar, Shamshad (2006), 'Shariah compliant corporate governance', a paper presented at the Monash Malaysia Conference in Malaysia, 27 November.

Asri, Mohamed and Fahmi, Mohamed (2004), 'Contribution of the Islamic worldview toward corporate governance', a paper at the International Islamic University, Malaysia, in 2004.

Basel Committee on Banking Supervision (2006a), *Enhancing Corporate Governance for Banking Institutions*, Basel: Bank for International Settlements.

Basel Committee on Banking Supervision (2006b), *Basel II: International Convergence of Capital Measurements and Capital Standards: A Revised Framework – Comprehensive Version*, Basel: Bank for International Settlements.

Chapra, M. and Ahmed, H. (2002), *Corporate Governance of Islamic Financial Institutions*, Jeddah: Islamic Development Bank.

El-Gamal, Mahmound A. (2005), 'Islamic bank corporate governance and regulation: a call for mutualisation', unpublished paper at Rice University, September.

Gooden, S. (2001), 'Participation of stakeholders in the corporate governance of Islamic financial institutions', *New Horizon*, 114: 12–15.

Grais, Wafik and Pellegrini, Matteo (2006a), 'Corporate governance in institutions offering Islamic financial services', World Bank Policy Research Working Paper 4052, Washington, DC: World Bank.

Grais, Wafik and Pellegrini, Matteo (2006b), 'Corporate governance and stakeholders' financial interests in institutions offering Islamic financial services', World Bank Policy Research Working Paper 4053, Washington, DC: World Bank.

Grais, Wafik and Pellegrini, Matteo (2006c), 'Corporate governance and Shariah compliance in institutions offering Islamic financial services', World Bank Policy Research Working Paper 4054, Washington, DC: World Bank.

Islamic Financial Services Board (2006), *Guiding Principles on Corporate Governance for Institutions Offering Only Islamic Financial Services (Excluding Islamic Insurance 'Takaful' Institutions and Islamic Mutual Funds)*, Kuala Lumpur: ISFB December.

Lewis, Mervyn (2005), 'Islamic corporate governance', *Review of Islamic Economics*, 9(1): 5–29.

Maali, B., Casson, P. and Napier, C. (2006), 'Social reporting by Islamic banks', *Abacus*, 42(2): 266–83.

Nienhaus, Volker (2007), 'Governance of Islamic banks', in M.K. Hassan and M.K. Lewis (eds), *Handbook of Islamic Banking*, Cheltenham, UK and Northampton, MA, USA: Edward Elgar, pp. 128–43.

Rebciz, Karim (2006), 'Corporate governance for conventional and Islamic banks in the MENA region', *The Arab Bank Review*, 8(1): 13–25.

Shamil Bank of Bahrain (2006), *Annual Report 2006*.

Suleiman, Nasser M. (2005), 'Corporate governance in Islamic banks', http://www.al-bab.com/arab/econ/nsbanks.htm.

APPENDIX 1: IFSB SEVEN GUIDING PRINCIPLES OF CORPORATE GOVERNANCE

1. IIFS shall establish a comprehensive governance policy framework which sets out the strategic roles and function of each organ of governance and mechanisms for balancing the IIFS's accountabilities to various stakeholders.
2. IIFS shall ensure that the reporting of their financial and non-financial information meets the requirements of international recognised accounting standards which are in compliance with *Shari'ah* rules and principles and are applicable to the Islamic financial services industry as recognised by the supervisory authorities of that country.
3. IIFS shall acknowledge IAHs' right to monitor the performance of their investments and the associated risks, and put into place adequate means to ensure that these rights are observed and exercised.
4. IIFS shall adopt a sound investment strategy which is appropriately aligned to the risk and return expectations of IAH (bearing in mind the distinction between restricted and unrestricted IAH), and be transparent in smoothing any returns.
5. IIFS shall have in place an appropriate mechanism for obtaining rulings from *Shari'ah* scholars, applying fatwa and monitoring *Shari'ah* compliance in all aspects of their products, operations and activities.
6. IIFS shall comply with *Shari'ah* rules and principles as expressed in the rulings of IIFS's *Shari'ah* scholars. The IIFS shall make these rulings available to the public.
7. IIFS shall make adequate and timely disclosure to IAH and the public of material and relevant information on the investment accounts that they manage.

Note: IIFS stands for 'institutions offering Islamic financial services'.

Source: Islamic Financial Services Board (IFSB), 2006.

PART III

The practice: operating Islamic financial institutions

8. Performance of Islamic banks and conventional banks

Mohamed Ariff, Mohammad K. Badar, Shamsher M. and Taufiq Hassan

1.0 INTRODUCTION

In this chapter an attempt is made for the first time to assess the financial performance of Islamic banks and conventional banks by choosing a matched sample of banks to assess their financial performance across the world over a lengthy period. Islamic banking is based on replacing the pre-fixed-interest-based bank deposit-cum-lending activities with risk-sharing and profit-sharing principles advocated by Islam, which in turn appears to be consistent with the social norms of pre-modern societies prior to the rise of interest-based-fractioning banking in the last 200 years, which refers to the fractional-reserve banking from the close of the 18th century. Risk- and profit-share principles in financial transactions have been with humanity for a long time and they are still practiced silently in most rural non-bank lending activities across the world. They have certainly been followed for a long time in Islamic countries, where lending practices reshaped the old pre-Islamic practices across the then known world by avoiding pre-fixed interest-based lending practices in preference of risk-share–profit-share principles. The modern banking practice of fractional lending and pre-fixed interest without risk-sharing developed over the last three centuries just around 1752 AD following the papal dictate lifting the Catholic ban on interest-based lending.[1]

For some 45 years since 1963 the old practice of financial transaction of risk-share–profit-share lending has come back to be formally organized in Islamic banking. As at 2008 this form of banking practice has become heavily institutionalized in some 76 countries, few of them in the heartlands of modern finance in Hong Kong, London, Melbourne, New York, Singapore and Zurich. These Islamic banks operate checking deposits and credit cards with no interest; accept savings deposits and pay a dividend each month after the deposit is made instead of pre-arranged interest income; and engage in other banking activities based on non-interest-based arrangements to invest clients' money, to arrange mortgage loans, provide letters of credit, and so on. The total assets in management in some 400 Islamic banks are estimated to be about US$3 trillion with equity capital of US$320 billion.[2] In one country, Malaysia, both Islamic banks and conventional banks operate this specialized form of banking side by side and the customer base has no religious basis. There, after 25 years since the start of this new form of banking, the total assets amount to about 12 percent of the total assets of all banks, although the world average is no more than 3 percent. Two countries have solely Islamic banks, and there are no conventional banks there: Iran and Sudan. These two cases are not included in this study as this study is about comparing both types of banks within the same economic environment.

An important public policy issue, now that Islamic banking is widely accepted, is whether this form of banking is as good as the conventional banks for people to do their banking business. Some have argued that Islamic banking is an agenda of the extreme Islamists.[3] Are Islamic banks equally welfare-promoting as conventional banks? If they are inferior in practice, then it requires that the banking regulators raise alarm about this form of banking.[4] If indeed the financial performance from alternative banking practices is at least similar to conventional banking, then it may be said that this new form of banking is not likely to be a less welfare-promoting form of banking than the 200-year-old modern conventional banking.[5] Some proponents of this new form of banking would have us believe that the financial performance of Islamic banks ought to be higher, and be more aligned with community interest, since lender and borrower are linked together to share risk and the rewards must thus be higher. These issues could only be settled by a careful experiment comparing the long-run performance of a matched sample of Islamic and conventional banks around the world.

The rest of the chapter is divided into four sections. In section 2 the reader will find that the performance of two forms of banking is about the same as measured by three different financial measures, namely cost efficiency, revenue efficiency and profit efficiency. The results are then tested and compared by controlling the size of banks – see section 3 – by controlling age and regions – see section 4. Conclusions and suggestions for further research are found in the last section.

2.0 REVIEW OF LITERATURE AND RATIO ANALYSIS

Financial ratio analysis is widely recognized and entrenched as a valid means of assessing the performance of economic entities. So the entrenched concepts in financial ratios may be used to make valid comparisons on this issue.[6] Financial ratios are still widely used, in fact mandated by regulators in policy-making situations, to evaluate financial performance. To analyze the cost, revenue and profit efficiency of the banks, a set of six critical financial ratios commonly applied were identified and used in our study. These ratios have been widely employed in the literature to assess the performance and efficiency of banking institutions (Akkas, 1994; Sabi, 1996; Abdus-Samad, 1999; Bashir, 2000; Hassan and Bashir, 2003; Islam, 2003; Halkos and Salamouris, 2004; Iqbal and Molyneux, 2005). These ratios are explained later in this chapter.[7]

Some studies attempted to explain regional differences in banking performance. Some of the studies used different methodology, though: Allen and Rai (1996), Berger and Humphrey (1997), Maudos et al. (2002). However, only few studies have examined revenue efficiency: Al-Shammari (2003), Brown and Skully (2005) and Ariff et al. (2008) assessed the financial performance of Islamic banks as cross-country comparisons. All these studies examined some selected ratios and not the six ratios that we plan to employ in this study.

2.1 Cost Efficiency Financial Ratios

Cost to income ratio (CTIR)

This ratio measures the overhead costs or costs of running the bank as a percentage of income generated before provisions for bad debt. Salaries and wages form the major cost element in this ratio. It is a measure of cost efficiency. The ratio improves when each dollar of income generated incurs less cost if the spread in the lending margins increases. In the case of the conventional banks as well as Islamic banks the items under this cost are the same, the most important one being the salaries, wages, rent, overheads, etc. Though it is best to minimize this ratio by reducing costs and increasing income, high volatility in trading income and therefore high variability in income can distort the value of this ratio. In summary, the lower the ratio, the better is the cost efficiency.

Net interest expenses/average assets (NIER)

The net interest expense of conventional banks is equivalent to income (dividends) declared to deposit holders in Islamic banks. It is the traditional margin between deposit and lending rates: in Islamic banks, this is the difference between the income (dividend) declared to the deposit holders and the income (profit share) from borrowers (*mudharibs*) in the loan book. The average assets in both types of banks have the same meaning, and are measured by averaging the end-period assets in two consecutive years. The ratio of these items is another cost efficiency ratio by expressing the expense per unit of assets. It measures the cost efficiency of the bank assets. The lower the ratio, meaning the lower the expense involved per unit of assets, the better is the cost efficiency.

2.2   Revenue Efficiency Financial Ratios

Net interest margin (NIM)

The net interest margin (NIM) ratio is the net interest income expressed as a percentage of earnings generated by a conventional bank's assets. As defined in sub-section 2.1, this has an equivalent item in Islamic banks although the item is based on profit share not interest income. The higher this ratio, the cheaper the funding or the higher the margin the bank is commanding. A higher margin means higher revenue efficiency. However, management should maintain the quality of assets by avoiding too high margins that may actually be associated with banks taking very high risk. This ratio is not adjusted for risk.

Other operating income/average assets (OPIR)

OPIR is calculated by dividing the other operating income by the average value of assets. It indicates the value of other operating income generated for every dollar of asset value: if for each dollar of asset more income is generated, this ratio goes up. The higher the income earned for every dollar of asset value, the higher the revenue efficiency. Unlike the operating income, other operating income is a relatively smaller percentage of the total income earned for most average-sized banks – it is proportionately larger for fee-based banking particularly of large banks – it is less volatile and is considered as a lower risk form of income.

2.3   Profit Efficiency Financial Ratios

Return on average assets (ROAA)

By and large profit ratios are used in assessments as the most important ratios since these ratios indicate the ability of an economic entity to earn income sufficient to compensate the capital providers to the banks. Return on average assets is the most important single ratio used for comparing profit efficiency and the operational performance of banks as it looks at the returns generated from the assets financed by the debt and equity providers to a bank. The (ROAA) ratio equals the net income after tax over the average of total assets. The higher the value of net income generated per dollar of asset value, the greater the profit efficiency.

Return on average equity (ROAE)

The shareholders' income earned per dollar of shareholders' asset is the return on average equity. This is a key ratio measuring overall performance from the point of view of shareowners, the owners of banks. Banks in most countries score very high on this ratio. Most of the times – economic recession being the exception – this ratio is around 10 25 percent for banks. The return on equity is a measure of the return on shareholder funds. This (ROAE) ratio equals the net income over the average total equity capital in the book at the end of two years. The higher the value of returns for every dollar of shareholders' equity, the greater is the profit efficiency. However, it should be noted that firms can manage their financial statements by reducing equity and increasing debts, thereby increasing the value of this ratio. With evidence on income-smoothing practices practised by managers in many countries, one needs to be cautious about the interpretation of this ratio in a given year although the average ratio over about five years is more likely to be reliable. This ratio can also be generated by multiplying the ROAA by the equity multiplier (EM).[8]

The numbers for computing these ratios are taken from financial statements over 1990/1 and 2005/6 as available in the year 2006/7 in the BankScope database. Despite the differences in accounting and reporting practices in different countries, this database provides standardized figures so that most of the items are comparable across time and space: also most journals accept this source as a reliable data source. We collected the data from this database, and verified the data for transcription errors and corrected them wherever possible. The line items for the ratios were identified, and the ratios themselves were identified using the database, if available.

We covered all the countries where there are few Islamic banks and matched for each of them a conventional bank of relatively the same size. In this way, we selected 80 banks falling into two samples of 37 Islamic banks and 43 conventional banks. Originally we selected 44 banks from each group, and then had to drop a number of Islamic banks and one conventional bank by imposing the criterion that the bank must have been in operation for at least seven years. With data over 16 years – we collected data over 17 years to set up an 'average' for some items so one year of data was needed for this – on 80 banks, we would have potentially 80×16 or 1280 items of data for each item: with 12 items of data for six ratios, the total data set is about 15,000 observations. Since some banks were incorporated in later years, we had less than this potential number of total observations in some of our tests.

Our analysis is made using the entire sample to study the overall behaviour first. Subsequently, we analyse the two samples separately to test the hypothesis about any difference in the financial performance of the two types of banks and by portioning the sample by size, age and regions as explained in the results section. Tests were done using t-tests as the number of observations is large enough. The one-way ANOVA test is also used. Critical values are used at 0.10 and 0.05 acceptance levels.

3.0   OVERALL RESULTS: ALL BANKS

In this section the reader is provided with descriptive statistics and tests of significance using all banks. The results over different time periods for the overall sample, conventional and Islamic banks are also presented. We also present the performance results over the period 1990–2005.

3.1   Cost, Revenue and Profit Efficiency of All Banks

First we present the overall results for all banks in Table 8.1 to assess the behaviour of the sample of commercial banks in this study. The statistics in this table may be used as a benchmark for the total sample. The ROAE is about 11 percent, which is roughly the average one would expect in the world banking system as a whole.

Similarly an ROAA of 1.35 percent is about what is documented in the banking literature as the return on earning assets in the test period. An operating income ratio of 2.9 percent is again about the level reported in the literature. Thus profit ratios and revenue ratios – see the last two columns for the numbers – indicate that the sample we have chosen is representative of the banking population in the world. For every dollar of assets, the net interest expense is about 4.18, meaning that this cost efficiency is about four times the asset value. Finally, the overall cost to income ratio of 58 indicates that to generate 100 dollars of income the cost incurred is 58 dollars. We have no comparable data from literature to cite a reference to this type of analysis.

Now we present the statistics for the two samples, conventional and Islamic banks: see Table 8.2. The statistics presented in Table 8.2 may be evaluated as to whether the two forms of banking have significant differences in the six performance parameters over the 16 years (1990/91–2005/6). It can be observed that the exception is the measure of ROAE: the Islamic banks appear to have a 2 percent higher return, 11.6 percent, to shareholders compared with the conventional banks' return to shareholders of 9.6 percent. However, as the t-tests of difference indicate, this 2 percent difference is not statistically significant at the 0.05 level. The return on all assets (ROAA) is slightly higher as well (1.41 and 1.27 percent) but again the t-statistics verify that the difference is not significant at the 0.05 acceptance

Table 8.1   All banks: cost, revenue and profit efficiency, 1990–2005

Category	Statistics	Cost Efficiency Ratios		Revenue Efficiency Ratios		Profit Efficiency Ratios	
		CTIR	NIER	NIM	OPIR	ROAA	ROAE
All Banks	N	80	80	80	80	80	80
	Mean	58.041	4.174	3.780	2.892	1.345	10.688
	Std. Deviation	20.170	3.313	2.517	3.447	1.699	16.604
	Maximum	105.486	19.550	15.360	16.156	9.907	69.197
	Minimum	24.093	0.745	−0.225	0.380	−3.049	−87.416

Note: The descriptive statistics are obtained using the Eviews program. Since the means and median values are very close, we report only the mean values.

Table 8.2   Conventional and Islamic banks: cost, revenue and profit efficiency

Category	Statistics	Cost Efficiency Ratios		Revenue Efficiency Ratios		Profit Efficiency Ratios	
		CTIR	NIER	NIM	OPIR	ROAA	ROAE
Conventional Banks	N	37	37	37	37	37	37
	Mean	58.165	4.097	3.919	2.449	1.274	9.614
	Std. Deviation	19.905	3.559	2.811	3.395	1.954	20.255
	Maximum	102.687	19.550	15.360	16.156	9.907	69.197
	Minimum	25.878	0.745	0.793	0.380	−3.049	−87.416
Islamic Banks	N	43	43	43	43	43	43
	Mean	57.935	4.240	3.660	3.272	1.405	11.611
	Std. Deviation	20.630	3.127	2.262	3.485	1.466	12.847
	Maximum	105.486	14.925	8.442	14.340	6.010	43.388
	Minimum	24.093	1.095	−0.225	0.423	−1.820	−22.918
Significance of t-test (2-tailed)*	Equal variance assumed	0.96	0.85	0.65	0.29	0.73	0.60
	Equal variance not Assumed	0.96	0.85	0.65	0.29	0.74	0.61

Note: * No significant differences between means of conventional versus Islamic banks at 0.05 percent level.

level. As for the revenue efficiency, the same conclusions are valid. The revenue efficiency ratios of 3.92 and 2.45 (conventional banks) are no different from the respective 3.66 and 3.27 (Islamic banks) at an acceptable probability level of 0.05. Finally, the same conclusion is suggested by the failure to reject the hypothesis of no difference for the two ratios on cost efficiency ratios, which are the cost-to-profit and cost-to-asset ratios. These ratios are: 57.94 and 4.24 (Islamic banks) and 58.165 and 4.10 (conventional banks).

Thus, the overall financial performance of both types of banks is similar over a recent 16-year period, although there is a slightly higher nonsignificant return to shareholders of 2 percent. Since the samples were taken from the same countries, this difference cannot be attributed to inflation differences, but to the way the two banks are managed. It is possibly driven by the difference in the process of earning returns. The Islamic banks declare a return to deposit holders after a month of using the deposits, and theory-wise, this declared amount depends on the income earned by the banks rather than the interest rate ruling in the market.

As we know the interest surprises produce the interest rate risk known as the gap risk in conventional banking, which requires careful hedging that incurs costs to conventional banks: Islamic banks have problems getting approval to hedge this gap risk from their supervisory boards. Perhaps the interest rate surprises to conventional banks reduce the conventional bank earnings by this 2 percent?

The null hypothesis of no difference in the two forms of banks cannot still be rejected. That means any criticism that the Islamic bank is a scam or welfare-reducing practice is at best not supported by these statistics as it produces similar returns to shareholders.

Researchers using unmatched samples and data from different periods have produced results contrary to ours. Examples of such studies are Iqbal and Molyneux (2005) and Hassan and Bashir (2003). Perhaps, the differences are due to different samples, or periods, or countries, and the small number of banks in each study. Our test data set is the largest, and is the only one to match the samples in the same economic and financial environment over a lengthy period. The other authors compare returns of banks in unmatched samples from other published studies, which procedure is fraught with error, although it is widely done for lack of data or difficulty in sourcing a matched sample data set.

As a summary of the above discussion, we present the mean ratio scores in a chart: see Figure 8.1.[9] Although the results are not statistically significant, the chart shows slight differences in all ratios between the groups of banks. It reveals that Islamic banks are slightly better in managing cost ratios as these ratios are lower than in conventional banks. Islamic banks appear to be more profit-efficient as their ROAA and ROAE ratios are higher

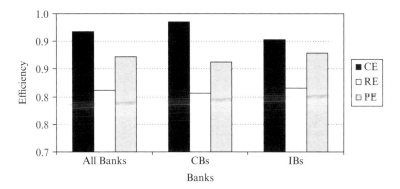

Figure 8.1   Average ratios of conventional, Islamic, and all banks

than those of conventional banks. In addition, Islamic banks also scored higher OPIR ratios than conventional banks. That means Islamic banks, on average, are slightly more revenue-efficient than conventional banks. However, conventional banks have slightly higher net interest margins (NIM) than Islamic banks and are exposed to more interest rate surprises.

3.2   Time Series Statistics on Cost, Revenue and Profit Efficiency

In order to provide a feel for the time series variations in the ratios for the two types of banks, we provide in two tables here the average statistics over the test period from 1990/91 to 2005/6. The findings reported in Table 8.3 suggest that all the performance ratios are unstable, and are quite volatile over the period of analysis. The CTIR improved in the last few years as the ratio decreased, which means that there is a learning curve for banks in being able to minimize their costs in the more recent years, perhaps due to cost-cutting measures in the wake of Basel II. The NIER ratio had the highest value in 1998, which means that the highest interest was paid for every dollar of asset value in that year. The values of NIM and OPIR ratios increased over time suggesting increasing revenue efficiency over time. ROAA improved significantly in 2003 and in later years. The negative ROAE ratio in 1999 is due to the extreme losses (-724.52) reported by a conventional bank (Bank Mandiri in Indonesia) in that year and other negative results scored by a few other banks in the wake of the political-cum-economic turmoil in Indonesia.

Table 8.3 presents the average results for conventional banks over the test. Similar to the findings for the 'all banks' group, results for the

Table 8.3   Cost, revenue and profit efficiency of conventional banks, 1990/1–2005/6

Year	Conventional Banks					
	Cost Efficiency Ratios		Revenue Efficiency Ratios		Profit Efficiency Ratios	
	CTIR	NIER	NIM	OPIR	ROAA	ROAE
16 (recent)	46.754	3.657	3.464	2.933	1.931	16.815
15	54.789	3.870	3.719	2.705	1.661	15.806
14	56.168	4.502	4.013	3.174	1.545	13.424
13	58.989	3.438	3.781	1.672	1.035	18.049
12	53.249	3.389	3.833	1.737	1.313	13.996
11	54.626	3.190	3.489	1.842	1.371	15.402
10	68.399	4.161	2.891	1.862	−0.097	−25.033
9	56.786	3.493	3.597	1.428	0.902	9.189
8	49.048	3.062	3.651	1.669	1.473	11.691
7	49.853	3.237	3.544	1.947	1.147	10.417
6	48.412	3.153	3.426	1.633	1.026	9.476
5	64.202	2.774	2.957	1.236	0.996	9.745
4	66.471	2.530	2.352	1.079	0.402	11.312
3	56.146	2.124	2.239	1.265	0.797	8.984
2	46.335	2.141	2.783	1.097	0.954	26.255
1	49.098	1.920	2.686	1.251	1.004	10.525

conventional banks are volatile over the period of analysis. The minimum 'best' CTIR ratios were 46.335 and 46.754 in 1991 and in 2005, respectively, which indicates the minimum costs for every dollar of net income, which is the best cost-efficiency scores in those years. The highest NIER value was observed in 2003, that is, the highest interest cost paid for every dollar of assets in this year. The revenue efficiency of conventional banks also improved in the last few years as shown by the increasing value of NIM and OPIR ratios.

The annual cost, revenue and profit efficiency ratios for Islamic banks are reported in Table 8.4. Similar to conventional banks, the cost efficiency of the Islamic banks also improved in the last few years as indicated by the declining value of CTIR ratio. This suggests that, on average, Islamic banks are learning slowly how to minimize their costs over time – the learning curve effect – probably by learning from experience of other similar banks. As indicated by the NIER ratio, the Islamic banks paid the least interest (dividend declared to savings deposit holders) costs in 1992 and the highest interest (dividend) costs in 1998. Although showing an upward

Table 8.4   Cost, revenue and profit efficiency of Islamic banks, 1992–2005

	Islamic Banks					
Year	Cost Efficiency Ratios		Revenue Efficiency Ratios		Profit Efficiency Ratios	
	CTIR	NIER	NIM	OPIR	ROAA	ROAE
14	43.905	3.236	4.652	2.210	2.779	23.710
13	51.325	2.993	3.342	2.286	1.812	16.593
12	52.179	3.698	3.316	3.160	1.788	15.364
11	57.119	3.878	3.361	2.718	1.182	11.587
10	65.956	3.947	4.075	2.530	1.042	9.388
9	57.028	3.715	4.014	2.425	1.282	12.975
8	63.922	3.954	3.656	2.618	0.772	8.256
7	55.442	5.145	4.045	2.973	0.281	1.367
6	67.423	3.838	4.247	2.128	0.666	−1.048
5	51.641	3.063	4.406	1.557	1.520	16.032
4	51.578	2.683	3.091	1.624	1.177	16.209
3	58.915	2.775	2.833	1.729	1.107	16.394
2	71.422	3.086	2.499	1.312	0.371	5.558
1	55.999	1.729	1.508	0.919	0.548	8.185

drift, indicating increasing revenue efficiency, the NIM and OPIR ratios are volatile over the years implying unstable revenue-generating capabilities of Islamic banks. However, ROAA and ROAE ratios are improving steadily since 2001 and they are slightly better than conventional bank ratios. The negative ROAE value in the year 1997 is an outcome of the extreme negative score by Dubai Islamic Bank (−233.09) and some other negative results in that year.

4.0   DOES EFFICIENCY CHANGE WITH SIZE, AGE AND LOCATION OF BANKS?

We extend our analysis in this section to do some robustness tests to see if the failure to reject the null hypothesis of no difference in performance is contingent upon other factors. The sample was reorganized according to the size of the banks – small versus big banks – to see if the alternative hypothesis holds for different-sized banks (see Kwan (2006); and Hassan and Bashir (2003) who studied conventional banks of same size). Similarly, we hypothesized that the learning effect may be evident by examining the data over the recent period versus data over earlier periods by splitting

Table 8.5   Cost, revenue and profit efficiency of big and small banks, 1990/1–2005/6

Size	Statistics	Cost Efficiency Ratios		Revenue Efficiency Ratios		Profit Efficiency Ratios	
		CTIR	NIER	NIM	OPIR	ROAA	ROAE
Big Banks	N	38	38	38	38	38	38
	Mean	54.327	3.604	3.518	2.472	1.379	11.909
	Std. Deviation	19.204	3.333	2.068	3.420	1.836	21.329
	Maximum	105.486	19.550	8.835	16.156	9.907	69.197
	Minimum	25.878	0.745	0.551	0.380	−3.049	−87.416
Small Banks	N	42	42	42	42	42	42
	Mean	61.402	4.690	4.016	3.271	1.314	9.589
	Std. Deviation	20.657	3.248	2.869	3.468	1.587	10.865
	Maximum	102.687	14.925	15.360	14.340	6.010	43.388
	Minimum	24.093	1.095	−0.225	0.423	−1.820	−13.263
T-Test Significance (2-tailed)*	Equal variance assumed	0.12	0.14	0.38	0.30	0.87	0.54
	Equal variance not assumed	0.12	0.15	0.37	0.30	0.87	0.55

Note: * No significant differences between means of big versus small banks at 0.05 percent level.

the data of each bank accordingly. It is possible that the acceptance of Islamic banking by the world's major banks has led very experienced banks in national settings to readily accept Islamic banking in recent years to increase their clientele.

Finally, Islamic banks are found in regions where the economies are at an early stage of development, and that would mean either that the banks are more profitable or that they would have captive clients. That would make a difference in performance. So, we divided the sample into banks in different parts of the world accordingly.

4.1   Big Versus Small Banks

Table 8.5 reports the average cost, revenue and profit ratios of big, small and all banks. It includes a summary of the t-tests of difference in efficiency ratios between big and small banks. The findings show no significant difference in the mean scores between big and small banks for all efficiency categories. Therefore, the null hypothesis that the cost, revenue and profit efficiency of big banks are not significantly different than those of small banks cannot be rejected. This evidence suggests that size of banks does not affect cost, revenue and profit efficiency, a result in line with the results previously presented in Table 8.2 for both types of banks.

The mean cost-efficiency ratios (CTIR and NIER) of big banks are 54.327 and 3.604, respectively, while the same ratios for small banks are 61.402 and 4.960, respectively. This indicates that big banks are slightly more cost-efficient, though not enough to be statistically significantly different to those small banks. However, the averages on revenue efficiency ratios (NIM and OPIR) indicate that small banks are slightly more revenue-efficient than big banks. This is contrary to intuition in that big banks, with cross-product clients giving them scope economics, should be more revenue-efficient especially given the scope economics in favour of big banks. The two important profit ratio scores (ROAA and ROAE) suggest that big banks are more profit-efficient than small banks.[10]

The annual values of cost, revenue and profit efficiency scores across time from years 1990 and 2005 for big banks are summarized in Table 8.6. There is no consistent trend in the scores over the 16-year period. The statistics indicate a decreasing trend in the CITR ratio however, which indicates cost-efficiency improvement. However, the NIER ratio scores are on an upwards trend, suggesting increasing interest expense for every dollar of asset value utilized, suggesting loss of control on this dimension. Similarly, the OPIR and NIM ratios are on an upwards trend indicating an increasing level of revenue efficiency. The ROAA and ROAE are unstable, which indicates unstable profit efficiency of big banks. The negative values of profit efficiency ratios in some years are due to extreme negative values scored by some banks as the consequence of the financial crisis that occurred around 1998–1999. Now we present the statistics for the small banks on all six ratios: see Table 8.7. The summary statistics would lead to the same conclusions for the small banks. There appear to be no pronounced trends. Minor changes appear. For example small banks appear to have improved their cost efficiency – see the first two columns of data – steadily over time. The value of 3.808 in 2005 in the second column indicates a rapid improvement for this ratio compared with the figure in 1990 of 2.50. The small banks appear to have a 50 percent improvement in this ratio over a 16-year period. Though the profit ratios were erratic over time, reversing trend sometimes, the achievements by small banks in the first five years of the 2000s are notable. A one-way ANOVA test suggests an improvement in this ratio as shown in the last column. However,

Table 8.6   *Time series statistics on cost, revenue and profit efficiency of big banks, 1990–2005*

Year	Cost Efficiency Ratios		Revenue Efficiency Ratios		Profit Efficiency Ratios	
Big Banks						
	CTIR	NIER	NIM	OPIR	ROAA	ROAE
16 (recent)	45.395	3.255	3.914	2.274	2.077	19.206
15	53.009	3.181	3.469	2.430	1.809	18.579
14	54.062	3.774	3.394	3.068	1.707	19.260
13	58.027	2.987	3.390	2.105	1.531	17.965
12	59.703	3.438	3.680	1.734	1.139	14.059
11	55.847	3.026	3.429	1.981	1.424	15.837
10	66.160	4.204	3.301	2.266	0.155	−15.144
9	56.087	3.533	3.505	1.928	0.465	3.492
8	58.431	3.198	3.885	1.822	0.885	2.521
7	50.684	2.907	3.795	1.804	1.176	12.240
6	49.829	2.565	2.642	1.551	0.990	12.367
5	62.119	2.243	1.977	1.408	0.940	12.059
4	68.690	1.954	2.000	1.172	0.878	11.229
3	56.090	1.745	1.750	0.993	0.597	9.690
2	48.058	1.824	2.134	1.030	0.786	31.151
1	49.098	1.630	2.225	1.115	0.886	11.874

the trend improvements are also observed in the case of big banks. That would suggest that the trend improvements are due more to the variables affecting the time series data rather than the banks being small or big. Hence, the general conclusion that the null is not rejected would also hold for the time series data set.

Given this observation, it would be meaningless to test if there are differences across small and big banks by types of banks.

4.2   Does Age of Banks Make a Difference?

In this sub-section results relating to age effect on the efficiency of conventional versus Islamic banks are reported. There are studies examining for example whether the age of banks is related to efficiency, while other studies used age as a conditioning factor for lower risk. The results relate to efficiencies in old and new Islamic and conventional banks.

Table 8.8 is a summary of average ratios and the test statistics on cost, revenue and profit efficiency of old and new conventional and old and

Table 8.7   Time series statistics on cost, revenue and profit efficiency of small banks, 1990/1–2005/6

	Small Banks					
Year	Cost Efficiency Ratios		Revenue Efficiency Ratios		Profit Efficiency Ratios	
	CTIR	NIER	NIM	OPIR	ROAA	ROAE
16 (recent)	44.683	3.808	4.236	3.178	2.733	21.391
15	57.959	3.666	3.581	2.556	2.059	13.649
14	57.545	4.351	3.871	3.260	1.873	10.039
13	63.222	4.292	3.721	2.320	1.091	11.664
12	58.334	3.916	4.240	2.558	2.116	9.185
11	56.779	3.868	4.072	2.290	1.420	12.553
10	72.805	3.921	3.233	2.216	0.596	−2.084
9	55.601	5.168	4.155	2.535	−1.977	6.764
8	61.225	3.751	4.035	1.995	1.431	8.210
7	51.582	3.472	4.134	1.717	1.593	14.025
6	51.817	3.435	4.074	1.747	1.234	12.728
5	76.284	3.368	3.943	1.478	1.156	12.815
4	86.998	3.840	2.998	1.213	−0.289	5.230
3	46.553	2.319	2.294	1.361	0.864	7.253
2	36.707	2.553	3.578	1.203	1.095	8.675
1	32.645	2.500	3.607	1.660	1.210	8.163

new Islamic banks. The findings show no significant differences between the cost efficiencies (CTIR and NIER) of old and new conventional and Islamic banks. The null hypothesis that the mean cost efficiency of old/new conventional banks is not different from the old/new Islamic banks cannot be rejected.

In contrast, the revenue efficiency (NIM ratio) of new conventional banks is significantly higher than new Islamic banks.[11] However, the null hypothesis of mean revenue efficiency of old conventional banks is significantly different than that of revenue efficiency of old Islamic banks cannot be rejected. That means we find support for mean difference between new conventional and new Islamic banks but not old conventional banks versus old Islamic banks. This is the only rejection of the null hypothesis of no difference so far.

In terms of profit efficiency, the table shows that there are no significant differences between conventional and Islamic banks based on their age. Hence, the null hypothesis is again not rejected, so there is no difference because of age of banks in both types of banks. We also accept the null

Table 8.8   *Average cost, revenue and profit efficiency of old and new conventional and Islamic banks, 1990/1–2005/6*

Age Category	Statistics	Cost Efficiency Ratios		Revenue Efficiency Ratios		Profit Efficiency Ratios	
		CTIR	NIER	NIM	OPIR	ROAA	ROAE
OCBs	N	27	27	27	27	27	27
	Mean	55.993	3.502	3.232	2.451	1.309	13.476
	Std. Deviation	21.015	3.630	2.067	3.746	1.867	13.537
	Maximum	102.687	19.550	8.835	16.156	9.907	69.197
	Minimum	25.878	0.745	0.793	0.380	−0.605	−8.083
OIBs	N	23	23	23	23	23	23
	Mean	56.347	3.535	3.541	2.254	1.439	12.531
	Std. Deviation	17.482	2.233	2.376	2.615	1.302	13.748
	Maximum	85.049	10.490	8.177	11.670	5.228	43.388
	Minimum	28.400	1.095	−0.225	0.425	−0.272	−22.918
NCBs	N	10	10	10	10	10	10
	Mean	64.027	5.703	5.774	2.445	1.181	−0.812
	Std. Deviation	16.017	2.942	3.746	2.360	2.277	30.759
	Maximum	88.910	12.345	15.360	8.935	5.855	17.512
	Minimum	46.253	2.672	2.377	0.760	−3.049	−87.416
NIBs	N	20	20	20	20	20	20
	Mean	59.762	5.051	3.796	4.444	1.366	10.553
	Std. Deviation	24.091	3.813	2.175	4.028	1.669	11.991
	Maximum	105.486	14.925	8.442	14.340	6.010	33.730
	Minimum	24.093	1.221	−0.110	0.423	−1.820	−13.263
One-way ANOVA Significant	Between groups	0.70	0.14	0.05*	0.14	0.98	0.12

Note: * The mean difference is significant at the 0.05 percent probability level.

hypotheses of no difference in means on profit efficiency ratios of new conventional banks and new Islamic banks. The mean efficiency scores show slight differences in the sub-groups of banks, though not amounting to a statistically important difference. Despite that, we could conjecture that old conventional banks are thus marginally better, because of a slightly higher value, in minimizing costs.

Table 8.9   *Average cost, revenue and profit efficiency of old and new banks*

Age Category	Statistics	Cost Efficiency Ratios		Revenue Efficiency Ratios		Profit Efficiency Ratios	
		CTIR	NIER	NIM	OPIR	ROAA	ROAE
Old	N	50	50	50	50	50	50
	Mean	56.156	3.517	3.374	2.360	1.369	13.041
	Std. Deviation	19.277	3.036	2.197	3.245	1.617	13.502
	Maximum	102.687	19.550	8.835	16.156	9.907	69.197
	Minimum	25.878	0.745	−0.225	0.380	−0.605	−22.918
New	N	30	30	30	30	30	30
	Mean	61.184	5.268	4.456	3.778	1.304	6.765
	Std. Deviation	21.542	3.509	2.891	3.644	1.855	20.433
	Maximum	105.486	14.925	15.360	14.340	6.010	33.730
	Minimum	24.093	1.221	−0.110	0.423	−3.049	−87.416
T-Test Significance (2-tailed)	Equal variance assumed	0.28	0.02*	0.06	0.08	0.87	0.10
	Equal variance not assumed	0.30	0.03*	0.08	0.09	0.88	0.14

Note: * The mean difference is significant at the 0.05 percent probability level.

Revenue and profit efficiency ratios as measured by OPIR and ROAE ratios are higher in old conventional banks. However, the revenue efficiency (NIM) is better in new conventional banks and the profit efficiency (ROAA) is better in old Islamic banks.

An interesting result needs highlighting. The new Islamic banks are better than new conventional banks in minimizing costs – see the cost ratios in the first two columns – which difference is due to the higher interest expenses of new conventional banks to compete with older banks. Surprisingly, even though new conventional banks are significantly better in respect to revenue efficiency, new Islamic banks are more profitable than new conventional banks. Because of the overall differences between the two types of banks, we regrouped the sample into merely old and new banks without separating them across types of banks. The results are shown in Table 8.9 on average cost, revenue and profit efficiency of old and new banks.

The findings reveal that there is significant difference in NIER, or cost efficiency, between old and new banks in our total sample. It indicates that old banks are more cost-efficient than new banks. The mean NIER score for old banks (3.517) is significantly lower than the ratio for new banks (5.268), thus the null hypothesis which suggests that the old banks are more cost-efficient than new banks cannot be rejected.[12] This indicates that old banks are significantly better than new banks in minimizing their interest expenses. That is also what one would predict from the learning effect hypothesis that makes older banks more skilled in controlling costs. This could also be due to attempts by the new banks to compete for the clients of old banks, in which case the cost control is not the aim, rather the market share of the new banks. However, there are no significant differences between old and new banks in respect to the revenue and profit efficiencies. That is, the market share strategy did not lead to tardiness in profit-seeking by new banks. Consequently, the two null hypotheses that the old banks are more revenue(profit)-efficient than new banks cannot be accepted.[13]

4.3   Does Location Contribute to Performance?

This section reports our test results on the impact of geography on the performance of conventional and Islamic banks. We divided the samples on banks into three regions: Africa, Asia and the Middle East and Turkey regions.

The regional test results are summarized in Table 8.10, separated as cost, revenue and profit efficiency ratios in Africa, Asia and the Middle East–Turkey. The findings show no significant differences in cost efficiency between banks in these regions (the computed p-values were 0.51 and 0.08 for the two cost efficiency ratios). The null hypothesis of no significant difference in average cost efficiency scores in the selected regions is not rejected. However, as the p-values for OPIR suggest, banks in Africa are relatively more revenue-efficient compared to banks in other regions. For every dollar of asset value, these banks generate about 4.6 dollars of other income, compared to 1.4 for Asia and 2.6 for the Middle East–Turkey region.[14]

The multiple comparison tests (Tukey HSD Post Hoc Test) show that there is significant difference in the mean scores of OPIR (revenue efficiency) between African and Asian banks. In the case of the ROAA ratio (profit efficiency), there is considerable difference between Asian banks and the banks in the Middle East–Turkey as the p-value of 0.052 is very close to the 0.05 significance level. On average, banks in Africa scored the highest mean for cost efficiency (CTIR, NIER), revenue efficiency (NIM, OPIR) and profit efficiency (ROAE). The banks in the Middle

Table 8.10   Cost, revenue and profit efficiency of banks in different regions

Region Category	Statistics	Cost Efficiency Ratios		Revenue Efficiency Ratios		Profit Efficiency Ratios	
		CTIR	NIER	NIM	OPIR	ROAA	ROAE
Africa	N	21	21	21	21	21	21
	Mean	61.782	5.550	4.173	4.675	1.181	12.635
	Std. Deviation	22.053	3.354	2.660	3.911	2.186	17.196
	Maximum	102.687	12.345	8.835	13.448	9.907	69.197
	Minimum	25.878	1.228	0.551	0.380	−1.820	−13.263
Asia	N	19	19	19	19	19	19
	Mean	59.111	3.457	3.618	1.409	0.644	4.646
	Std. Deviation	20.359	1.819	2.127	0.739	1.251	24.218
	Maximum	93.473	8.761	8.148	3.405	3.303	33.730
	Minimum	25.410	1.760	0.793	0.425	−3.049	−87.416
Middle East and Turkey	N	40	40	40	40	40	40
	Mean	55.570	3.791	3.650	2.660	1.763	12.535
	Std. Deviation	19.210	3.676	2.647	3.624	1.497	10.620
	Maximum	105.486	19.550	15.360	16.156	6.010	33.293
	Minimum	24.093	0.745	−0.225	0.423	−0.605	−22.918
One-way ANOVA Significance	Between groups	0.51	0.08	0.71	0.01*	0.052	0.19

Note: * The mean difference is significant at the 0.05 percent level.

East–Turkey reported the highest profit efficiency measured as the ROAE ratio. The ROAE is almost 3 percentage points higher in Africa. As suggested in an earlier section, this may in fact reflect the higher riskiness of banking operations in Africa as well as the monopoly profits that are likely to be higher in that region with a low level of banking penetration, thus, a low level of competition.

Meanwhile, banks in the Middle East–Turkey reported the lowest cost efficiency (CTIR) and Asian banks also reported the lowest cost efficiency (NIER), revenue efficiency (NIM, OPIR) and profit efficiency (ROAA and ROAE) ratios. Although the differences are not statistically significant, these results reveal that African banks rank at the top, Asian banks rank at the bottom, and banks in the Middle East–Turkey rank in the middle in respect to cost, revenue and profit efficiency.

As there is need for further and different analyses to disentangle these differences, one could merely speculate that these significant differences arise from banking concentration and thus monopoly profits in some regions have lower competition than in others.

Next, we examine if the Islamic banks have similar results across the two types of banking in this study: see Table 8.11. The findings show no significant differences in cost, revenue and profit efficiencies between conventional and Islamic banks in the selected regions. The one exception is a significant difference in the revenue efficiency, OPIR. According to the multiple comparison tests, the OPIR ratio is very close to the 0.05 significance level because of the big difference between African Islamic and Asian conventional banks. On average, conventional banks in Africa had better cost (CTIR) and profit efficiency (ROAA and ROAE) than the Islamic banks. Meanwhile, African Islamic banks had lower cost efficiency (NIER) but higher revenue efficiency (NIM, OPIR) compared to Asian and Middle East Islamic banks. The Islamic banks in the Middle East–Turkey had the highest profit efficiency measured by ROAA compared to Islamic banks in Africa and Asia.

The conventional banks in the Middle East–Turkey were more cost-(CTIR and NIER) and profit-(using ROAE) efficient than their counterparts in Asia and Africa. The Asian Islamic banks scored the lowest mean of NIER ratios (better cost efficiency) and Islamic banks in the Middle East–Turkey scored the lowest mean NIM ratio suggesting better revenue efficiency. Asian conventional banks had poor revenue and scored the lowest mean of OPIR and profit ratios of ROAA and ROAE efficiencies. Thus, Islamic banks in Africa are at the top of the list of these sub-groups followed by African conventional banks, whereas conventional banks in Asia are at the bottom of the list.

These results would have us believe that there are regional differences in financial efficiencies of both the conventional and Islamic banks. A significant difference between the African and Asian banks is surprising in that common belief is that the Asian banking system is well-regulated. If our results here are valid – we believe these are robust results – this common belief is not correct in that for some well-regulated Asian banking systems, there are many that are badly regulated. Finally, the Middle-Eastern banks are essentially banks managed by Western country banks, which brought their expertise and run these banks although some local banking groups have had good success in some locations in more open economies such as Bahrain and Kuwait. Thus, the financial performance of Islamic and conventional banks does have significant differences across where the banks are located. But the age and size of banks matter not!

Table 8.11   *Cost, revenue and profit efficiency of conventional versus Islamic banks by regions*

Region Category	Statistics	Cost Efficiency Ratios		Revenue Efficiency Ratios		Profit Efficiency Ratios	
		CTIR	NIER	NIM	OPIR	ROAA	ROAE
African CBs	N	10	10	10	10	10	10
	Mean	61.379	5.072	4.134	4.020	1.695	14.098
	Std. Deviation	25.082	3.191	2.854	4.095	2.968	20.475
	Maximum	102.687	12.345	8.835	13.448	9.907	69.197
	Minimum	25.878	1.228	1.198	0.380	−0.029	−1.754
African IBs	N	11	11	11	11	11	11
	Mean	62.148	5.986	4.208	5.270	0.713	11.306
	Std. Deviation	20.154	3.591	2.612	3.831	1.060	14.491
	Maximum	92.385	11.893	8.442	11.670	1.672	43.388
	Minimum	34.636	1.263	0.551	0.927	−1.820	−13.263
Asian CBs	N	9	9	9	9	9	9
	Mean	61.260	3.537	3.587	1.152	0.186	−2.745
	Std. Deviation	16.923	1.291	2.156	0.410	1.345	32.652
	Maximum	88.311	5.523	7.996	2.007	1.655	17.512
	Minimum	36.953	1.885	0.793	0.690	−3.049	−87.416
Asian IBs	N	10	10	10	10	10	10
	Mean	57.176	3.385	3.646	1.640	1.056	11.297
	Std. Deviation	23.784	2.264	2.216	0.904	1.059	11.026
	Maximum	93.473	8.761	8.148	3.405	3.303	33.730
	Minimum	25.410	1.760	1.720	0.425	−0.552	0.491
Middle East and Turkey CBs	N	18	18	18	18	18	18
	Mean	54.832	3.834	3.965	2.225	1.585	13.303
	Std. Deviation	18.662	4.455	3.186	3.613	1.317	6.165
	Maximum	98.278	19.550	15.360	16.156	5.855	25.545
	Minimum	32.178	0.745	1.130	0.457	−0.605	3.563
Middle East and Turkey IBs	N	22	22	22	22	22	22
	Mean	56.174	3.756	3.392	3.016	1.910	11.907
	Std. Deviation	20.064	3.004	2.155	3.677	1.645	13.334
	Maximum	105.486	14.925	8.177	14.340	6.010	33.293
	Minimum	24.093	1.095	−0.225	0.423	−0.590	−22.918
One-way ANOVA Sig.*	Between groups	0.91	0.37	0.95	0.053	0.09	0.23

Note: * Significance at 0.05 percent level.

5.0   CONCLUSION

This chapter aimed to address the public welfare issue of whether or not the newly-emergent Islamic banking based on risk-share–profit-share principles in financial transactions does have historical experience to warrant its further promotion. If this new niche banking is less efficient than the conventional banks, it raises the question as to whether its continued promotion is welfare-enhancing for societies being served by them. To do this we selected matched samples of banks from both types of banks operating in the same countries so that the factors affecting the two types of banks in the 16-year period are identical. This enables us to test if there are significant differences in the two groups' financial performance as measured by three pairs of financial ratios widely recognized as proven ratios in other studies. We subjected the tests to age, size and location differences to reveal consistent differences produced by age or size or country locations. The data set covers about 15,000 items of information collected mainly from the BankScope financial statements relating to 16 years prior to the onset of the 2008 world financial crisis. The maintained hypothesis is that there is no difference in financial performance of the two types of banks.

The results discussed and as confirmed by robust test statistics reveal that the two forms of banking appear to score just about the same values on all six financial ratios computed from data over the test period, despite testing for age and size as likely factors for differences in performance. That is, overwhelmingly, the two bank types appear to be similar in performance, although the return on equity of Islamic banks is consistently a modest 2 percentage points higher, but not enough to be accorded statistical significance to that difference. The only dimension on which the banks are different is on location. African banks appear to be more efficient than the Middle-Eastern, which in turn are yet more efficient than the Asian banks in some of the aspects of efficiency. To us, it is more to do with lack of competition and higher risk in countries that result in higher returns. These differences are not across the Islamic banks alone, but also across the conventional banks as well.

The conclusion we endorse is that this new form of banking after 45 years since its advent is a healthy alternative to the conventional banking for the clientele who want this ethics-based lending and wish to avoid banking on pre-fixed interest rates and the one-sided contract of not sharing in the risk of borrowers to earn returns on bank lending. That this similarity could be due to the careful design of Islamic banking with the same accounting and central bank oversights (in most cases) with an additional layer of supervision by the *Shari'ah* board is an alternative explanation. The strict regulatory regime perhaps injects an element of conservatism that may account for the Islamic banks not breaking into more risky banking practices and tending to be as conservative as the mainstream commercial banks that we included in our study. Also, the similarity may well be due to the desire of the Islamic banks at their early stage of growth over the 45 years not to pose a threat to the conventional banks, in order at a later stage to truly transform themselves by sharing more of the profits now going to the shareholders to the depositors. This is a likely explanation because Islamic banks have in recent years been criticized as trying to copy conventional bank practices with only cosmetic changes, and that these are not yet true profit-sharing banks. As more data become available in a few years, this study should be replicated to ensure that the conclusions are still valid for taking future policy initiatives.

NOTES

1. It is fascinating to note the impact of Luther's reform in the then Germanic nations, where the ban on interest-based lending slowly evaporated and that led to the Germanic people developing the modern banking practices before it spread to Holland even before the Catholic Church's ban on interest was lifted in 1752. Further, the so-called Islamic banking practice of not permitting interest-based lending actually existed in the pre-Islamic period. Islam's scriptural ban on usury as excessive interest was a heritage of humanity for a long time before the advent of Islam as is also verified in similar bans found in the world scriptures of Christianity and Hinduism as well as in the Torah of Jews. More broadly it was the norm of humanity to lend on risk-share and profit-share principles prior to the rise of modern banking about 200 years ago. There has been vehement opposition to fractional reserve modern banking as one that enables money to be created out of thin air.

2. The total assets of Islamic banks were just about equal to the total assets of the fourth largest bank in the world in 2006 (before the decline of bank assets due to the World Financial Crisis in 2008). At that time they represented less than 1 percent of the total assets of all banks in the world. This emphasizes the early stage growth potential of this new form of banking. Also, one should take into account that there is a group of clients who would not lend by imposing pre-fixed interest in financial transactions as they truly believe that such a form of financial transaction is sinful. Thus, this form of banking is a growing niche market to cater to the needs of this clientele. Common sense dictates that a large lender lending on the basis of profit-share is predictably better off than taking the interest in bank deposits, which are no bigger than inflation in most countries, including the developed ones: the 90-year history of the bank deposit rate in the US indicated that it is just about 0.5 percent higher than the inflation rate!

3. The august journal, the *Belgium Journal of Inquiry*, has an article that a politician has written giving the slant that Islamic banking is promoted by extremists.

4. The year 2002 is important in that after five years of careful study initiated by the renowned banker, Eddie George, the Bank of England changed the laws to permit the establishment of Islamic banks in the United Kingdom. Since then the speed at which regulators in other financial centres are approving applications to operate this new form of banking has doubled. More big banks are establishing units within conventional banks to enter this banking system.

5. One writer (Saleem, 2007) has called Islamic banks a 'scam' without any analytical evidence to back the claim.
6. Financial ratio analysis has been criticized in recent years as to whether it is a robust method in comparison with other methods such as the production efficiency measures (DEA; Malmquist; Stochastic Frontier; etc.). However, a vast body of literature exists based on financial ratio analysis and various laws also give recognition to this form of analysis as being recognised for public policy-making purposes. Besides, for comparison, it is a good method.
7. The average and across time measures of these ratios were calculated by the authors based on the BankScope database and definitions of these ratios.
8. The EM is a leverage factor. EM = Total Assets/Total Equity Capital. If a bank had no leverage (a pure equity bank), its ROAA and ROAE would be equal.
9. The CTIR ratio is given in a special graph because it has a very different scale. Although statistics are not included here, we find that these results based on financial ratios are bound to be similar using the DEA Malmquist measures of total factor productivity. The Islamic banks are more profit- and revenue-efficient in measures using production efficiency ratios. Those results are shown in a working paper presented in the 14th Global Finance Conference in 2007 in Melbourne: see Ariff et al. (2008) in the conference web site.
10. The one-way ANOVA tests rejected the hypotheses.
11. However, NIM ratio is part of the revenue efficiency measure. The one-way ANOVA tests suggest that there is no significant difference in the mean scores of the OPIR (the other revenue efficiency measure) in both banking streams based on their age.
12. Lower NIER means better cost efficiency in respect to interest expenses minimization.
13. As there is no significant difference in CTIR, the t-test also rejects the null hypothesis which claims that the 'overall' cost efficiency in old banks is significantly higher than new banks.
14. However, the NIM and ROAE do support the hypotheses that there are no significant differences in mean revenue and profit-efficiency scores between banks in the selected regions. This can be explained by the different inputs of NIM and OPIR ratios even though both are indicating revenue efficiency and the different inputs of ROAA and ROAE even though both are indicating profit efficiency. Perhaps, this limitation is among the weaknesses of financial ratio analysis in assessing efficiency. In frontier analysis, however, analysts do not face such a contradiction because cost efficiency, for example, is represented in one figure and cannot be in multiple figures as ratios.

REFERENCES

Ariff, M., M. Bader, M. Shamsher and Taufiq Hassan (2008), Cost, revenue, and profit efficiency of Islamic versus conventional banks: international evidence using data envelopment analysis, *Islamic Economic Studies*, 15 (2), 23–76.

Abdus-Samad (1999), Relative performance of conventional banking vis-à-vis Islamic banking in Malaysia, *IIUM Journal of Economics and Management*, 7 (1), 1–25.

Akkas, A. (1994), Relative efficiency of the conventional and Islamic banking systems in financing investment, Unpublished doctoral dissertation, Dhaka University, Bangladesh.

Allen, L. and A. Rai (1996), Operational efficiency in banking: an international comparison, *Journal of Banking and Finance*, 20 (4), 655–672.

Al-Shammari, S. (2003), Structure–conduct–performance and the efficiency of GCC banking markets, PhD thesis, University of Wales, Bangor, UK.

Bader, M., M. Ariff, M. Shamsher and H. Taufiq (2007), Cost, revenue, and profit efficiency of Islamic versus conventional banks: international evidence using data envelopment analysis, *Islamic Economics Studies*, 15 (2): 23–76.

Bashir, M. (2000), Risk and profitability measures in Islamic banks: the case of two Sudanese banks, *Islamic Economic Studies*, 6 (2), 1–24.

Berger, A.N. and D.B. Humphrey (1997), Efficiency of financial institutions: international survey and directions for future research, *European Journal of Operational Research*, 98, 175–212.

Brown, K. and M. Skully (2005), Islamic banks: a cross-country study of cost efficiency performance, accounting, commerce and finance, *The Islamic Perspective Journal*, 8 (1–2), 43–79.

Halkos, G.E. and D.S. Salamouris (2004), Efficiency measurement of the Greek commercial banks with the use of financial ratios: a data envelopment analysis approach, *Management Accounting Research*, 15 (2), 201–224.

Iqbal, M. and P. Molyneux (2005), *Thirty Years of Islamic Banking: History, Performance, and Prospects*, New York: Palgrave Macmillan.

Islam, M.M. (2003), Development and performance of domestic and foreign banks in GCC countries, *Managerial Finance*, 29 (2/3).

Kwan, S.H. (2006), The X-efficiency of commercial banks in Hong Kong, *Journal of Banking and Finance*, 30 (4), 1127–1147.

Maudos, J., J. Pastor, F. Perez and J. Quesada (2002), Cost and profit efficiency in European banks, *Journal of International Financial Markets Institutions and Money*, 12, 33–58.

Sabi, M. (1996), Comparative analysis of foreign and domestic bank operation in Hungary, *Journal of Comparative Economics*, 22, 179–188.

Saleem, M. (2007), *Islamic Banking: A $200 Million Scam*, No publisher mentioned in source Amazon.com.

APPENDIX: SUMMARY TABLE OF OUR ANALYSIS

Table 8A.1   Summary of financial ratios results

Banks	Cost Efficiency Ratios		Revenue Efficiency Ratios		Profit Efficiency Ratios	
Bank Category	CTIR	NIER	NIM	OPIR	ROAA	ROAE
All Banks	58.041	4.174	3.780	2.892	1.345	10.688
Conventional Banks (CBs)	58.165	4.097	3.919	2.449	1.274	9.614
Islamic Banks (IBs)	57.935	4.240	3.660	3.272	1.405	11.611
Big Banks	54.327	3.604	3.518	2.472	1.379	11.909
Small Banks	61.402	4.690	4.016	3.271	1.314	9.589
Big CBs	50.763	3.553	3.163	2.725	1.295	10.768
Big IBs	57.534	3.649	3.837	2.245	1.454	12.936
Small CBs	65.177	4.612	4.635	2.188	1.441	6.870
Small IBs	58.284	4.754	3.505	4.166	1.362	10.460
Old Banks	56.156	3.517	3.374	2.360	1.369	13.041
New Banks	61.184	5.268	4.456	3.778	1.304	6.765
Old CBs	55.993	3.502	3.232	2.451	1.309	13.476
Old IBs	56.347	3.535	3.541	2.254	1.439	12.531
New CBs	64.027	5.703	5.774	2.445	1.181	−0.812
New IBs	59.672	5.051	3.796	4.444	1.366	10.553
African Banks	61.782	5.550	4.173	4.675	1.181	12.635
Asian Banks	59.111	3.457	3.618	1.409	0.644	4.646
Middle East & Turkey (ME&T) Banks	55.570	3.791	3.650	2.660	1.763	12.535
African CBs	61.379	5.072	4.134	4.020	1.695	14.098
African IBs	62.148	5.986	4.208	5.270	0.713	11.306
Asian CBs	61.260	3.537	3.587	1.152	0.186	−2.745
Asian IBs	57.176	3.385	3.646	1.640	1.056	11.297
ME&T CBs	54.832	3.834	3.965	2.225	1.585	13.303
ME&T IBs	56.174	3.756	3.392	3.016	1.910	11.907

9. *Shari'ah*-consistent investment vehicles in Malaysia

Kabir Hassan and Eric Girard

1.0 INTRODUCTION

Islamic finance offers unique but alternative financial system based on religious doctrine. The industry has been growing tremendously at an average 15–17 per cent rate over the last years. Total asset value is expected to be $2.8 trillion in 2015 compared to $1.4 trillion in 2010 and only $700 billion in 2005 (IFSB Website 2005). Islamic finance is prevalent in all dimensions of financial services: debt and capital markets including mutual funds, insurance, asset management, structured and project financing and derivatives. The Islamic finance market is mainly concentrated in Islamic countries of the Middle East, North Africa and South-east Asia, but it is gaining popularity in non-Muslim and Muslim-minority countries such as the US, UK, and Europe and India.

Malaysia is the first Islamic country to have its own Islam-based stock exchange, the Bursa Malaysia Berhad. This subset of the country's main stock market was launched on March 18, 2005. The exchange lists equities, derivatives and offshore markets – but only those that adhere to Islamic tenets. For example, companies cannot actively seek revenues from interest income, gambling, life insurance, tobacco, or alcohol. In short, Malaysia has done what no other country has done – accommodated the tenets of Islamic law in its economy and its stock market by setting up separate listings. These companies allow the devout to invest with a conscience and help foster the Islamic economy.

This Malaysian system would not work in many other areas of the world. But it gives tens of millions of Muslim investors a unique solution to today's rapidly changing financial markets. There are over 1.5 billion Muslims in the world today, representing 24 percent of the world's population. Key developments like Malaysia's Bursa Berhad help to bring them into modern society while addressing their religious needs. The *Shari'ah* Index was launched in April 1999 to meet the demands from local and foreign investors who seek to invest in securities which are consistent with the Islamic principles of *Shari'ah.* Investors seeking to make investments based on *Shari'ah* principles now have a benchmark towards making better informed decisions. The *Shari'ah* Index is a weighted-average index with components comprising the securities from the Main Board which have been approved by the SAC. The index tracks the performance of these *Shari'ah*-approved securities and is regularly updated to reflect changes in the SAC's *Shari'ah*-approved list of companies.

Malaysia's Islamic investing sector is growing faster than any other Muslim countries. Its corporate world is finding Islamic modes of financing more and more appealing. Portfolio managers have a limited exposure to individual emerging stock markets – i.e., usually, investments in emerging markets are limited to a mere 20 percent of global portfolios and follow the weights of an emerging market index (Henry, 2000b). Within these broad divisions, the asset manager would usually be given discretion to allocate his or her portfolio among individual country and/or industry securities based on their risk, return and correlation characteristics. For portfolio investors, Malaysia provides a unique place for *Shari'ah*-compliant investing opportunity. This chapter seeks to provide in-depth understanding of the stock price discovery in the Malaysian stock market with specific focus on *Shari'ah*-compliant and non-*Shari'ah*-compliant stocks – i.e., accessibility, investment process, restrictions, liquidity, information discovery and risk–return generating process. Our study identifies the leading risk factors when investing in Malaysia and in its *Shari'ah* versus non-*Shari'ah* stock markets. As a result, it has important implications for pricing *Shari'ah*-compliant and non-*Shari'ah*-compliant equities, determining the cost of equity in Malaysia, and understanding the arguments for or against including Malaysia and its *Shari'ah*-compliant stock sector as a separate asset class within a global asset allocation strategy.

Specifically, this chapter investigates if there is a cost to Islamic investing by analyzing the difference in returns and risk exposure between Malaysian *Shari'ah*-consistent (S) and non-*Shari'ah*-consistent (NS) stocks. Our findings indicate that *Shari'ah*-consistent stocks return approximately the same as non-*Shari'ah*-consistent stocks. While we cannot find any difference in fundamental exposure between the two categories of stocks, we uncover significant differences in the way local and global risk factors affect each category of stocks.

2.0 THE FUNDAMENTALS OF ISLAMIC INVESTING

Islamic alternatives to traditional investment tools have been driven by the fact that such tools do not conform to the Islamic standards. There has been a growing desire to have funds in which profits are not based on *riba*, or interest, which is rejected in Islam. The Muslim faith deems that profit should come as a result of efforts; this is not the case in interest dominated investments. In addition, there is a desire for investment portfolios which are morally purified. Thus investments in companies that do not comply with Muslims' moral orientations are not permitted and are eliminated from the portfolio. To ensure compliance with the forgoing condition, Islamic mutual funds are governed by *Shari'ah* advisory boards whose role is mainly to give assurance that money is managed within the framework of Islamic laws (Hassan, 2001, 2002).

An Islamic mutual fund is similar to a 'conventional' mutual fund in many ways. However, unlike its 'conventional' counterpart, an Islamic mutual fund must conform to *Shari'ah* investment precepts. The *Shari'ah* encourages the use of profit-sharing and partnership schemes, and forbids *riba* (interest), *maysir* (gambling and pure games of chance) and *gharar* (selling something that is not owned or that cannot be described in accurate detail in terms of type, size and amount) (El-Gamal, 2000). The *Shari'ah* guidelines and principles govern several aspects of an Islamic mutual fund, including its asset allocation (portfolio screening), investment and trading practices, and income distribution (purification).

When selecting investments for their portfolio (asset allocation), conventional mutual funds can freely choose between debt-bearing investments and profit-bearing investments, and invest across the spectrum of all available industries. An Islamic mutual fund, however, must set up screens in order to select those companies that meet its qualitative and quantitative criteria set out by *Shari'ah* guidelines. Qualitative screens are used to filter out companies or securities based on *riba, maysir* or *gharar*, referenced earlier, or other business practices considered unethical by *Shari'ah* including, for example, selling alcohol, or engaging in biotechnology using aborted embryos and human cloning. Thus, excluded from Islamic-approved securities are fixed income instruments such as corporate bonds, treasury bonds and bills, certificates of deposit (CDs), preferred stocks, warrants and some derivatives (e.g., options), etc. Moreover, Islamic mutual funds cannot trade on margin; in other words, they cannot use interest-paying debt to finance their investments. They are also not permitted to engage in sale and repurchase agreements (i.e., repos or buy-backs). These transactions are considered akin to indirect interest charges.

The basis upon which an Islamic mutual fund operates must also be *Shari'ah*-compliant – i.e., its invested funds must be liberated from interest-based debt or speculation. Traditional funds that rely heavily on interest-based debt to finance their activities are not compliant with Islamic law. In addition, Islamic fund managers are not allowed to speculate. An Islamic economic unit is expected to assume risk after making a proper assessment of such risk with the help of information. Only in the absence of information or under conditions of uncertainty is speculation akin to a game of chance and considered reprehensible.

On another front, most scholars allow partially 'contaminated' earning income to be cleansed or purified. This means that investment can be made in stocks of companies with a tolerable (i.e., kept at a minimum proportion) amount of interest income or with tolerable revenues from unacceptable business activities if all 'impure' earnings are 'cleansed' by giving them away to designated charities. If, for example, the company has 8 percent interest-related income, then 8 percent of every dividend payment must be given away to 'purify' the fund earnings. Cleansing capital gains, however, remains debatable. Some scholars argue that this is not necessary since the change in the stock price does not really reflect interest, while others suggest that it is safer and more equitable to purify earnings made from selling shares as well. This purification process is done either by the fund manager before any distribution of income, or by reporting the necessary financial ratios for investors to purify their earnings on their own. Some researchers affirm that the fund ought to encompass a clear procedure and techniques of sorting out interest-based income and other sources of contaminated profits from the portfolio.

Another form of purification is *zakat*. *Zakat* is a form of charity paid on personal wealth (exceeding a minimum amount called *nisab*) held idle for one lunar year. The rate of *zakat* differs with the type of the asset, 2.5 percent being the rate on most forms of monetary wealth and earned income. *Zakat* calculation on investment profits, however, is still controversial. In addition, such calculation is complicated given the intricacies of the timing of the portfolio incomes and capital gains. Recipients of *zakat* are clearly identified in Islamic jurisprudence and include charities and other bodies identified by the funds' supervisory boards.

In addition to the above principles, other pillars have been identified in the literature as promoting socially responsible business practices. Shareholder advocacy refers to the mechanism of involving shareholders in positively influencing corporate behavior. Shareholders in the Islamic environment are not merely concerned with higher returns on their investment, but they also have a proactive role given their position as corporate owners. Constant monitoring and timely reporting are also needed to ensure that the companies included in the portfolio continuously meet the guidelines for Islamic investing. Often company shares are dropped from a certain fund after information about a violation is reported.

3.0 LITERATURE REVIEW OF ISLAMIC INVESTING

Kreander et al. (2000) analyze 40 SRI funds from seven countries using a matching approach. The countries included are Belgium (1), Germany (4), the Netherlands (2), Norway (2), Sweden (11), Switzerland (2) and the UK (18). The authors apply four criteria for the matching procedure: age, size, country and investment universe of the fund. Like most of the earlier studies, they use Jensen's alpha, the Sharpe ratio and the Treynor ratio as performance measures. In the regression equation for Jensen's alpha a measure for market timing is included. As market timing of the fund management can significantly bias the estimation of Jensen's alpha this is an important improvement compared to earlier studies. The statistical tests concerning the differences in the performance measures show that the Sharpe and Treynor ratios of the conventional funds are slightly higher but not significant whereas the Jensen's alpha of the SRI funds is higher but only at the 10 percent significance level. The authors conclude that SRI and conventional funds exhibit a very similar performance.

Cointegration test and Jobson-Korkie significance test of performance from 1986:1 to 1995:12 using US data revealed interesting results. After testing for stationarity of the data, the cointegration test was performed to investigate the long-term relationship between the socially responsible funds and their peers. The results conclude that there is no cointegration between the funds which indicates that the process of screening tends to isolate the socially responsible funds' behavior from their peers. Furthermore, the Sharpe ratio is higher for the 11 peer funds; however, for the Jobson-Korkie test, statistics of the null hypotheses of equality between peer and socially responsible funds could not be rejected, implying that the performance of both funds is equal.

Bello (2005) investigates empirically the extent to which the ethical and moral screening of companies affects the level of diversification and overall performance of socially responsible stock mutual funds. He uses 42 socially responsible funds with 84 conventional funds and returns on the S&P 500, three-month Treasury bills, and monthly return data on the DSI 400 as benchmarks for both socially and non-socially responsible assets. Applying the two-sample Wilcoxon rank-sum test, Jensen's alpha, Sharpe ratio and excess standard deviation adjusted return, he finds the following. Socially responsible funds are not significantly different from conventional funds for alpha and eSDAR. Conventional funds significantly underperform their socially responsible peers for Sharpe ratio, portfolio diversification represented by residual variance shows the two groups of funds are not significantly different, and there is no significant correlation between alpha and residual variance for each of the two groups of funds or for the combined sample.

Bauer et al. (2005), in their study aimed first, to investigate whether there is evidence on the difference in performance between ethical compared to non-ethical investment, and second, to examine the claims that ethical investment is small-cap oriented. In their paper, they utilize the four factor model for both domestic and international investments for ethical versus non-ethical mutual funds from 1992:11 to 2003:4 in Australia. In addition, they examine the data against home bias and time sensitivity by dividing the data into three periods. They conclude that there is no statistically significant difference in return between ethical and conventional mutual funds both domestically and internationally. Ethical domestic investment is small-cap oriented and in general, ethical investment has less exposure to the market than conventional funds. There is strong evidence of home bias for international ethical funds. The ethical funds underperformed in the market due to the overall sentiment of a bearish market in the first period, while in the second period they outperformed the conventional funds; moreover, for the last period there was no significant difference. The study concludes that there is no penalty for ethical investors.

Geczm et al. (2003), tested whether investing in socially responsible investment cost more than investing in their counterpart using CAPM and the Fama-French three-factor model and Carhart four-factor model. They constructed their own fund running from July 1963 through December 2001 on a monthly basis. The results indicate that when investors use CAPM as their choice of asset ignoring managerial skill it costs as little as 1 to 2 basis points. On the other hand, using Fama-French and Carhart models or inculcating managerial skills the investment in socially responsible investment will be significantly costlier and reach 30 basis points.

The literature on Islamic investing, a subset of ethical investing, is still at its infancy. The following articles best describe the stage of current research on faith-based Islamic investing. Ahmed and Ibrahim (2002) investigate the performance of KLSI (Islamically approved securities) with comparison to KLCI (conventional) for the period 1999–2002. They use various methodologies to investigate the performance measured by risk and return of both indexes. The techniques used are adjusted Sharpe ratio, Treynor Index, adjusted Jensen Alpha and t-test for comparing means. They divide the sample into three periods: overall, growing from 1999:4 to 2000:2 and declining from 2000:3 to 2002:1. In comparing raw returns and risk for all the periods they conclude that for the overall and declining periods the return is low for KLSI while for the growing period KLSI slightly outperforms the market. For risk, KLCI is riskier for all the periods. When comparing the means the results were statistically insignificant for all the periods. In addition, using different measures of risk adjusted return only in the growing periods KLSI appears to be higher than KLCI. They argue that the underperformance of the KLSI might be because the market is dominated by non-Muslims as well as the lower existence of Muslim investment in *Shari'ah*-approved securities. Moreover, it can be said that the shortness of the period could be a reason for such results.

Hassan (2002) empirically examines the issues of market efficiency and the time-varying risk–return relationship for the Dow Jones Islamic Market index (DJIM) over the 1996–2000 period. His paper employs serial correlation, variance ratio and Dickey Fuller tests to examine the market efficiency of the DJIM. The results show that DJIM returns are normally distributed and the returns show that DJIM returns are efficient. The paper also examines calendar anomalies of the DJIM. The results show that there is no turn-of-calendar-year, turn-of-financial-year or month effect on DJIM returns. Utilizing a GARCH framework, the paper examines volatility of the DJIM returns and finds a significant positive relationship between conditional volatility and DJIM equity index returns.

Hakim and Rashidian (2004a) employ a co-integration and causality analysis to examine the relationship between the DJIM, Wilshire 5000 Index and the risk-free rate proxied by the three month Treasury bill over the time period 1999–2002. They find no correlation between the DJIM and the Wilshire 5000 Index, or the three month Treasury bill. The results also show that the changes in the DJIM are not caused by either the Wilshire 5000 Index or the three month Treasury bill. They conclude that the filtering criteria adopted to eliminate non-compliant firms leads to an Islamic index with unique risk–return characteristics unaffected by the broad equity market. Hakim and Rashidian (2004b) use a capital asset pricing model (CAPM) to examine to what extent a *Shari'ah*-compliant index is correlated with the Dow Jones World Index (DJW) and Dow Jones Sustainability World Index (DJS) or green index. Their results show that the DJIM has done relatively well compared to the DJW, but has underperformed in relation to the DJS.

Hussein and Omran (2005) study the performance Islamic index in Dow Jones against the Dow Jones index in three periods, namely, the entire period, bull period and the bear period. They perform few analytical and statistical techniques to calculate the risk adjusted return for monthly data from 1995:12 to 2003:6. They use raw return, Sharpe ratio, Jensen Alpha and Treynor risk adjusted formulas, while they use parametric t-statistics and non-parametric Wilcoxson signed-rank test to test whether the Islamic index has abnormal return. Moreover, they apply cumulative abnormal return and buy-and-hold abnormal returns to investigate the long-run performance of the indexes as well as the wealth relative as a performance measure. The results suggest that the Islamic index outperformed the non-Islamic index both in the entire and bull periods while the opposite is true for the bear period although it was not statistically significant in the bear period. In addition the wealth relative indicates that $1 invested in both the whole and bull periods will yield $1.16 and $1.27 respectively, while it will yield $0.9 in the bear period. The main reasons pointed out for the outperforming and underperforming are twofold. First, the most profitable firms borrow the least; this is true since it is one of the screening methods of DJIM to exclude companies with more than 33 percent of debt. Second, the events of September 11 might cause Islamic investment to be less popular and also the exclusion of alcoholic firms from the Islamic index, since they are among the best performers during the bear market period.

Elfakhani et al. (2005) examine Islamic mutual funds and the fundamentals of investing in such venues. They explore the dynamics of Islamic mutual funds, their governance and control, and marketing and distribution. They present the results of a study verifying whether the application of the Islamic investment guidelines in asset allocation and portfolio selection has had a downside effect on investors' wealth in terms of risk-adjusted returns relative to the market benchmark. Considering the overall sample of 46 Islamic mutual funds, the total number of outperforming funds ranges between 29 funds (63 percent of the sample) and 11 funds (24 percent), depending on the used performance measure and market benchmark. In terms of fund category, four of the eight fund categories outperform their benchmarks regardless of what performance measure is used. Moreover, the ANOVA statistical test shows that no statistically significant disparity exists for the performance of the funds compared to all used indexes. Therefore, a conclusion of their study is that the behavior of Islamic mutual funds does not differ from that of other conventional funds, with some *Shari'ah* compliant mutual funds outperforming their benchmarks and others underperforming them.

Hassan et al. (2005) use the Treynor-Mazury (TM) model to measure the security-selection ability and market-timing ability of Islamic mutual fund managers. Their results show that the American Equity Fund, the European Equity Fund, the combined Emerging Fund and the Technology Fund all have positive security selection, but only the Emerging Equity Fund has positive selectivity that is statistically significant. The remaining three funds (i.e., Global, Asian and Malaysian funds) have negative selectivity performance during the same period. This is not so surprising as the results may be dominated by the Asian crisis, while Western funds are less affected during the same sampling period. In particular, the Asian Equity Fund performs very badly as the intercept is statistically and significantly negative at the 1 percent level. However, other results show that the Asian Equity Fund has a significant positive market timing performance; all remaining funds have negative market timing performance, particularly the European and the combined Emerging Funds that are statistically significant at the 5 percent level. This observation is confirmed by the negative correlations reported in the table except for the Asian fund.

Hassan and Tag el-din (2005) adapt duration dependence tests to analyze Islamic mutual funds of the DJIM. The fundamental idea of the tests comes from survival analysis frequently used by engineers and biostatisticians. According to the theoretical rational speculative bubbles model, if bubbles do not exist, runs of positive excess returns should not display the duration dependence. To render this implication testable, returns are transformed into series on positive and negative observed excess returns. Then, the authors examine the probability that a run – a sequence of observations of the same sign – of positive excess return ends has positive dependence or negative hazard function with the length of the run. This approach is reliable and robust since duration dependence is not affected by fundamental price movements and is more unique to bubbles unlike the traditional measures of detecting bubbles such as autocorrelation, skewness or kurtosis. They use both weekly and monthly data of the DJIM and the American Stock Exchange (AMANX and AMAGX) to test for the speculative bubbles in these markets. Their results show that none of the weekly and monthly returns of AMANX, AMAGX and the DJIM show statistically significant evidence of speculative bubbles during our sample periods.

Girard and Hassan (2009) examine FTSE indices using data from January 1999 to December 2006. Their findings suggest that the behavior of FTSE Islamic indices does not differ from that of their conventional counterparts, with some indices outperforming their conventional counterparts and others underperforming them. Overall, similar reward to risk and diversification benefits exist for both types of index. Controlling performance for style and time variability, they find that Islamic indices are growth focused and conventional indices are value focused. After controlling for market risk, size, book-to-market, momentum, local and global factors, they conclude that the difference in return between Islamic and conventional indices is not significant. Their findings suggest that the difference in performance of Islamic indices as compared to conventional indices is attributed to style differences between the two types of series. The multivariate cointegration analysis suggests that both the Islamic and conventional groups are integrated for the overall period.

4.0 DATA AND EMPIRICAL ANALYSIS

Our study of the Malaysian market starts in 1999:01 with the creation of the *Shari'ah* Index and ends in 2006:12. Monthly US dollar MSCI world index prices, local index prices, and US T-bill returns are retrieved from Datastream. US dollar-denominated stock prices, market value, book-to-price ratio, value traded and investability weighs are obtained from the Emerging Markets Database and cross-checked with Datastream. Economic, financial and political data are obtained from the International Country Risk Guide.

4.1 Economic Performance, Equity Returns and Global Allocation Implications

We first compare the macroeconomic characteristics of the Malaysian economy with those of the USA. As shown in panel A of Table 9.1, Malaysia's economy expanded at 5.32 percent over the past five years, more than 2 percent above the US economy. The growth of the Malaysian economy has been fueled by the increase of foreign money into the Malaysian economy – i.e., the ratio of foreign debt to GDP is well above 40 percent, and foreign direct investment in Malaysia reached $5.7 billion in 2006, a 12 percent increase from 2005. Malaysia's current account surplus is approximately 8.76 percent of GDP, the US current account deficit exceeds 5 percent of GDP. Thus, Malaysia's income has been increasingly greater than its spending – i.e., the nation is producing more goods, services and construction than its residents have purchased – and the difference was purchased by foreigners. The Exchange Rate Stability figures show the appreciation or depreciation of a currency against the US dollar (against the Euro in the case of the US). Since Malaysia pegged the ringgit to the US dollar until the end of 2006, this is shown by the figures in Table 9.1 which provide evidence that the ringgit has stayed at par with the US dollar since 1999.

Given the increase in export productivity, and the reserve accumulation (the liquidity ratios for Malaysia are 5 to 6 times greater than those of the USA), Malaysia should be facing inflationary pressures. So far, Malaysia is able to control inflation pressures through administrative controls on interest rates and the exchange rate – the inflation rate (2.3 percent per annum from 2002 to 2006) is lower than the US inflation rate. The newly floating currency will certainly put inflationary pressures on the Malaysian economy.

Finally, the Malaysian stock market has cumulated 11.13 percent from 1999 to the end of 2002, and 33.71 percent from 2003 to 2006. These figures

Table 9.1   Macro statistics

Panel A: Return and economic performance

	Malaysia		United States	
	1999–2002	2003–2006	1999–2002	2003–2006
Buy-and-Hold Return (%)	11.13	33.79	−38.70	50.30
Budget Balance as % GDP	−3.27	−4.25	0.78	−3.22
Current Account as % of GDP	7.35	8.76	−3.55	−5.58
Current Account as % of SGX (Singapore Exchange)	6.97	7.01	−25.69	−43.20
Debt Service Ratio	7.41	5.26	25.99	20.98
Exchange Rate Stability	0.80	0.81	−3.09	−7.71
GDP per Head of Population	$3,850.15	$4,640.60	$34,536.79	$39,102.17
Real GDP Growth	4.90	5.32	3.03	3.26
Inflation	2.32	2.27	2.59	2.72
International Liquidity	5.79	6.29	0.83	0.68
Total Foreign Debt as % GDP	48.59	44.31	9.44	34.89

Panel B: Risk ratings

	Malaysia		United States	
	1999–2002	2003–2006	1999–2002	2003–2006
Composite Risk Rating	74.99	78.78	81.30	76.10
Economic Risk Rating	39.79	40.96	40.85	38.66
Real Annual GDP Growth	7.89	9.40	7.95	8.41
GDP per Head of Population	2.31	2.27	4.97	5.00
Annual Inflation Rate	9.33	9.48	9.43	9.42
Budget Balance as a Percentage of GDP	6.21	5.44	8.13	6.05
Current Account Balance as a Percentage of GDP	14.05	14.38	10.39	9.78
Financial Risk Rating	41.40	41.52	35.54	32.24
Current Account as a Percentage of SGX*	13.04	12.85	9.73	7.95
Foreign Debt Service as a Percentage of SGX*	9.50	9.74	7.00	7.67
Exchange Rate Stability	9.98	10.00	8.81	8.93
Foreign Debt as a Percentage of GDP	5.55	5.77	9.50	7.20
Net Liquidity as Months of Import Cover	3.32	3.16	0.50	0.50

Table 9.1   (continued)

	Malaysia		United States	
	1999–2002	2003–2006	1999–2002	2003–2006
Political Risk Rating	68.75	75.02	86.16	81.25
Government Stability	10.27	10.34	10.79	9.34
Socioeconomic Conditions	6.73	9.03	9.92	8.44
Investment Profile	7.64	8.90	11.01	11.69
Internal Conflict	9.72	10.48	10.72	10.29
External Conflict	10.25	10.43	7.90	7.65
Corruption	2.79	2.45	4.00	4.46
Military in Politics	5.00	5.00	5.67	4.29
Religious Tensions	4.00	4.00	5.61	5.27
Law & Order	3.08	3.67	5.90	5.00
Ethnic Tensions	4.00	4.00	4.90	5.00
Democratic Accountability	2.27	3.73	5.58	5.82
Bureaucracy Quality	3.00	3.00	4.00	4.00

* Statistically different.

are in line with its economic performance. For instance, the US economy has grown on average at a real rate of 3 percent from 1999 to 2006, which is approximately half the growth in the Malaysian economy. In addition, a dollar invested in the US market in 1999 would have returned about half the dollar invested in the Malaysian market in 2006.

If we take a closer look at the composite, economic, financial and political ICRG composite rating, we find that Malaysia's overall composite, economic, financial and political risk ratings have improved throughout the 1999–2006 period (Table 9.1, panel B). Furthermore, Malaysia's economic (with the exception of poverty measured by GDP per Head of Population) and financial ratings are higher than those of the US. However, political risk remains much lower than those of the US. For instance, panel B shows that, as compared to the US, Malaysia is still plagued by issues of corruption, religious and ethnic tensions, lack of rule of law, poor democratic accountability and low bureaucracy quality.

We further investigate if Malaysia can be considered as individual asset classes. Further, we differentiate in our investigation between *Shari'ah*-consistent (S, thereafter) and non-*Shari'ah*-consistent (NS, thereafter) securities. Portfolio managers have a limited exposure to individual emerging stock markets – i.e., usually, investments in emerging markets are limited to a mere 20 percent of global portfolios and follow the weights of an emerging market index (Henry, 2000a). Within these broad divisions, the asset manager would usually be given discretion to allocate his or her portfolio among individual country and/or industry securities based on their risk, return and correlation characteristics.

Table 9.2 shows the monthly returns and risks for Malaysia, Malaysia S, Malaysia NS, and eight commonly followed indexes – MSCI USA, IFCG Asia, IFCG Europe, IFCG MEA, IFCG Latin America, IFCG Emerging Composite, MSCI EAFE, and the MSCI WORLD indices. First, the familiar pattern of higher emerging market returns (means) and high risks (standard deviations) compared to the developed countries indices (USA, EAFE) is evident. Second, along with fairly impressive returns over the past eight years, Malaysia's stock market also demonstrated exceptionally higher volatility as compared to the developed countries Indices (USA, EAFE).

However, while individual returns and risks are clearly important for international portfolio allocation, key additional ingredients are the correlations among country returns. We report the (monthly) return correlation relationships based on US dollar adjusted returns in colums 7 to 9 in Table 9.2. We can see that S and NS series are strongly correlated with each other (0.97) and weakly correlated with other emerging markets (0.40 and 0.39, respectively) as well as with developed markets (0.39 and 0.34, respectively). Thus, it seems that fund managers still have an ability to achieve 'gross' diversification gains by including the Malaysian market in a global strategic allocation portfolio.

The effect of the low correlations on the potential gains from simple country-by-country diversification is shown in Figure 9.1. Figure 9.1 compares the efficient mean–variance of returns frontier, based on monthly country index returns, for the 1999–2006 period with the inclusion of Malaysia S, Malaysia NS and without Malaysia; the other asset classes are EM Asia, EM Europe, EM Latin America, EM MEA, MSCI USA and MSCI EAFE. It can be seen that gains from including Malaysia in a country-by-country diversification are present during the 1999–2006 period. Further, the S series provides more reward to risk than the NS series.

4.2   Firm Characteristics

4.2.1   *Shari'ah*-consistent (S) and non-*Shari'ah*-consistent (NS) stocks
In Table 9.3, we provide information on descriptive Malaysian market and firm statistics (the number of stocks included in EMDB, the number of deletions, investability,[1] market and firms size, liquidity, returns and standard deviation, betas,[2] and multiples). We retrieve our firm data from the Emerging Market Data Bank (EMDB).[3] We select all investable and

Table 9.2   Markets statistics (1999–2006)

	No. of companies	Median Size (Billions)	Median Monthly Value Traded (Billions)**	Return (%)	Std Dev. (%)	Cor. between Mal. Series	Cor. with Em. Mkts	Cor. with Dev. Mkts	PE	PB	DY (%)
Malaysia All Stocks	243	$103.5	$2.7	0.91	9.21	n/a	0.38	0.35	13.30	2.14	1.80
Malaysia (Shari'ah-compliant stocks)	85	$40.0	$0.9	0.98	9.41	0.97	0.40	0.39	15.01	1.86	1.74
Malaysia (non-Shari'ah-compliant stocks)	158	$63.5	$1.8	0.86	9.14	0.97	0.38	0.34	11.65	2.36	1.84
IFCG Asia (excluding Malaysia)*	996	$683.1	$98.5	0.39	6.76	n/a	0.60	0.65	77.74	2.08	1.68
IFCG Europe*	194	$157.0	$16.9	1.84	9.10	n/a	0.48	0.51	17.08	1.71	1.88
IFCG Middle East and Africa*	333	$235.6	$23.2	0.86	5.89	n/a	0.42	0.53	16.91	2.58	3.08
IFCG Latin America*	286	$257.1	$11.3	1.19	8.34	n/a	0.55	0.77	15.55	1.43	3.19
IFCG Composite*	1755	$1,273.8	$142.8	0.76	6.18	n/a	1	0.54	21.29	1.84	2.18
MSCI USA	n/a	>$10,000	n/a	0.70	4.12	n/a	0.52	0.82	16.30	2.10	3.10
MSCI EAFE	n/a	>$10,000	n/a	0.45	4.18	n/a	0.57	0.82	n/a	n/a	n/a
MSCI WORLD	n/a	>$30,000	n/a	0.56	3.91	n/a	0.54	1	n/a	n/a	n/a

Notes: *IFCG and MSCI consist of at least 60% of the total market capitalization and liquidity of the stocks traded in the country/region.
** Median per month and per company.
PE = price earnings; PB = price to book ratio; DY = dividend yield; IFC = International Finance Corporation; MSCI = Morgan Stanley Composite Index; EAFE = East Asia and the Far East.

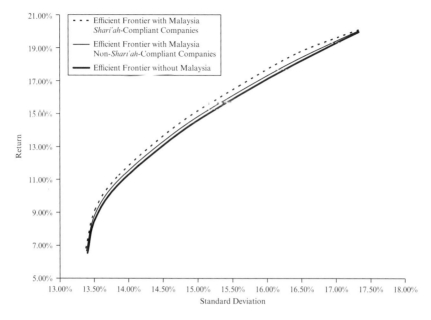

Figure 9.1   Efficient frontiers (1999–2006)

non-investable firms traded in China from 1999:01 until 2006:12. We use the US dollar as the standard to make the average returns comparable across market segments.[4] Stocks are included in our sample as they become available and delisted stocks are also included for the period during which they were traded. Not all firms are retained in the final sample. The deciding criterion for retention is that stock return series must have at least two years of data. Data imperfections such as missing values and recording errors are handled by dropping the firm for the particular month of data imperfection but retaining it as part of the sample.

Our sample consists of the 220 largest and most liquid stocks traded in Malaysia – i.e., a maximum of 22 non-investable and 198 investable companies traded from 1999 to 2006. Out of these 220 companies, 53 were delisted during that period. Finally, out of the 220 companies, 72 are S and 148 are NS. If Malaysian investability weight averages about 50 percent, S stock are more investable than NS stocks. Our sample consists of more than 70 percent of the total capitalization and liquidity (measured by the value traded) of the Malaysian stock market.

The buy-and-hold return (geometric return) is higher for S stock versus NS stocks (78.39 percent for S stocks, and 48.67 percent for NS stocks). Additionally S stocks are slightly more risky, measured by the standard

Table 9.3   Malaysian equity market characteristics

	Descriptive	*Shari'ah* Companies	Non-*Shari'ah* Companies
General	Median Number of Stocks Traded in the Malaysian Stock Markets	876	
	Median Number of Stocks available in the Malaysian EMDB Universe	243	
	Number of Stocks Retained	72	148
	Number of New Stocks	36	71
	Number of Stocks Delisted	32	21
	Number of Investable Malaysian Stocks (Investable weight>0)	66	132
	Number of Non-Investable Malaysian Stocks (Investable weight=0)	6	16
	Median Investable Weight (%)	53.5	48.0
Returns (%)	Average Monthly Return for Malaysian Stocks ($US)	0.98	0.86
	Cumulated Return for Malaysian Stocks ($US)	88.59	77.55
	Buy-and-Hold Return for Malaysian Stocks ($US)	78.39	48.67
	Monthly Standard Deviation of Malaysian Stocks' Returns	9.41	9.14
	Average Monthly Return for the MSCI 'FREE' WORLD Index ($US)	0.58	
	Cumulated Return for the MSCI 'FREE' WORLD Index ($US)	14.54	
	Buy-and-Hold Return for the MSCI 'FREE' WORLD Index ($US)	7.30	
	Monthly Standard Deviation of MSCI 'FREE' WORLD Index's Return	4.17	
	Average Monthly 90-days Treasury Bill Return	0.26	
	Cumulated Return for the 90-days Treasury Bill	23.42	
	Buy-and-Hold Return for the 90-days Treasury Bill	26.34	
Betas	Median Local Beta (relative to IFCG Malaysia)	1.15	1.31
	Maximum Local Beta	2.20	3.17
	Minimum Local Beta	0.32	0.15

Table 9.3   (continued)

	Descriptive	*Shari'ah* Companies	Non-*Shari'ah* Companies
Betas	Median Global Beta (relative to MSCI World)	1.15	1.20
	Maximum Global Beta	2.35	2.89
	Minimum Global Beta	−0.01	−0.04
Size	Median M. Cap. Of the Malaysian Market ($\times 10^6$)	$152,517.73	
	Median M. Cap. Of the Malaysian EMDB Sample ($\times 10^6$)	$103,454.50	
	Median M. Cap. For Malaysian Companies Traded in EMDB ($\times 10^6$)	$612.91	$1,125.40
Multiples	Median PE for all Stocks Traded in the Malaysian Stock Markets	20.24	
	Median PE for all Stocks Traded in the Malaysian EMDB Universe	13.30	
	Median Price to Earnings Multiple	15.01	11.65
	Median PB for all Stocks Traded in the Malaysian Stock Markets	n.a.	
	Median PB for all Stocks Traded in the Malaysian EMDB Universe	2.14	
	Median Price to Book Multiple	1.86	2.36
Liquidity	Median Monthly Value Traded in the Stock Markets ($\times 10^6$)	$3,966.20	
	Median Market Capitalization of the EMDB Sample ($\times 10^6$)	$2,702.43	
	Median Value Traded in the EMDB Universe per company ($\times 10^6$)	$12.46	$21.75
Dividend Yield (%)	Median DY for all Stocks Traded in the Malaysian Stock Markets	1.76	
	Median DY for all Stocks Traded in the Malaysian EMDB Universe	1.80	
	Median Dividend Yield	1.74	1.84

deviation, than NS stocks. However, S stocks have slightly lower (local and global) betas than NS stocks. Interestingly, NS stocks are larger and more of the growth type than S stocks – i.e., the median monthly market capitalization is $1,125 ($612.91) billion for NS (S) stock and PB is 2.36 (186) for NS (S) stocks.

In sum, the Malaysian market shows similar patterns to other emerging markets – i.e., higher market returns from 1999 to 2006, higher risk measured by the standard deviations of returns. These higher standard deviation figures are associated with puzzling features. Firstly, multiples and dividend yields are somewhat in the same vein as what is observed in the US (the median PEs and PBs are around 13.3× and 2.14×, respectively; the dividend yield is slightly less than 2 percent); second, the return differential between S and NS stocks cannot be totally explained by their exposure to value and size. Indeed, we established that during the 1999–2006 period, large value stocks significantly outperformed small growth stock. Since NS are larger than S stocks, NS stocks should return more than S stocks.

Since *Shari'ah* screens exclude companies from particular industries, we narrow our description of the Malaysian market by reporting descriptive statistics by economic sector in Table 9.4. NS and S stocks have very different risk/return inter- and intra-sector performance (−0.94 to 2.64 percent returns, and 6.1 to 19.08 percent standard deviations). In addition, S stocks have their largest concentration in industrials – a sector with smaller stocks and high multiples; while NS stocks have their largest concentration in financials – a sector characterized by larger companies, low multiples, high value traded and higher beta. The last two columns of Table 9.5 show the coefficients and standard error of the follow regression:

$$RP_i = \sum_{n=1}^{10} \beta_i D_i + \varepsilon_i \qquad (9.1)$$

where RP_i are the risk premia for each stock and D_i are dummy variables for each sector the stocks belong to. The β_i indicate the impact of a sector on the return of S and NS stock series. For instance, S stocks series are significantly affected by the stocks belonging to consumer staples, industrials, telecommunication services and utilities; NS stock series are significantly dependent on the stocks making the consumer discretionary, financial, industrial and utilities sectors. In sum, it is quite evident that the difference in performance between S and NS stock series is narrowly related to the difference in sector allocation.

4.2.2 Fundamental risk premiums

We investigate the sign and significance of five well-established firm-specific risk factors – i.e., fundamental risk premiums. For this, we use all stocks traded in Malaysia from 1999:01 to 2006:12 and proceed by carefully following the methodology described in Rouwenhorst (1999). That is, at the beginning of each month, stocks with available ranking information are sorted into three portfolios (top 30 percent, middle 40 percent,

Table 9.4 Shari'ah *and non-*Shari'ah *stocks statistics by economic sector*

Sector		No. of Stocks	Weight (%)	Ret (%)	Std Dev (%)	Size	VT	PE	PBV	IW (%)	Beta L	Beta W	β (sector influence)	Std. error
Cons. D.	NS	26	17.57	0.95	13.90	773.25	19.81	28.70	1.74	51.26	1.16	1.01	0.009539	0.003762
	S	6	8.33	0.30	10.17	532.53	10.82	15.49	1.69	33.20	1.05	0.88	0.002996	0.006947
Cons. S.	NS	9	6.08	-0.05	11.07	917.74	14.95	31.47	7.32	36.03	1.05	0.95	0.000474	0.006044
	S	12	16.67	1.80	8.65	951.01	16.72	14.18	2.78	49.57	0.77	0.77	0.018001	0.003428
Energy	NS	4	2.70	1.35	12.96	291.24	10.76	18.29	2.93	29.15	1.63	1.86	0.013538	0.014496
	S	2	2.78	0.15	6.10	695.24	4.76	9.51	1.73	52.93	0.56	0.07	0.001479	0.009102
Financial	NS	45	30.41	1.34	14.31	1072.79	23.45	0.01	1.37	52.73	1.48	1.41	0.013427	0.003162
	S	12	16.67	0.05	14.71	245.89	5.94	11.08	0.86	59.71	1.34	1.29	0.000512	0.007207
Health C.	NS	3	2.03	1.97	19.08	122.43	4.35	4.38	3.09	73.38	1.69	1.48	0.019710	0.023686
	S	0	0											
Industrials	NS	29	19.59	1.19	16.44	930.96	16.75	8.40	3.59	49.41	1.40	1.16	0.011912	0.004634
	S	26	36.11	1.52	16.57	337.25	14.04	14.98	1.41	67.26	1.45	1.41	0.005196	0.005024
Inf. Tech.	NS	6	4.05	-0.94	14.89	176.00	8.71	50.69	1.78	55.11	1.53	1.48	0.009393	0.012291
	S	3	4.17	0.45	15.93	613.87	16.72	17.94	3.29	60.17	1.22	1.73	0.004485	0.013783
Materials	NS	17	11.49	0.19	17.03	108.06	4.70	4.09	0.97	59.18	1.24	1.36	0.001941	0.007739
	S	7	9.72	0.56	16.57	316.36	3.47	22.89	1.99	50.52	1.04	1.21	0.005647	0.007917
Tel. Serv.	NS	4	2.70	1.52	14.29	5095.76	88.69	13.33	2.85	41.49	1.33	1.23	0.015181	0.010518
	S	1	1.39	2.64	10.26	1096.95	23.59	20.51	2.74	33.48	1.06	0.99	0.026439	0.014381
Utilities	NS	5	3.38	0.99	9.41	2810.08	37.16	19.26	1.74	41.50	1.00	0.92	0.009881	0.004545
	S	3	4.17	0.88	6.61	1976.42	19.40	16.47	2.00	43.58	0.86	0.93	0.008828	0.004405

Table 9.5   Fama and French factors in Malaysia

Data	Average (%)	Standard Error	t-stat
Low Local Beta	1.092		
High Local Beta	0.758		
HML Local Beta	−0.335	0.0089	−0.375
Low Global Beta	0.999		
High Global Beta	0.822		
HML (Global Beta)	−0.177	0.0085	−0.210
Small	−0.373		
Big	1.768		
SMB	−2.142	0.0067	−3.211**
Growth	−0.305		
Value	1.734		
HML_BP	2.039	0.0053	3.850**
Loser	0.616		
Winner	1.136		
WML	0.520	0.0055	0.953

**Significant at 0.05 level.

bottom 30 percent) based on local beta, global beta, the natural logarithm of market value measured in US dollars, and the book-to-price ratio. For each sorting and within each group, returns of these stocks are then averaged. The difference between the top and bottom local beta-sorted portfolios provides a 'local beta premium', the difference between the top and bottom global beta-sorted portfolios provides a 'global beta premium', the difference between the bottom and top size-sorted portfolios provides a size premium, and the difference between the top and the bottom book-to-price portfolios provides a value premium.

Finally, momentum portfolios are formed by sorting all stocks with available information at the beginning of each month on prior six month returns ('month −7' to 'month −2'). The top and bottom 5 percent are eliminated, the remaining are ranked into three portfolios (high 30 percent, middle 40 percent, bottom 30 percent) and returns are averaged within each group. The difference between the top tier (winners) and the bottom tier (losers) provides a monthly momentum premium.

In Table 9.5, we report the value of each premium for the overall period. Local and global beta premia are negative, indicating that high (local or global) beta stocks underperform low beta stocks from 1999 to 2006.

Although not significant, this negative difference raises questions about the validity of a constant beta to value Malaysian stocks.

The value premium is significantly positive, indicating that value firms outperform growth firms. However the size premium is significantly negative, indicating that small firms underperform large firms. This latter 'anomalous' finding clearly indicates the presence of return-generating dynamics in Malaysia above and beyond those found in the developed markets. Studies abound on the return-generating process of stocks traded in emerging equity markets and there is a dichotomy in findings on whether the factors driving the return-generating process in emerging and developed economies are similar or different. For instance, Fama and French (1998), Patel (1998), Rouwenhorst (1999), and Barry et al. (2002) argue that risk premiums in emerging markets exhibit the same characteristics as those in developed markets[5] – i.e., they display significant momentum, small stocks outperform large stocks and value stocks outperform growth stocks. On the other hand, Claessens et al. (1998) and Girard and Omran (2007) describe mixed results for the relationship between fundamental attributes and returns in emerging markets. These authors find, in some instances, a positive relationship between size and returns, and a positive relationship between price-to-book value and returns. Both results are contrary to the conventional belief that small and value firms are riskier, but the researchers make cogent arguments to explain their findings.[6] The momentum premium is not significantly positive, indicating that past winners do not significantly outperform past losers.

4.3   Differences in Return-Generating Processes between S and NS stocks

4.3.1   Forecasting Malaysia S and NS stocks' returns with micro and macro information

In this section, we test the forecasting ability of a conditional multifactor model that takes into consideration micro factors as well as macro local and global factors. We then compare it to simpler nested forecasting models. We use a methodology similar to Griffin (2002) to examine alternative factor models' ability to explain time-series variation in Malaysian S and NS stock returns.

We first run regressions for individual stock returns[7] over the whole sample (1999–2006). The results are reported in Table 9.6. We observe that the F-statistic fails to reject the null hypothesis that alphas are jointly equal to zero for all models. Thus, we can not reject any of the models' specifications.

F-statistics for the R^2 suggest a significant relationship between stock return and the factors used in each model. Furthermore, R^2, a measure of goodness-of-fit, ranks the conditional 5-factor model as the best for both periods. For instance, the R^2 for the conditional model is 0.765 as

*Table 9.6   Regression of individual stock excess returns, model fit,
              specifications and forecast errors*

Model	Fit	Shari'ah-Compliant	Non-Shari'ah-Compliant	Spec-ification	Shari'ah-Compliant	Non-Shari'ah-Compliant
Unconditional	R Square	0.410	0.270	Alpha	0.015	−0.005
CAPM	Std. Error	0.147	0.098	Std. Error	0.019	0.016
	F-stat	7.807**	7.492**	F-stat	0.613	0.108
	Forecast Evaluation	2001–2006	2001–2006			
	Out the sample MAE	8.06%	6.72%			
Unconditional	R Square	0.431	0.323	Alpha	0.015	−0.004
2-factor CAPM	Std. Error	0.146	0.096	Std. Error	0.019	0.016
	F-stat	8.716**	11.295**	F-stat	0.568	0.054
	Forecast Evaluation	2001–2006	2001–2006			
	Out the sample MAE	7.89%	6.50%			
Unconditional	R Square	0.607	0.515	Alpha	0.005	0.004
5-factor CAPM	Std. Error	0.120	0.086	Std. Error	0.055	0.084
	F-stat	25.428**	36.200**	F-stat	0.009	0.002
	Forecast Evaluation	2001–2006	2001–2006			
	Out the sample MAE	6.61%	5.44%			
Conditional	R Square	0.788	0.765	Alpha	0.022	0.036
5-factor CAPM	Std. Error	0.110	0.081	Std. Error	0.096	0.129
	F-stat	51.267**	89.712**	F-stat	0.053	0.079
	Forecast Evaluation	2001–2006	2001–2006			
	Out the sample MAE	4.65%	3.49%			

Notes:

α-alpha.
Unconditional CAPM: $r_{i,t} = \alpha_i + \beta_{1,i} r_{Malaysia,t} + \varepsilon_{i,t}$

Unconditional 2-factor CAPM: $r_{i,t} = \alpha_i + \beta_{1,i} r_{Malaysia,t} + \beta_{2,i} r_{World,t} + \varepsilon_{i,t}$

Table 9.6   (continued)

Unconditional 5-factor CAPM:

$$r_{i,t} = \alpha_i + \beta_{1,i}r_{Malaysia,t} + \beta_{2,i}r_{World,t} + \beta_{3,i}SMB_t + \beta_{4,i}HMLBP_t + \beta_{5,i}MOM_t + \varepsilon_{i,t}$$

Conditional 5-factor CAPM:

$$r_{i,t} = \alpha_i + \beta_{1,i}r_{Malaysia,t} + \beta_{2,i}r_{World,t} + \beta_{3,i}SMB_t + \beta_{4,i}HMLBP_t + \beta_{5,i}MOM_t$$
$$+ Z_{t-1}(\beta'_{1,i}r_{Malaysia,t} + \beta'_{2,i}r_{World,t} + \beta'_{3,i}SMB_t + \beta'_{4,i}HMLBP_t + \beta'_{5,i}MOM_t) + \varepsilon_{i,t}$$

$r_{i,t}$, $r_{Malaysia,t}$, and $r_{World,t}$ are risk premia. SMB is the size premium, $HMLBP$ is the value premium, MOM is the momentum premium, and IP is the investable premium. Z_{t-1} are instruments consisting of local and global variables. Local risk factors (lagged 1 month) are the risk factors for Malaysia's economic, financial, and political risk ratings $((1+\%$ change in risk rating$)^{-1}-1)$. Global factors (lagged 1 month) are the risk factors for GDP-weighted world political, economic and financial risk ratings in the G7 countries.
**Significant at 0.05 level.

compared to next best model with an R^2 of 0.607 (unconditional 6-factor model) – i.e., an increase in proportion of explained variance by conditioning local and global variables of 26.03 percent.

Next, as in Griffin (2002), we examine the forecasting ability of each model by estimating a two-year rolling regressions and multiply the estimated regression betas by the average factor return over the entire data period prior to the forecast to calculate the next month's expected return estimates. Then, we evaluate the mean absolute error (MAE) for each month and each stock. Again, we run our forecast for the S and NS stocks for the 2001–2006 period. Our results indicate that, for both series, the error forecast is approximately divided by 2 when the conditional 5-factor model is used rather than the unconditional one-factor model and it indicates the increasing relevance of time-varying macro factors in estimating expected returns or cost of capital in Malaysia. Forecasting error is less for NS stocks than S stocks.

In conclusion, results show that a factor model conditioned by the change in global and local factors provides a greater explanatory power. We also notice that micro factors cannot be ignored and that global factors are getting increasingly important in explaining the return-generating process of Malaysian stock returns.

4.3.2   Local, global and fixed effects attribution analysis
Rouwenhorst (1999) shows that emerging markets were isolated from world markets from 1982 to 1995; Griffin (2002) shows that practical applications of Fama and French's three-factor model, such as cost of capital calculations and performance evaluations, are best performed on a country-specific

basis. There is no evidence that global risk factors can account for the excess returns of emerging market stocks from 1982 to 1999. However, the first three sections of our study still show that (1) S and NS stocks returns are increasingly correlated to the world capital markets' returns and (2) changes in Malaysian risk ratings are also increasingly related to the changes in global economic, financial and political ratings. This is in line with the findings of Bekaert and Harvey (1997), who demonstrate that co-movement between emerging market country returns has increased over time.

$$r_{i,t} = \alpha_i + \beta_{1,i} r_{Malaysia,t} + \beta_{2,i} r_{World,t} + \beta_{3,i} SMB_t + \beta_{4,i} HMLBP_t + \beta_{5,i} MOM_t$$

$$+ Z_{t-1} (\beta'_{1,i} r_{Malaysia,t} + \beta'_{2,i} r_{World,t} + \beta'_{3,i} SMB_t + \beta'_{4,i} HMLBP_t$$

$$+ \beta'_{5,i} MOM_t) + \varepsilon_{i,t} \tag{9.2}$$

We further investigate the impact of the change in local and global factors in the pricing of S and NS stocks. Accordingly, we use the conditional 5-factor model tested in the previous section as an attribution tool to analyze the degree to which changes in conditioned (local and global effects) and unconditioned (fixed effects) factors can explain Malaysian stock returns variations.

We test the local and global exposure of S and NS stocks with the following conditional multifactor model:

Where $r_{Malaysia,t}$, and $r_{World,t}$ are risk premia.[8] *SMB* is the size premium, *HMLBP* is the value premium, *MOM* is the momentum premium, Z_{t-1} are instruments consisting of local and global variables. Local risk factors (lagged 1 month) are the change in risk ratings for Malaysia's economic, financial, and political risk ratings. Global factors (lagged 1 month) are the percent change for GDP-weighted world political, economic and financial risk ratings. We orthogonalize the sector effect from the stock risk premia by using the residuals of equation (9.1) for $r_{i,t}$. The results of equation (9.2) are summarized in Table 9.7 for S and NS stocks.

A summary of the results of equation (9.2) for S and NS stocks are presented in Table 9.7. The unconditioned factors are the market risk, world risk, size, value and momentum premiums; the sign of the coefficient associated with each of these variables provides information on the composition of our sample. The negative coefficients associated with the value factors and the positive coefficient associated with the size factor indicate that the NS and S stocks included in our sample are dominated by larger growth stocks, which returns are significantly sensitive to changes in global economic, financial and political risk, as well as to changes to local economic, financial and political risk.

Table 9.7 Stocks excess returns attribution – local, global and fixed influences

	Shari'ah-Compliant			Non-Shari'ah-Compliant		
	Coefficient	t-Statistic	Standardized Coefficient (absolute value)			Standardized Coefficient (absolute value)
Intercept	−0.001	−0.182		−0.005*	−2.132	
Market Risk Premium (RPM)	1.023**	14.517	0.52	1.043**	21.473	0.530
RPM × Local ECON	1.752	0.366	0.04	−4.125	−1.346	0.060
RPM × Local FIN	3.497	0.422	0.01	−6.321	−1.081	0.045
RPM × Local POL	20.684**	2.131	0.10	−1.820	−0.323	0.006
RPM × Global ECON	7.750	0.622	0.03	22.174**	2.577	0.120
RPM × Global FIN	−4.625	−1.854	0.09	0.340	0.192	0.005
RPM × Global POL	23.190**	3.658	0.14	1.342	0.309	0.001
World Risk Premium (RPW)	−0.063	−0.888	0.04	−0.025	−0.516	0.018
RPW × Local ECON	3.309	0.645	0.01	−2.594	−0.735	0.011
RPW × Local FIN	−42.559	−1.266	0.06	−4.058	−0.315	0.002
RPW × Local POL	9.499	0.984	0.04	7.967	1.239	0.045
RPW × Global ECON	16.503	1.257	0.05	14.075	1.498	0.064
RPW × Global FIN	3.659	1.196	0.04	−2.310	−1.095	0.036
RPW × Global POL	−3.815	−1.145	0.03	−0.489	−0.201	0.003
Size Factor (SMB)	0.323**	2.615	0.13	0.247**	3.277	0.167
SMB × Local ECON	−13.783	−1.764	0.07	0.065	0.012	0.000
SMB × Local FIN	−12.425	−1.260	0.05	−17.816**	−2.822	0.147
SMB × Local POL	9.968	0.646	0.01	14.332*	2.049	0.125
SMB × Global ECON	34.022*	2.132	0.09	2.648	0.279	0.002

Table 9.7   (continued)

	Shari'ah-Compliant			Non-Shari'ah-Compliant		
	Coeffi-cient	t-Statistic	Stand-ardized Coeffi-cient (absolute value)			Stand-ardized Coeffi-cient (absolute value)
SMB × Global FIN	8.926*	2.180	0.11	−1.673	−0.514	0.028
SMB × Global POL	8.392	0.946	0.02	7.124	1.217	0.058
Value Factor (HML-BM)	−0.174	−1.211	0.06	−0.385**	−3.998	0.162
HML-BM × Local ECON	−21.087*	−2.236	0.12	−11.301	−1.692	0.075
HML-BM × Local FIN	−23.661	−1.159	0.04	−37.556**	−2.814	0.136
HML-BM × Local POL	30.170	1.318	0.07	26.347**	2.615	0.143
HML-BM × Global ECON	37.332	1.575	0.07	26.547	1.684	0.083
HML-BM × Global FIN	8.244	1.476	0.06	2.349	0.551	0.019
HML-BM × Global POL	23.328	1.748	0.09	1.410	0.154	0.002
Momentum Factor (WML)	0.033	0.542	0.02	−0.049	−1.093	0.034
WML × Local ECON	−0.738	−0.236	0.03	−7.345**	−3.147	0.179
WML × Local FIN	6.034	0.776	0.03	−18.088**	−3.501	0.190
WML × Local POL	10.830	1.665	0.08	−0.622	−0.144	0.003
WML × Global ECON	4.465	0.653	0.01	7.742	1.823	0.090
WML × Global FIN	2.962	0.886	0.02	−0.701	−0.289	0.005
WML × Global POL	7.330	1.248	0.05	3.472	0.854	0.024
Sum			2.43			2.62

Table 9.7   (continued)

Risk Influence Attribution	Percentage of 2.43 standard response in the dependent variable	Percentage of 2.62 standard response in the dependent variable
Local Risk Influence	31.57	44.60
Economic Risk Influence	11.52	12.41
Financial Risk Influence	7.94	19.87
Political Risk Influence	12.11	12.32
Global Risk Influence	37.14	20.61
Economic Risk Influence	10.47	13.71
Financial Risk Influence	13.08	3.54
Political Risk Influence	13.59	3.35
Fixed Risk Factors Influence	31.30	34.80

Notes: *Significant at 0.10 level. **Significant at 0.05 level.

The conditioned factors indicate how these stocks are responding to the changes in global and local risk factors. For instance, S stock returns are positively correlated to their market and this positive relationship is affected by changes in local and global political risk. In the same vein, NS stock returns are positively correlated to their market and this positive relationship is affected by changes in global economic risk. The unconditional variable (market and world premium, SMB, HML-BP and WML) indicate the composition of S and NS series – i.e., S stock series are sensitive to local market changes, are mostly comprised of smaller companies; NS stocks are sensitive to local market changes, are comprised of larger stocks than the S series, and are more 'value'-oriented. Further, S and NS stocks are never affected by the same conditioning variables. For instance, all 'S' stocks are significantly conditioned by only local and global political factors. Larger 'S' stocks are sensitive to changes in global financial and economic conditions, and growth-oriented 'S' stocks are significantly impacted by the changes in local economic variables. All 'NS' stocks are significantly affected by changes in global economic ratings. Larger and growth (smaller and value) 'NS' stocks tend to be more sensitive to changes in local financial (political) ratings. Further, loser 'NS' stocks are conditioned by changes in local financial and economic ratings.

We then turn our attention to the standardized coefficients, which provide information about the impact of each independent variable on stock returns. For instance, an increase in one standard deviation in the Malaysian market return provides a 0.520 standard deviation increase in S stock returns and 0.53 standard deviation increase in NS stock returns. The sum of the absolute value of the standardized coefficients is equal to 2.43 for S stocks and 2.62 for NS stocks, which means that if there were a 1 standard deviation shock in each independent variable then it would lead to a cumulated impact of 2.43 standard deviation on S stock returns and 2.62 standard deviation on NS stock returns.

Next, we combine local, global and unconditioned effects, and conclude on their relative impact on S and NS stock returns. We compute the standardized coefficients, then take their absolute value and determine the relative impact of a change in global, local and fixed variables on stock return variations each year. We find that local factors explain 31.57 (44.6) percent of the change in S (NS) stock returns while global factors explain 37.14 (20.61) percent of stock return variations for S (NS) stocks.

We observe that local and global risks have homogenous impacts on S stock. However NS stock returns are most sensitive to local financial risk – i.e., 19.87 percent of the stock return standard shocks are explained by changes in local financial risk – followed by local economic (12.41 percent) and political (12.32 percent) risks, and global economic (13.71 percent) risk. Global financial and political risks have limited impacts on NS stocks – i.e., changes in global financial and political risks only lead to 3.54 percent and 3.35 percent of the changes in NS stock returns. In sum, from 1999 to 2006, more than 65 percent of the variations in S and NS stock returns are explained by shocks in global and local economic, financial and political risks. In addition, while S stocks tend to be uniformly affected by local and global risk factors, NS stocks are mostly sensitive to local factors since almost half the variations in NS returns can be explained by variations in local economic, financial and political variables.

This result has important implications on the pricing of Malaysian equity, and evaluating the cost of equity of Malaysian firms: A model failing to condition firms' fundamentals with local and global changes in economic, financial and political risks would miss out at least 65 percent of the sources of stock return variations and, thus, will fail to fairly value Malaysian stock intrinsic prices and estimate the cost of equity.

5.0 CONCLUSION

Islamic finance is a growth industry and provides an alternative asset class for investors. In South Asia, Malaysia has been a leader in promoting this sector. Malaysia is also growing and has its own unique characteristics. This study attempts to identify the leading risk factors when investing in Malaysia and its *Shari'ah* (S) and non-*Shari'ah* capital (NS) markets. As a result, it has important implications for pricing S and NS equities in Malaysia, determining the cost of equity in Malaysia, and understanding the arguments for or against including Malaysian S and NS as separate asset classes within a global asset allocation strategy. We examine the notion that S and NS stocks represent separate asset classes.

First, we assess the empirical evidence indicating the S and NS stocks inclusion within Malaysian capital market. We find that gains from including S stocks outweigh NS stocks over all risk–return ranges. There is a significant advantage to including S stocks for Malaysian investors during the 2001–2006 period. Second, we explore the notion of a difference in risk exposure between S and NS at macro and micro levels. For this, we test a multifactor expression that include micro factors conditioned by time-varying macro factors, and conclude that both types of risk factors are instrumental in describing the return-generating process of S and NS equities. We find that S stocks are influenced more by local and global factors than NS stocks. Overall, this chapter seeks to provide in-depth understanding of the stock price discovery in Malaysian S and NS stocks – i.e., accessibility, investment process, restrictions, liquidity and risk–return generating process.

NOTES

1. Investable stocks are determined by their 'investable weight', the percentage of foreign ownership authorized for each stock. In fact, this value changes throughout the study – e.g., a stock might have an investable weight of 10 percent in 1993 and 90 percent in 2006.
2. Local (global) betas are computed by regressing each stock dollar's returns on the IFCG China (MSCI World) index returns. These value weighted indices are also dollar-denominated. One lag of the index return is included to allow for a delayed response due to non-synchronous trading. Betas are computed with a minimum of two years and a maximum of five years of historical monthly returns.
3. EMDB is a Standard and Poors product which provides quality information about emerging markets. However, it does not constitute a random sample of emerging market stocks. Indeed, as Rouwenhorst (1999) argues, the database is biased toward larger and more liquid firms (selection bias).
4. All returns series are converted into US dollars using the exchange rates provided by EMDB.
5. See, for example, Fama and French (1992 and 1996) which show that high beta, small, value and high momentum firms have higher cross-sectional risk premiums in developed markets.

6. These explanations include a liquidity premium for value stocks in emerging markets, market growth resulting from an increase in number of firms rather than an increase in value (Harvey and Roper, 1999), low leverage of small firms due to capital market imperfections in emerging markets (Girard and Omran, 2007), and market segmentation of nascent markets because of market microstructure and regulatory and tax regimes (Classens et al., 1998).
7. All sector effects are orthogonalized from nominal returns using equation (9.1).
8. All sector effects are orthogonalized from nominal returns using equation (9.1).

REFERENCES

Ahmed, Z. and H. Ibrahim (2002), A study of the performance of the KLSE Syariah index. *Malaysian Management Journal*, 6, 25–34.

Barry, C.B., E. Golgreyer, L. Lockwood and M. Rodriguez (2002), Robustness of size and value effects in emerging equity markets, 1985–2000. *Emerging Markets Review*, 3, 1–30.

Bauer, R., K. Koedijk and R. Otten (2005), International evidence on ethical mutual fund performance and investment style. *Journal of Banking and Finance*, 29, 1751–1767.

Bekaert, G. and C. Harvey (1997), Emerging equity market volatility. *Journal of Financial Economics*, 43 (1), 29–78.

Bello, Z. (2005), Socially responsible investing and portfolio diversification. *The Journal of Financial Research*, 28, 41–57.

Claessens, S., S. Dasgupta and J. Glen (1998), The cross section of stock returns: evidence from emerging markets. *Emerging Markets Quarterly*, 2, 4–13.

Elfakhani, S., M.K. Hassan and Y. Sidani (2005), Comparative performance of Islamic versus secular mutual funds. Paper presented at the 12th Economic Research Forum Conference in Cairo, Egypt, on December 19–21.

El-Gamal, M.A. (2000), *A Basic Guide to Contemporary Islamic Banking and Finance*. http://www.ruf.rice.edu/~elgamal/files/primer.pdf, accessed in November 2005.

Fama, E.F. and K.R. French (1992), The cross-section of expected stock returns. *Journal of Finance*, 47(2), 1225–48.

Fama, E.F. and K.R. French (1996), Multifactor explanations of asset pricing anomalies. *Journal of Finance*, 51, 55–84.

Fama, E.F. and K.R. French (1998), Value versus growth: the international evidence. *Journal of Finance*, 53, 890–943.

Geczym C., R. Stambaugh and D. Levin (2003), Investing in socially responsible mutual funds. Working Paper, University of Pennsylvania.

Griffin, J. (2002), Are the Fama and French factors global or country specific? *Review of Financial Studies*, 15, 783–803.

Hakim, S. and M. Rashidian (2004a), Risk and return of Islamic stock market indexes. Paper presented at the International Seminar of Non-bank Financial Institutions: Islamic Alternatives, Kuala Lumpur, Malaysia.

Hakim, S. and M. Rashidian (2004b), How costly is investor's compliance to Sharia? Paper presented at the 11th Economic Research Forum Annual Conference in Sharjah, U.A.E. on December 14–16, Beirut, Lebanon.

Harvey, C. and A. Roper (1999), 'The Asian bet', in Alison Harwood, Robert E.

Litan and Michael Pomerleano (eds), *The Crisis in Emerging Financial Markets*, Brookings Institution Press, pp. 29–115.

Hassan, M.K. (2001), Nuances of Islamic mutual funds. *Islamic Horizons*, 30 (3), 16–18.

Hassan, M.K. (2002), Risk, return and volatility of faith-based investing: the case of the Dow Jones Islamic Index. Paper in Proceedings of 5th Harvard University Forum on Islamic Finance, Harvard University.

Hassan, M.K. and S.I. Tag el-Din (2005), Speculative bubbles in Islamic stock market-empirical assessment. MIHE Working Paper, Leicester, UK.

Henry, P. (2000a), Stock market liberalization, economic reform, and emerging market equity prices. *Journal of Finance*, 55(2), 529–564.

Henry, P. (2000b), Do stock market liberalizations cause investment booms? *Journal of Financial Economics*, 58, 301–334.

Hussein, Khaled and Mohammed Omran (2005). 'Ethical investment revisited: evidence from Dow Jones Islamic Indexes', *The Journal of Investing*, 14, 105–124.

Kreander, N., R. Gray, D. Power and C. Sinclair (2000), The financial performance of European ethical funds 1996–1998. *Journal of Accounting and Finance*, 1, 3–22.

Patel, S. (1998), Cross-sectional variation in emerging markets equity returns. January 1988–March 1997, *Emerging Markets Quarterly*, 2, 57–70.

Rouwenhorst, K.G. (1999), Local return factors and turnover in emerging stock markets. *Journal of Finance*, 54, 1439–1464.

10. *Takaful* insurance: concept, history and development challenges

Syed Othman Alhabshi and
Shaikh Hamzah Razak

1.0 INTRODUCTION

Takaful is derived from its Arabic root word '*kafala*' which literally means 'to guarantee'. In terms of usage and implication, the term *kafala* certainly denotes the agreement by one party to indemnify another for any liability that has been pre-agreed upon.

Conventional insurance companies operate on the basis of a guarantee to the policy holders that they would undertake to compensate them against any loss incurred as per their contract. In this sense there is no material difference between the practices of a conventional insurance to those of the *takaful* operators (we mean Islamic insurance companies). Both are dealing with indemnifying their customers and paying out compensation for the losses incurred by the customers. What then are the real differences between conventional insurance and *takaful* that have led to the separate, dramatic development of the latter industry the world over in the last four decades? Are these differences based on the concept and principles or simply operational?

Unlike Islamic banking that basically meanders away from the usury or *riba* in order to make the products and operations *Shari'ah*-compliant, *takaful* can easily avoid *riba* by investing in non-*riba*-based instruments that have been developed by the Islamic banks and the Islamic capital and money markets. What else are the main differences between conventional insurance and *takaful*? In order to fully appreciate what *takaful* entails and how it operates that it becomes *Shari'ah*-compliant, we need to fully understand the underlying principles that have been employed to formulate a concept of *takaful* that is not only *Shari'ah*-compliant but operational as a business concern as well.

Before we dwell into the *Shari'ah* principles that make *takaful* different from conventional insurance, it would be better appreciated if we understand some of the traditional or tribal ancient Arab practices that were akin to the *takaful* operations today. This chapter will therefore expound these principles from the practices that have been endorsed to be *Shari'ah*-compliant by the Holy Prophet Muhammad (peace and blessings of Allah be upon him) himself and fully supported by the Quranic injunctions. We shall also illustrate the concepts and principles employed by modern *takaful* operators in order to operationalise their models. The chapter will not be complete if we do not briefly point out some of the issues and challenges that still plague these models and the industry as a whole.

2.0   PRE-ISLAMIC PRACTICES OF THE CONCEPT OF KAFALA

The concept of *kafala* was in vogue well before the advent of Islam as it is generally known that the ancient Arabs practiced a strong tribal system that was based upon the pride of lineage and ancestry. There was no compromise when the good name of one's ancestors was being ridiculed or defamed. One would fight to the death to defend the pride of one's ancestry or lineage.

Such an heroic act was handed down to the members of the tribe. Any member of the tribe had the right to be protected not only by his or her immediate family members but rather by the whole tribe which was much larger in number by far than the immediate family in the absence of a central state that could govern these tribes. What is more interesting to note is that the member of the tribe had to be protected whether he or she was in the right or not. Consequently, tribal wars were very common and once started, they never ended. The hatred and revenge would go down generation after generation. Thus we see how important and dear the concept of *kafala* was to such a society.

When a member of the tribe had committed a murder, for instance, it could lead to one of two consequences. Either tribal war would break out to avenge the death of the tribal member, or settlement would be reached by paying what is called 'blood money'. The money that was used to compensate the loss of life came from the tribal fund which was collected from among the members. The concept was such that the tribal fund formed was based on outright donations by the members of the tribe. Once the donation was collected, there was no refund allowed. The fund was used mainly to settle compensation that was required when tribal disputes occured. It could also be collected when a dispute had occurred or whenever the fund was depleted. This practice was known as '*Al-Aqilah*'.

In tribal life, each tribe was united as one unit and the loss of its members was considered as the loss of the entire tribe. If a tribe lost any member, it received compensation for that loss from the tribe which was responsible for that loss. On the other hand, if a tribe killed anyone belonging to the other tribe, it compensated the whole tribe by paying blood money for that loss.

According to this ancient Arab custom (perhaps also customs of the Eastern Mediterranean cultures), the entire tribe was held responsible for the payment of blood money to the tribe or the relatives of the killed. This co-operation on the part of the whole group or the community to mutually share the burden of any of its members reflects the spirit of mutuality in *takaful*.

In essence, the object of blood money is to secure protection against the danger to which each and every member of the tribe is equally exposed, and to eliminate a common danger which may fall upon any member of the tribe at any time. Accordingly, the tribe jointly contributed to meet the loss (in blood money) which might fall upon any of them. In other words, it is mutual coverage of accidental loss by the community exposed to a common danger. It can be said that the payment of blood money is an obvious example of mutual insurance, wherein the whole community stood guarantee against the loss to any of its members in the form of blood money. This communal enterprise was social in character but economic in consequence.[1]

> The underlying principle in mutual insurance is that the individual members are themselves the insurers as well as the insured.[2]

2.1 Principle of Mutuality and Islam

In the pre-Islamic period, payment of blood money by the family or tribe of the killer as compensation to the family or tribe of killed was commonplace. The individual killer was generally responsible for the payment of the compensation. However, the common practice was for his family or tribe to pay the compensation. As the members of each tribe were closely related and united to face the common dangers of desert life, they developed an extreme sense of loyalty to their tribe. Each tribe tried to protect and safeguard the life and property of its members. Gradually, this group loyalty and the interdependence of its members developed into mutuality and manifested itself in the form of collective responsibility of the tribe to pay compensation for the killing of a member of another tribe by one of its own members. The payment could be in the form of cash or kind, such as camels.

Theoretically, it was the personal responsibility of the killer to make this payment, but, in practice, ultimate responsibility lay on the community. This was reflected in the behaviour of the tribesmen when any of their members was killed by a member of another tribe. All of them, individually as well as collectively, felt duty bound to avenge the death of their associate by killing the killer or any member of the killer's tribe. As Watt put it, 'though it is preferable to inflict the penalty on the person responsible for the death or injury, it may be inflicted on any member of the clan or tribe instead of him. It is thus clear that ultimately the responsibility both for the original act, and exacting vengeance is communal'.[3]

The principle of compensation in cash or kind for the death or injury to any person greatly helped to eliminate or, at least, reduce the tribal warfare and family feuds which lasted for years and caused enormous loss of life and property. This custom had four outstanding benefits for the people of Arabia as follows:

1. it reduced bloodshed and blood-feuds in the country;
2. it replaced individual responsibility with the ultimate collective responsibility of the tribe for the actions of its members, and thus helped achieve social security for individual members of each tribe;
3. it reduced the financial burden of the individual by transferring it to the group; and
4. it developed a spirit of co-operation and brotherhood among the members as reflected in mutuality to share the individual burden amongst the group.[4]

3.0   THE PRACTICE AFTER THE ADVENT OF ISLAM

When Islam came, the same practice was continued due to its virtues and benefits as is evident from the Quranic injunction quoted below:

> O ye who believe! The law of equality is prescribed to you in cases of murder: The free for the free, the slave for the slave, the woman for the woman. But if any remission is made by the brother of the slain, then grant any reasonable demand, and compensate him with handsome gratitude. This is a concession and a Mercy from your Lord. After this whoever exceeds the limits shall be in grave penalty.[5]

This verse clearly supports the practice of paying compensation in terms of blood money or *al-diyah* although the law of equality allows revenge only to the same extent. It is mainly intended to mitigate the horrors of the pre-Islamic custom of retaliation and revenge. In order to meet the strict claims of justice, equality is prescribed, with a strong recommendation for mercy and forgiveness. Thus, Islam helped to reduce the severity of punishment and the terrible consequences of the pagan custom of retaliation, by adopting and improving the pre-Islamic custom of compensation for the relatives or the family of the killed. It enjoined upon the believers not to waste human lives in retaliation, but to let the law take its course, and if the aggrieved party agreed to a reasonable compensation, brotherly love is better than retaliation.

> Never should a believer kill a believer; but (if it so happens) by mistake, (compensation is due): If one (so) kills a Believer, it is ordained that he should free a believing slave, and pay compensation to the deceased family, unless they remit it freely. If the deceased belonged to a people at war with you, and he was a believer, the freeing of a believing slave (is enough). If he belonged to a people with whom ye have a treaty of mutual alliance, compensation should be paid to his family, and a believing slave be freed. For those who find this beyond their means, (is prescribed) a fast for two months running: by way of repentance to God: for God hath all knowledge and all wisdom.[6]

In the same way, Islam mitigated the horrors of the pre-Islamic custom of retaliation in wounds and injuries by prescribing the law of equality in all such cases. 'We ordained therein for them: Life for life, eye for eye, nose for nose, ear for ear, tooth for tooth, and wounds equal for wounds. But if any one remits retaliation as charity, it shall be an act of atonement for himself.'[7] Again forgiveness and mercy, instead of retaliation, is being strongly recommended in all such cases in order to avoid bloodshed in the community.

The Islamic acceptance is further reinforced by the Holy Prophet (peace and blessings of Allah be upon him) in the following *hadith*:

> Narrated by Abu Huraira (may Allah be pleased with him): Two women of Hudail fought each other and one hit the other with a stone. The stone hit her in the belly and she had been pregnant and the unborn child was killed. They both took the matter before the Holy Prophet (s.a.w.), and he ruled that the blood money was due to her relatives for what she had in her womb as a male or female slave of the highest quality. Hamal ibn Nagigha said: 'O messenger of God! Will I be penalized for a being that has not drank or eaten or made a sound nor even come into existence?' At that the Messenger of God (peace and blessings be upon him) said: 'He is a brother of those who tell fortunes.'[8]

What can be learnt from this *hadith* is that compensation for life is permitted and that the value or quantum must be agreed upon and the money must come from the family of the party that committed the killing or murder.

The same provision is included in the First Islamic constitution of Medina upon the migration of the Holy Prophet (peace and blessings be upon him). Through the practice of *al-Diyah* or blood money, the money was supposed to be paid mutually by the *Aqilah* (the close relatives of the killer) to the heir of the deceased (victim).[9] In view of the support by the tribe, the murderer was exempted from criminal prosecution even though the relatives were unable to pay.

The above injunctions are further supported by the following *hadith* which in essence calls for uplifting the hardships of others instead of pressing charges although law of equality allows such revenge to take place as in the above-quoted verse.

> 'Narrated by Abu Huraira (may Allah be pleased with him). . . the Holy Prophet (peace and blessings be upon him) said: whosoever removes a worldly hardship from a believer, Allah will remove from him one of the hardships in the day of judgment. Whosoever alleviates from one, Allah will alleviate his lot in this world and the next'.[10]

The companion Sayyidina Umar ibn al-Khattab (may Allah be pleased with him) directed all districts of the State to list the name of the Muslim brothers-in-arms and the people who owed each other to contribute blood money in the event of any manslaughter committed by anyone of their own tribe.

By the end of the eighth century, the Muslims had developed marine science, marine navigation and had built a strong naval unit in the Mediterranean. Abdur Al-Rahman laid the basis of the first naval unit in Muslim Spain. He appointed his first Chamberlain, Tammam, as its head. Tammam thus became the first Muslim Admiral in Europe. Under Abdur Al-Rahman III, the Arab navy became the most powerful in the Western Mediterranean. The fact remains, however, that Spain under Islam reached economic and cultural heights unattained before, and its capital vied with Constantinople and Baghdad as a world centre of grandeur, affluence, learning and enlightenment. Arab writers styled Cordova the 'bride of all Andalus' and an Anglo-Saxon nun called it the 'Jewel of the world'.[11]

It is during these voyages that the merchants felt the need for insurance to cover their losses through the perils in the sea. Based on the principle of 'helping one another' they contributed to a fund prior to starting their voyage and used it to compensate any of them who incurred losses. This was the start of the marine insurance which of course has been much modified today.

The principle that these Muslim merchants employed as is enjoined by the Holy Quran is based on the verse that reads, 'Help ye one another in righteousness and piety, but help ye not one another in sin and rancor'.[12] This principle of helping one another is amply demonstrated by the practice of *aqilah* of the pre-Islamic period and hence it became acceptable to Islam.

3.1 Concept of *Takaful*

We can discern from the above account of the pre-Islamic practices that *takaful* is based upon a mutual intention of protecting one another against common dangers. This is possible if the members of the group feel for themselves as much as they feel for the others. So much so, if any one of them is inflicted with any harm or danger, the whole group feels the pain. In this way, the whole group or community will feel obliged and responsible to help one another so that the burden is not shouldered by any one person but by each and every member of the group or community. If anyone is inflicted with harm the whole group or community feels it. By working as a group in facing the risks or dangers, the burden becomes much lighter. The bigger the size of the group the lighter is the burden or liability.

Such a feeling of responsibility is being reinforced by the Islamic teachings as found in the following injunctions:

> Help one another in righteousness and piety, but help ye not one another in sin and rancour.[13]

> Allah will always help His servant for as long as he helps others.[14]

> The place of relationships and feelings of people with faith, between each other, is just like the body; when one of its parts is afflicted with pain, then the rest of the body will be affected.[15]

> One true Muslim (Mu'min) and another true Muslim (Mu'min) is just like a building whereby every part in it strengthens the other part.[16]

> By my life, which is in Allah's power, nobody will enter Paradise if he does not protect his neighbour who is in distress.[17]

Based on the above, the principles of *takaful* are as follows:

- Policyholders co-operate among themselves for their common good.
- Every policyholder pays his subscription to help those that need assistance.
- Losses are divided and liabilities spread according to the community pooling system.

- Uncertainty is eliminated in respect of subscription and compensation.
- It does not derive advantage at the cost of others.

Essentially *takaful* is a cooperative insurance where members are those who face the same risk or danger of incurring losses and who willingly contribute a certain sum of money which knowingly will be used to compensate those members of the group who incur such losses. As in the case of ancient Arab tribal custom, every member of the tribe faces the same danger of being inflicted harm by another tribe which is at war with them.

In the case of motor policy, for instance, everyone who drives a vehicle on the road faces the danger or risk of meeting with an accident. The most logical thing to do is to invite these people who face the common danger to form a group and contribute a sum of money which can be used to compensate any of the members who incur losses due to an accident. The same principle is applied to marine, fire, etc.

3.2 The Difference Between *Takaful* and Conventional Insurance

In conventional insurance, the company sells a policy to the insured who would pay a premium for the risk he or she agrees to be indemnified by the company or insurer. The policy will not only determine the kind of risk that is covered but also the kinds of risks that are excluded, the period of coverage for the indemnity, the limit of compensation that the insured will get, and sometimes the limit of damage or loss that the company will not be responsible for. When the insured has incurred a loss that arises from an event that is defined by the policy, the company will pay or cover the losses incurred. If nothing happens during the period under cover, the company takes all the money or premium that has been paid up front.

It is clear from the conventional practice that the contract is one of sale and purchase. The company sells the policy to the insured at a price which is the premium. The company then basically takes chances that it will indemnify the insured up to some limit based on the premium that has been paid. However, the insured does not get any benefit except an undertaking as stated in the policy that the company will take care of his or her losses when the risk materializes. If the risk does not materialize during the period under cover, the company takes all the premium and the insured gets nothing.

Based on the above practice, the Muslim jurists are unanimous in concluding that while the objective of the insurance is good, the manner in which it is being conducted is not *Shari'ah*-compliant. The first objection is the presence of the element of chance taken by the company. Of course this is done on the basis of some historical knowledge about the probability of an event happening which follows the law of large numbers. However, a game of chance necessarily creates an ambiguous situation. There is no certainty in the outcome of the contract. Ambiguity is something that is not acceptable in Islam mainly because any of the two parties will be exposed to injustices. Ambiguity and uncertainty of this type is called *al-Gharar* which when present in any contract will cause the contract to be void.

The second objection is the element of *al-Maisir* or gambling that arises out of the chance phenomenon that exists in the contract. The insured takes a chance to protect himself from the risk that he is facing. He is quite prepared to lose the premium if the risk does not materialize. But if the risk materializes, he will get much more than the premium he has paid. This situation of getting something more than what one pays for that is based on chance is called gambling and is prohibited by *Shari'ah*.

The third element is *riba* or usury that is present in the form of returns from the investment of the insurance fund. Obviously, most of the investments are placed in interest-based instruments and hence is prohibited by the *Shari'ah*.

These are the three main objections raised by the Muslim jurists which make it necessary for them to formulate models that will be *Shari'ah*-compliant. The main reason is because *takaful* or insurance is a necessity and is beneficial to the community. Based on the following *hadith*, it is clear that it is better to leave behind wealth that would enable your loved ones to lead a good life than to leave them with nothing to depend on.

> Narrated by Amer ibn Sa'd who said that his father Abi Waqas said: 'In the year of the Holy Prophet's final pilgrimage I was taken seriously ill and the Holy Prophet (peace and blessings of Allah be upon him) used to visit me to enquire about my health. I told him: "I am beset with illness and I am wealthy but have no inheritors except one daughter. Should I give two-thirds of my property to charity?" He replied "No". I asked: "Half then?" He said "No" then he added: "one-third, and one-third is a great deal. It is better to leave your inheritors wealthy rather than to leave them in poverty and obliged to beg from others."'[18]

Similarly the next *hadith* even reinforces the need to take every precaution to secure our property instead of just leave it to chance and hope that Allah will protect it. We should not just leave the fate of our children or property to chance. We should work hard to secure them and only then we leave their safety to the will of the Almighty Allah.

> Anas bin Malik (May Allah be pleased with him) narrated that the Holy Prophet (peace and blessings of Allah be upon him) told a Bedwin Arab who

left his camel untied trusting to the will of Allah Almighty to tie the camel first then leave it to Allah Almighty.[19]

3.3 Formulation of *Takaful* Operations

Takaful operators then have to conduct their business in a way that is *Shari'ah*-compliant by avoiding the three prohibited elements above that will make the operations void. The easiest part is to avoid *riba*, by investing the *takaful* fund in non-interest-bearing instruments. The question is how to avoid the first two, i.e. *al-Gharar* or ambiguity and uncertainty and *al-Maisir* or gambling.

If we refer to the Quranic injunction quoted above[20] on the principle of *Ta'awun* which is to help one another in righteousness and piety, we then can invite people, especially those who face the same danger or take the same risk, to come together and form a group that will be willing to help one another. In other words, if anyone among them incurs a loss caused by an event that has been agreed upon, all the members of the group will contribute to compensate this unfortunate individual. Based on this understanding, a fund can be created from the contributions of each member on the basis of donation or *tabarru'* which comes from the same root word as *al-birr* or righteousness as is used in the verse of the Quran quoted above. This probably is the most important concept that has been applied in all *takaful* models.

Based on the above concept and the principles of *Ta'awun* and *tabarru'*, the company then is simply the operator who invites people who face the same risk to form that group. The company is not selling a policy, as such which will give rise to the prohibited elements of *al-Gharar* and *al-Maisir*. Rather the company is an operator who makes arrangements for the group to come together and agree not only to contribute to the fund but also at the same time agree to donate at least part of the fund to any member of the group who has become a victim of any peril or mishap that has been identified earlier.

This is exactly what the ancient Arab tribal system did. So did the Muslim merchants of the eighth century who collected a sum of money as a donation to be used as compensation to any of them who faced some mishap and incurred losses. There is complete transparency in this case to avoid all ambiguities or chances. Thus the company does not own the fund but the ownership of the fund remains with the policy holders or participants as they are called by the *takaful* industry.

In this sense, the company is not taking the risk, but it is the group of participants who bear the risk and are mutually covering each other. The company is only a trustee acting on behalf of the participants to manage the operation of the *takaful* business. As such, the company does not have any right to the *takaful* benefits. However, as an operator or manager of the *takaful* business, the company is the entrepreneur or *mudharib* whilst the participants are the provider of capital or *rabbul mal* as in the case of the *mudharabah* concept. In this sense, the profits made from the business can be shared by both parties at a pre-agreed ratio.

Based on the above concept, there are at least two ways that the company can operate as a business. The first is to employ the *mudharabah* or profit-sharing model. The second is to employ the *wakala* or agency model. There are other models such as the modified *mudharabah* model and *wakala-waqf* model which are the variants of the two basic models.

3.4   *Mudharabah* Model

The *mudharabah* model consists of two parties, namely the provider of capital or *rabbul mal* on the one hand, and the entrepreneur or *mudharib* who provides the management expertise and entrepreneurial acumen to the business, on the other. These two parties will share the profits after deducting all the expenses to conduct the business, at a pre-agreed ratio. However, in case of a loss, it is only the provider of capital who assumes the losses. The entrepreneur does not assume any liability in case of a loss because he or she has already provided the expertise without any payment.

The *mudharabah* or profit-sharing model as employed by the *takaful* operators is where the company operates as an entrepreneur or *mudharib*, utilizing its expertise in the general management of the company, underwriting the policies and investing the funds. General management also include functions such as product development, marketing, human resources, corporate planning, compliance and governance, etc. The contributions paid by the participants are deemed to belong to the participants, and hence they as a group are considered to be the provider of capital or *rabbul mal* in the *mudharabah* model. The profit arising out of the whole operation after deducting the expenses incurred to conduct the business is to be divided between the company and the participants at a pre-agreed ratio. In some cases, the cost of doing business is deducted from the share of the profits to the entrepreneur.

The question is that the management and staff of the company are salary earners and hence are not in sync with the concept of entrepreneur in the *mudharabah* model. It should be clarified that they are paid out of the shareholders' fund and not out of the income of the business. Hence, they represent the entrepreneur in the *mudharabah* model. Alternatively, the management expenses are being deducted from the share of gross profits to the shareholders. In other words, the total profit from the investment and underwriting surplus is being shared according to the pre-agreed ratio. It is from the share of the profit to the shareholders that the management expenses are being deducted. In this way, whether the management expenses are being borne by the shareholders from the shareholders' fund or from the share of the profit, the consequence is the same.

With this conception, the company then has the right to the share of the profits not only from the investment income of the *takaful* fund accumulated from the participants' contributions but also from conducting the business.

In any *takaful* operation, whether the company employs the *mudharabah* or *wakala* model, there are basically three funds; namely the shareholders' fund, the *takaful* fund comprising the participants' account and *tabarru'* or donation, or the participants' special account (PSA). Whilst the shareholders' fund literally belongs to the shareholders, the *takaful* fund actually comes from the participants' contributions and hence belongs to the participants. The allocation of the participants' contributions into these two funds is done based on actuarial studies. For products with a higher risk or claims ratio, a higher proportion of the contribution will be placed in the *tabarru'* fund to ensure that there is enough fund to cover the claims. It is only when the product has a lower risk or claims ratio that a higher proportion of the contribution will be allocated to the *takaful* fund.

Given these three funds, there should be two main sources of income to the *takaful* company, namely the investment income and the underwriting surplus. The investment income from the shareholders' fund will obviously go back to the shareholders. Logically, as an entrepreneur, the company has the right to a share in the investment income from the participants' account and *tabarru'* funds or the participants' special account. What seems to be contentious is the underwriting surplus.

One view is that the surplus from the underwriting activity cannot be shared by the company because it is a donation by the participant to pay out the claims. There is another view that the underwriting activity is done by the company with all its expertise and hence it should be able to have a share of it as a provider of that expertise.

However, the general view seems to be that the surplus should not be paid out to the participants either, since they have already donated the amount for the purpose of paying out the claims. Under the principle of *tabarru'* or donation, the donor has completely given away his or her right to the property or wealth that he or she has donated and therefore cannot receive any benefit from it.

The question may be raised as to how he or she can receive the claim payment to the loss that he or she incurs in the process. The concept here is that every individual participant pledges to help others with his or her own donation. His or her donation is meant for others and not for him/herself. With a large number of participants, it is possible that he or she

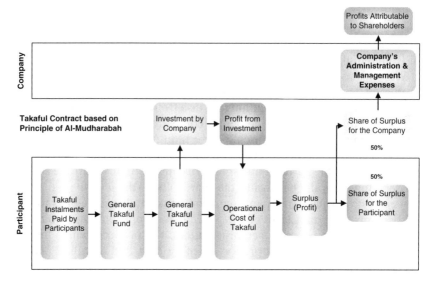

Source: INCEIF's Part II Specialized Module for *Takaful* on Managing *Takaful*
          Institutions.

Figure 10.1   Mudharabah *model – general* takaful

does not receive his money back, but whatever he or she receives will be the
donations made by others.

3.5   General *Takaful* Business

For conventional insurance, there are basically two categories, namely,
general and life. The same is true in *takaful* where there is the general, but
instead of life it is called family *takaful*. The general *takaful* business deals
mainly with specific contingencies such as fire, accident and theft. General
takaful normally covers a specific short period of one year and is to be
renewed annually to ensure its validity.

In the case of the general *takaful* business under the *mudharabah*
model, the company shares the profits from investments as well from
the underwriting surplus. However, all the administrative and management expenses are deducted from the company's share of the profits and
surplus. In the case of the modified *mudharabah* model for general *takaful*
the commissions to intermediaries and management expenses are paid
from the *takaful* fund. The company shares the profit and the underwriting
surplus with the participants. Figure 10.1 shows the *mudharabah* model
and Figure 10.2 gives the modified *mudharabah* model. These are just

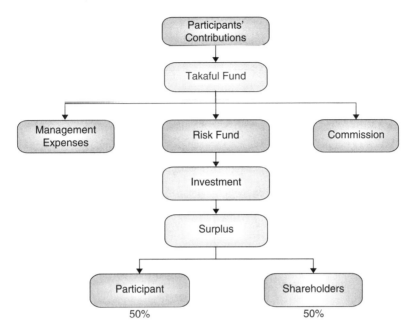

Source: INCEIF's Part II Specialized Module for *Takaful* on Managing *Takaful* Institutions.

Figure 10.2   Modified mudharabah *model – general* takaful

examples of how the models have been employed. Since the *mudharabah* model is not the dominating model at the moment, the examples given here cannot be taken as universally practiced.

3.6   Family *Takaful* Business

A life insurance contract insures the life of a person. Once it is sold, the company is liable to pay only upon the policy holder's death. Since the majority of the jurists do not approve that life insurance as defined here is *Shari'ah*-compliant, the *takaful* companies use the term family *takaful* instead. Family *takaful*, unlike life insurance, does not insure the life of the person who buys the policy. Instead, it is meant to provide a lump sum payment to the family of the deceased, to help them survive for some time without much sacrifice in lifestyle.

For the family *takaful* business under the *mudharabah* model, the company does not share the underwriting surplus but returns it to the participants to be accumulated to build the fund. The company only shares

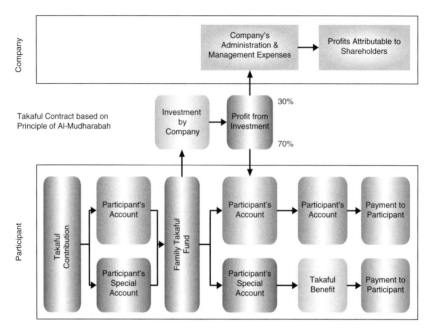

Source: INCEIF's Part II Specialized Module for *Takaful* on Managing *Takaful* Institutions.

Figure 10.3   Mudharabah *model – family* takaful

the investment profits and deducts all administrative and management expenses from the shareholders' share of the profits from investment.

Under the modified *mudharabah* model, the company shares not only the investment income from both the participants' accounts and the participants' special accounts but deducts the commission and management expenses from the participant's special accounts. Of course the share of the profits for the company under the modified *mudharabah* model is smaller compared to those of the *mudharabah* model. The Figures 10.3 and 10.4 are just examples of how the *mudharabah* and modified *mudharabah* models for the family *takaful* business are being employed. They are not universally practiced as most of the companies in operation today are employing the *wakala* model.

Wakala model

The *wakala* model is currently the most commonly used model in most countries. Although the *takaful* companies which were established in the 1980s employed the *mudharabah* or the modified *mudharabah* models, the

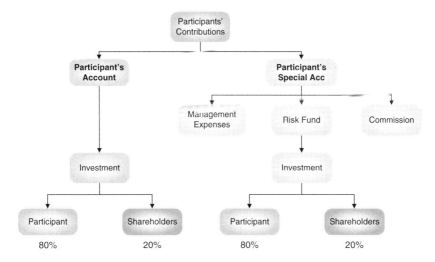

Source: INCEIF's Part II Specialized Module for *Takaful* on Managing *Takaful* Institutions.

Figure 10.4   Modified mudharabah *model – family* takaful

newly established companies in the last three or four years have chosen to employ the *wakala* model.

Wakala, which literally means agency, employs the *Shari'ah* principle of providing a service for a fee or *ujr*. In a *wakala* model, the *takaful* operator acts as the agent on behalf of the participants. The operator is paid a pre-agreed management fee for the services rendered in respect of underwriting, management and investment of the fund. The operator does not share in the underwriting surplus. This is mainly because the contributions by the participants allocated to the participants' special accounts are based on *tabarru'* or voluntary donation which according to *Shari'ah* cannot benefit the contributor any more. The proceeds from the underwriting surplus are being ploughed back into the fund.

In underwriting, the *takaful* operator acts as an agent on behalf of the participants to manage the *takaful* fund. Any liabilities for risks underwritten are borne by the fund and any surplus arising therefrom belongs exclusively to the participants. The operator is not liable for any deficit of the fund. The operator is being paid a management fee termed as *wakala* fee which is usually a percentage of the contributions paid by the participants. This is normally deducted upfront from the contributions.

As for the management of the investment activities of the fund, the operator is also paid a *wakala* fee based on an agreed percentage. Alternatively,

the operator may take a share of the profit if it considers the service provided as part of the expert service to manage the fund. When the fund is
still very small, the company may opt to do it in-house. Obviously, when
the fund has grown very big, the operator may need to outsource the
responsibility of managing the fund to an outside party. This approach
would certainly attract additional costs to the company, otherwise.

3.7   General *takaful* business

The contributions from participants for the general *takaful* business under
the *wakala* model are put into the General Risk Investment Account
(GRIA) which is also known as the General Fund. Upon receipt of the
contributions from the participants, the company charges a *wakala* fee for
managing this fund. Part of the contributions in GRIA is then placed in
the *Ta'awuni* Account Pool (TAP) that has front- and back-end charges as
allocations for benefits/reserves, claims, servicing, management expenses
and commission (Expense Fund, Risk Fund and Special Fund). The
TAP is essentially another name for the *tabarru'* fund that is used for the
payment of claims. Any surpluses in TAP will be put back into the GRIA.
The company will charge a surplus administration fee for this activity. The
balance of the surplus is put back into the GRIA. The profit received from
investment activities is returned to GRIA after deducting the investment
performance fee. The net surplus shall be shared at some predetermined
ratio between participant and company (see Figure 10.5).

Family *Takaful* Business

Family *takaful* business under the *wakala* model allocates contributions from participants into two separate accounts, namely the Personal
Investment Account (PIA) and Personal Investment Risk Account (PRIA)
at a ratio based on the various products offered. PRIA is for protection
whilst PIA is for protection and investment. The company charges a
wakala fee for managing the family fund. The fee varies from product to
product. Part of the contributions in PRIA and PIA will be put into the
Ta'awuni Account Pool (TAP) that has front- and back-end charges as
allocations for benefits, reserves, claims, servicing management expenses
and commissions (expense fund, risk fund and special fund) (Figure 10.6).

Any surplus in TAP is put back into the respective PRIA and PIA. The
company charges a certain percentage as surplus administration fee for
this activity. The balance is put back into PRIA and PIA respectively.
The profits from investment activities are returned to PRIA and PIA after
deducting an investment performance fee. The net surplus is shared at a
ratio of 50:50 or better between the participants and the company.

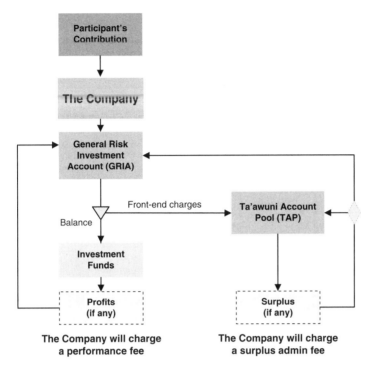

Source: INCEIF's Part II Specialized Module for *Takaful* on Managing *Takaful* Institutions.

Figure 10.5 Wakala *model – general business*

Wakala-waqf model

The *Wakala-Waqf* model (Figure 10.7) was started in South Africa and later was copied by Pakistan's first *takaful* company. The main reason why the *waqf* element is introduced into an otherwise pure *wakala* model is because of the nature of the *tabarru'* fund which has a very specific use, namely to pay claims. The term *tabarru'* itself implies that the participant who contributes has given up his or her right to any claim on his or her contribution. This concept is akin to the concept of *waqf* whereby once a person declares to give away a certain property for *waqf* he or she has severed all ties to the property. Immediately the property belongs to Allah and hence a trustee has to be set up to administer the property. The same is true in this *wakala-waqf* model. Once the participant declares that he or she has given away part of his or her contribution as *tabarru'*, a trustee has to be established in which case it is the *takaful* operator.

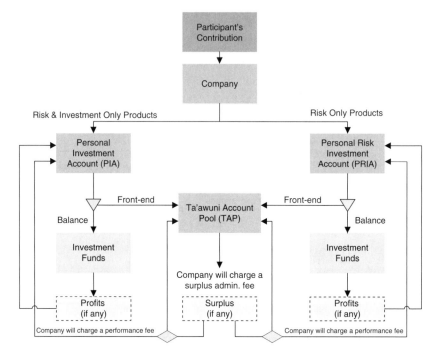

Source: INCEIF's Part II Specialized Module for *Takaful* on Managing *Takaful*
           Institutions.

Figure 10.6   Wakala *model* – family *takaful*

The main difference between the *wakala* model and the *wakala-waqf*
model is the existence of the *waqf* fund. The *waqf* fund is to be used solely
to pay out claims. To start the fund, the company has to pay the seed
money. The fund will then be built over time through contributions made
by the participants. If at any time the fund is insufficient to cover the
claims, the company will have to extend an interest-free loan which will be
paid back when the fund can afford it.

The participants will pay the *takaful* operator the contributions, based
on the product taken up by the participants from among the general
business. The contributions are credited to the general *takaful* fund as
tabarru' in the participants' special account (PSA). Any person will be
acknowledged as a member of the *waqf* fund if he or she signs the pro-
posal form, contributes to the *waqf* fund and subscribes to the policy
documents.

The *waqf* fund shall work to achieve the following objectives:

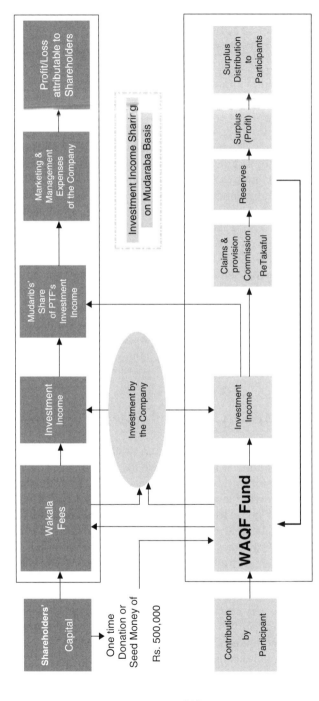

Source: INCEIF's Part II Specialized Module for *Takaful* on Managing *Takaful* Institutions.

Figure 10.7 Wakala-Waqf *model – general* takaful

1. To pay compensation to its members in the event of losses, mishap or damage.
2. To extend benefits to its members strictly in accordance with the *waqf* deed.
3. To donate to charities approved by the *Shari'ah* Supervisory Board.

The *Waqf* fund will lay down the rules for distribution of its funds to the beneficiaries and will decide how much compensation should be given to a subscriber or member . The *waqf* will become owner of all contributions and has the right to act as a legal entity as per its terms for investment, compensations and dealings with the surplus amounts

From among the above models, the most common now is the *wakala* model and some of its variants, which are being employed by almost all the new *takaful* operators. The *mudharabah* model and its variants will soon be left out as it is more advantageous for the operators to employ the *wakala* model. The obvious strength is in the *wakala* fee that the company gets upfront without having to do anything else. As in the *mudharabah* model, the surplus may neither be shared by the participants nor by the shareholders.

The other advantage is the possibility of sharing some of the profits that have been earned through investment or even underwriting. In the above case, the company earns from both sources as a performance fee. This is indeed possible and *Shari'ah*-compliant, depending on how they are viewed.

4.0 DEVELOPMENT OF THE *TAKAFUL* INDUSTRY

The *takaful* industry is only 30 years old, from when the first company was established in 1979 in Sudan. After about two decades, it has proven to be the fastest growing sector of the insurance market with an unprecedented double-digit rate of growth for some sustainable number of years.[21] 'Based on the 2007 Oliver Wyman Report, the potential premium for *takaful* worldwide, is at least USD20 billion. The report also estimates that up to 20% of the *takaful* revenues originated from non-Muslim customers. . . . Currently there are more than 250 *takaful* operators worldwide.'[22] The participation of established conventional players in the UK, US and Germany in establishing both the *takaful* and *retakaful* companies within their group is indeed a very crucial contributor to the growth of the *takaful* industry worldwide. *Retakaful* is a form used to refer to reinsurance taken by *takaful* insurance company to manage the risk.

In addition, the global demand for *takaful* products continues to grow as a consequence of the phenomenal growth of various components in the

Islamic financial system especially the Islamic banking and capital market sectors. This is evidenced by the tremendous growth in Islamic financing and mortgages in the Islamic banking sector and increasing popularity of *sukuk* issuance in the Islamic capital market.[23]

The industry is further supported by progress in the regulatory sphere in the last two years. The Islamic Financial Services Board (IFSB), in collaboration with the International Association of Insurance Supervisors is actively involved in the development of standards applicable to *takaful*. They are also looking at the corporate governance standard to cover key issues in the *takaful* business including rights and obligations of stakeholders in *takaful* operations.[24]

5.0   FUTURE CHALLENGES

Despite the past accomplishments and strong momentum for future growth, there are at least three challenges that need to be addressed.

First is the limited size and capacity. Despite the relatively rapid growth, the industry is still very small compared to the conventional insurance market. Participants' contributions stood at USD2 billion, accounting for only 1 per cent of USD3.7 trillion global insurance premiums in 2006. The *takaful* assets are estimated to be around USD20 billion, in contrast to the Islamic banking assets of USD500 billion. The *takaful* sector grows at relatively slower pace than the *sukuk* market which is growing at about 40 per cent. *Takaful* players are relatively small with the largest *takaful* company having total assets of only USD3 billion. Being young and new, many *takaful* operators also lack the capacity, capabilities and expertise to manage businesses with large and complex risks.[25]

Second is the low penetration rate. Although Muslims account for at least 22 per cent of the world population, *takaful* contribution in Muslim countries constitutes only 1 per cent of the total global insurance premium. This shows the strong latent demand for *takaful* products and services within the Muslim world if only they view *takaful* protection as an important tool for risk mitigation.[26]

Third is the lack of *retakaful* support and capacity. Adequate support from strong *retakaful* companies is vital for the *takaful* sector in risk mitigation, capital relief provision and building of essential technical capabilities in managing risks. 'Currently there are about 10 to 15 *retakaful* companies available to support over 250 *takaful* operators worldwide.'[27] Until now, most *takaful* and even the *retakaful* operators have had to depend on conventional reinsurers. This does not augur well with the need to cater for the unique principles of *takaful* products.

A number of strategies can be considered for planning and implementation.

First, there is a strong need to build a more globalized *takaful* industry through greater connectivity across jurisdictions. *Takaful* operators need to give a sufficient emphasis on cross-border interlinkages at the regional and international levels. This will not only widen the market but more importantly expose it to the different challenges to build strength and competitiveness.

Second, efforts towards concerted branding for *takaful* have to be initiated and developed. By concerted branding the appeal of *takaful* could be enhanced in the global community. The *takaful* principles of mutuality, transparency and cooperation could be further popularized to spearhead unique products for the global community.

Third, *Shari'ah* has to be positioned as an enabler for greater linkages of *takaful* markets globally. Research and training in *Shari'ah* and *Shari'ah*-related issues and fields may be one approach to spread the influence of *Shari'ah* and *takaful* in all markets that *takaful* can serve. The acute shortage of human talent cannot be ignored at all.

Fourth, *takaful*, as is the case with any business that deals with a huge number of clients, must surely be well-equipped with an infrastructure that could help expedite processes and improve accuracy to mitigate risks in these areas. It is not only the physical infrastructures including IT that are needed, but also the regulatory framework must be further strengthened.

Fifth, *takaful* should not be looked at merely as a business concern but should also locate in areas where socio-economic assistance is definitely needed. Corporate social responsibility could be employed as a means of reaching out to assist in community improvement.

6.0 CONCLUSION

The future of *takaful* is not bleak at all. Indeed it is very bright. Within a short 30 years or so, *takaful* has become a growing force in financial circles. However, it requires not just the operators, but rather the combined efforts of all the relevant parties – the regulators, market participants, *Shari'ah* scholars and the international community at large – to play their roles.

NOTES

1. Muhammad Muslehuddin (1969), *Insurance and Islamic Law*, Lahore, p. 15.
2. Morgan, T.W. (1933), *Porter's Law of Insurance*, London, p. 47.
3. Watt, W.M. (1956), *Muhammad at Medina*, Oxford, p. 262 quoted by Muhammad Muslehuddin, op. cit., p. 27.
4. Afzalaur Rahman (1979), *Economic Doctrines of Islam Volume 4, Banking and Insurance*, The Muslim Schools Trust, London, pp. 65–69.
5. *Quran: Surah Al Baqarah* (2): verse 178.
6. *Quran: Surah An-Nisaa* (4) verse 91.
7. *Quran: Surah Al-Maidah* (5) verse 48.
8. Zidan, A. and Zidan, D. (2002), *Mokhtaser Sahih Muslim*, A.S. Nordeen, Kuala Lumpur. *Hadith* 1034, p. 231.
9. Billah, M.M. (2007), *Applied Islamic Law of Trade and Finance*, Sweet & Maxwell Asia, Petaling Jaya. 3rd ed, pp. 125–200.
10. *Sahih Muslim* (English), *Kitab al-Birr*, *Hadith* No. 59.
11. Hitti, Philip K. (1969), *Makers of Arab History*, London, pp. 69–71.
12. *Quran*: *Surah Al-Maidah* (5): 3.
13. *Quran: Surah Al-Maidah* (5): 3.
14. Narrated by Imam Ahmad Ibn Hanbal and Imam Abu Daud.
15. Narrated by Imam al-Bukhari and Imam Muslim.
16. Narrated by Imam al-Bukhari and Imam Muslim.
17. Narrated by Imam Ahmad bin Hanbal.
18. Ibid. *Sahih Muslim* (English), *Kitab al-Birr, Hadith* No. 984.
19. Ibid. *Hadith* No. 59.
20. *Quran: Surah Al-Maidah* (5): verse 3.
21. Keynote Address by Dato' Muhammad bin Ibrahim, Assistant Governor, Central Bank of Malaysia, at the International Takaful Summit, 'Global Takaful Industry: Moving to the Next Level of Excellence', Jumeirah Carlton Hotel London, 16 July 2008.
22. Ibid., p. 1.
23. Ibid., p. 2.
24. Ibid., p. 2.
25. Ibid., p. 2.
26. Ibid., p. 3.
27. Ibid., p. 3.

PART IV

A debate on the issue of reward for parting with capital

11. Usury and its critics: from the Middle Ages to modernity

Constant Mews and Adrian Walsh

1.0 HISTORICAL MEANING OF USURY AND INTEREST

While it is common in discussions of Islamic finance to translate *riba* as interest, we wish to argue that it is better understood through the notion of usury since it was understood this way not just in the Christian Middle Ages but even at the time of Adam Smith in his *The Wealth of Nations* (1776). We also argue that the person responsible for changing attitudes towards usury (and for confusing our understanding of the word) was Jeremy Bentham, whose *Defence of Usury* (1787) would have a huge impact in shaping a tendency not just to trivialize the notion of usury, but to promote a tendency in the West to divorce financial behaviour from ethical concerns.

While their debate about usury has already attracted comment (Hollander 1999; Mews and Ibrahim 2007; Walsh and Lynch 2008), it deserves to be placed within a larger context. Bentham's ideas would eventually lead to the abolition of the usury laws in Britain in 1854, making London the global financial centre that it still is today. One could argue that when Britain's law-makers first acknowledged the legitimacy of Islamic financial contracts in 2002, they were unwittingly recognizing the validity of a system of financial ethics that had in fact underpinned the European economy for more than six hundred years until its abolition.

This chapter explores a parallel movement to Islamic finance in the European tradition. It is the fruit of collaboration between a historian of medieval Christian thought, and a philosopher concerned with contemporary financial ethics. In its first part, we shall explore classical understandings of usury starting from the work of Thomas Aquinas in the 13th century to that of Adam Smith in the 18th century. Its second part will consider how Jeremy Bentham, in writing his *Defence of Usury* against Adam Smith, created confusion in our understanding of the term, making it much more difficult to develop a system of financial ethics that can be related to that of Islamic law. Therein lies the rise of banking, by erasing the distinction between interest and usury (if we may call this excessive interest), with no ethical underpinning that has led to the banks becoming a dominant institution over the last two centuries. Once its aim to make more money with no ethical boundaries took a sinister turn – with the abolition of a distinction between usury and interest that has been around for a long time and the abolition of the separation of banking from insurance and investment in 1999 – the stage was set for a momentous world financial crisis that has reduced nations' ability to create wealth and prosperity for its peoples in 2007–08.

2.0   CONFLATING INTEREST AND USURY

There is a common tendency in books about Islamic finance not to recognize the semantic distinction between usury and interest widely known in historical writings in Western tradition. Certainly some scholars, like Iqbal and Mirakhor (2007, 69–76) in their recent *Introduction to Islamic Finance*, and Persky (2007) in a study titled 'From usury to interest', are aware that there has been a transition from one word to another, but without explaining why this should have happened. Confusion about the meaning of usury is deep-rooted and widespread. The *Oxford English Dictionary* (1989), for example, defines usury as initially 'the fact or practice of lending money at interest', but comments that it later means 'the practice of charging, taking, or contracting to receive, excessive or illegal rates of interest for money on loan', as well as mentioning its archaic meaning as any premium or interest on a loan. Little wonder we are confused. Any lawyer would observe that this range of meanings makes usury far too slippery a notion to be useful in law, let alone to be an adequate translation of *riba*.

What makes an excessive interest rate? The same dictionary illustrates the so-called 'modern' meaning of usury by referring to Jeremy Bentham's description of usury (1787) as 'the taking of greater interest than the law allows or [. . .] the taking of a greater interest than is usual for me to give and take'. Bentham had a vested interest in describing usury in this way, without any awareness of its classical meaning. Very simply, Bentham did not explain the traditional meaning of usury (*usura* in Latin) as much more than simply lending money at interest; it was the demanding of payment (by extension excess payment itself) that disturbed the natural justice and equality that should prevail between lender and borrower. By contrast, the word interest (*interesse* in Latin) derived from a term in Roman law to mean legitimate compensation to the lender for a loan (Noonan 1957,

112). Usury has thus always referred to the illegitimate demanding of money beyond the principal, or in the plural (*usurae* in Latin) as moneys demanded in this way.

The tendency to confuse usury and interest is widespread, as is the erroneous claim that the Protestant reformation introduced a change in the meaning of usury. As Kerridge observes in his important study, *Usury, Interest and the Reformation* (2002, 1):

> To make matters worse, most dictionaries turn a blind eye to the inconvenient fact that John Calvin and others favoured and used an entirely different set of words and terms in which to discuss the subject [usury], and this new terminology has, more often than not, been jumbled together with the old, making confusion worse confounded. This confusion, spread by R. H. Tawney, has crept into countless history books . . . Such error, constantly repeated at every turn over scores and scores of years, cannot be overcome by uttering a casual sentence or two; it must be torn up by the roots, which can be accomplished only by a full exposition of Christian teachings on the matter.

Kerridge (2002, 5) quotes a 16th-century definition to illustrate his theme: 'Usury and trewe interest be things as contrary as falshod is to truth.' Even Adam Smith distinguishes clearly between the notion of interest as legitimate compensation to a lender, and usury, which was always illegitimate as it involved a lender demanding money over and above any reasonable compensation for the loan, purely for the sake of profit.

In the Hebrew Bible, usury is condemned as a form of injustice between rich and poor, the same position taken by Islam in its scripture. To quote Exodus 22:25: 'If you lend money to any of my people, to any poor man among you, you must not play the usurer with him; you must not demand interest from him.' Christian thinkers found in the New Testament an even more challenging injunction in Luke 6:35: 'Lend, hoping for nothing in return.' Yet the practice of charging interest on loans was completely admissible in Roman law, and remained common practice throughout the medieval period, much to the distress of Christian moralists. Unlike Islam, Christianity did not develop in a mercantile context, and thus had no need to develop any sophisticated ethics of finance, at least in its first thousand years.

Only with the rapid economic development of the 12th century, when Europe started to become aware of the sophistication of the Islamic world in both commerce and ideas, did this begin to change. An insatiable demand for credit and thus exorbitant interest rates from money lenders, many of whom were Jews, permitted to lend at interest to non-Jews, according to Deut. 23:20–21 (Nelson 1949), prompted Christian reformers to advocate a system of financial ethics that avoided usury, a process not unlike the way Islamic finance has evolved as a reaction to perceived abuses in an established system imposed by the colonizing Western powers that introduced modern banking to the Islamic world. Like Islamic financial theory, Christian financial ethics too took time to evolve. Initially, in the mid-12th century, even educated theologians and canon lawyers with little understanding of business, viewed usury simply as theft. Peter Lombard condemned usury just on the authority of the Bible. Gratian defined it simply as any money demanded in return for a loan, above the principal; any more was theft.

Yet it was clearly insufficient to construct a financial system simply on Biblical exhortations. By the mid 13th century, a system of contracts was developed by lawyers that respected the core principle that any contract had to avoid usury, while giving legitimate compensation to a lender (as in Roman laws that survived to a later period). Theologians reflected on the principles involved (Noonan 1957; Langholm 1992). The preferred way of making an investment was through partnership in sharing the risk involved. As Thomas Aquinas observes in his *Summa Theologiae* IIa. iiae. q. 78.2 (Aquinas, 1985, 245), in a partnership there is no transfer of ownership, and thus the person offering money can legitimately claim his or her share of the profit. Collecting usury was morally wrong because no risk was shared. While it was usury to make money simply by advancing money for goods that would be resold for a higher price at a later date, it was legitimate to do so if there was an element of uncertainty involved (Kaye 2005, 36–37). In a census contract, credit could be offered in return for the right to a share in profits over a fixed term, so long as it was perceived that there was a legitimate equivalence between the money transferred and the profits acquired.

3.0 EARLY RESPONSE TO USURY AND INTEREST

While canon lawyers invariably differed on the legitimacy of particular contracts (just like their Islamic equivalents), theologians like Thomas Aquinas focused more on the larger question of usury as a particular form of injustice, relying more on philosophical reasoning than Biblical authority. In particular he was inspired by Aristotle's discussion of justice in commercial relationships in book 5 of the *Ethics* and the *Politics*. For Thomas the core principle of any financial transaction is equality: 'What is equally useful to both should not involve more of a burden for one than for the other and any contract between two parties should, therefore, be based on an equality of material exchange' (q.77.1; 1985, 215). Thomas debates the possibility that usury is not a sin, but then responds that to make money while lending money, 'sets up an inequality which is contrary to justice' (q.78.1; 1985, 235). If there was a loan, something had to be transferred; the borrower was duty bound to return what he had borrowed but no more. He recognizes, however, that 'Somebody who makes a loan is within his rights to settle terms of compensation for the loss of any advantage which he is entitled to enjoy, for this does not amount to selling the use of money, but is a question of avoiding loss' (q.78.2; 1985, 243).

Thomas is aware that civil law tolerates a measure of usury, 'to accommodate imperfect men who would be severely disadvantaged if all sins were strictly prohibited by suitable sanctions. Human law, therefore, allows the taking of usury, not because it deems this to be just but because to do otherwise would impose undue restrictions on many people' (q. 78.1; 1985, 239). He evaluates usury around a notion of equity and equilibrium that has to be estimated, in the same way as a just price, rather than basing it on strict equality, as Gratian had done (Kaye 2002). Implicit in his reasoning is a sense that a compromise sometimes has to be drawn between tolerating a modest degree of usury and rejecting larger usury that is manifestly unjust.

Canon lawyers, like their Islamic equivalents, were needed to guarantee the legal authenticity of any financial transaction. Inevitably there were suspicions that certain practices might involve usury. In the mid 14th century, an international financial crisis, which precipitated the collapse of many prominent Italian banking families, prompted many Italian towns to develop *monte comune* – effectively local community credit agencies, which raised money by imposing loans in return for payments of the order of 5 per cent (Armstrong 2003, 40–45). A system originally intended to help the poor, turned into a useful financial device for the city. Although lawyers argued that payments made in return for forced loans need not be usurious, the system of investing in communal debt was clearly open to abuse.

In the 16th century, many reformers were appalled by the legal devices used to escape usury. As Kerridge (2002) argues, far from allowing usury, they insisted that usury should not taint financial relationships, while recognizing that the role of interest, limited to a fixed amount, was to give legitimate compensation to a lender. Thus, an English law of 1571 prohibited usury, but created a legal ceiling of 10 per cent interest that gradually reduced to 5 per cent by the time of Adam Smith. The difficulty with this system is that although interest was still technically viewed as compensation, it also became an instrument of profit. By the 17th and early 18th centuries, the emergence of speculators ('projectors' as they were called) was creating an increasing divide between the theoretical equality upheld by the anti-usury law and the opportunities available through financial speculation.

Adam Smith was not simply the advocate of a free market. He was a moral philosopher, brought up to value very classical ideals of moderation and balance in ethical behaviour (Paganelli 2003). While he valued the importance of individual initiative in maximizing the wealth of any nation, he was also profoundly aware of the need for the state to maintain prohibition against usury – in Great Britain then set at 5 per cent – to ensure that credit could be available to the sober-minded, but that it could not be exploited by 'speculators and projectors' who took excessive risks by demanding excessive rates of interest in the hope of lending money on a profitable but dangerous venture. As Hollander (1999) argues, Smith's arguments against usury were based on suspicion of unnecessarily risky speculation – attitudes that have much in common with traditional Islamic distrust of both *gharar* and *riba*. Smith comments in passing that the complete prohibition of *riba* in 'Mahometan' countries led in practice to exorbitant unofficial rates of interest of 100 per cent. Whether or not his information was correct, his broader message was that while some level of compensation is necessary for any credit agency, a prohibition on usury must remain, for the sake of developing true productivity – not simply the profits of any particular bank.

4.0   THE WORLD OF USURY ACCORDING TO JEREMY BENTHAM

Jeremy Bentham, by contrast with Adam Smith, saw nothing wrong with speculation. Unlike Smith, he could not see usury as an assault against natural justice, and saw no reason for the state to establish what might constitute usury. It would be Bentham's way of thinking rather than that of Adam Smith that would in fact shape the modern world.

Bentham's defence of usury was part of a broader philosophical outlook known as utilitarianism. Unlike the Aristotelian ethical frameworks, which became foundations for an integrated value system into both Christianity and Islam, and that judges behaviour in terms of ideal values or virtues, Bentham held that questions of the rightness or wrongness of an action were settled with reference to the extent to which it maximized pleasure. He famously suggested that human beings are under the dominion of two sovereign masters, pleasure and pain, and goodness involved increasing pleasure and decreasing pain. Accordingly, it is the consequences in terms of pleasure and pain that determine the moral status of any human action. In such a philosophy earlier notions of natural balance or natural equilibrium had little place, being regarded as nothing more than pre-modern superstitions. The point of philosophy was in fact to question what society took to be natural and instead consider whether a practice increased or decreased the sum total of pleasure in that society. Their consequential effects were all that mattered.

We find this lack of interest in intellectual traditions prominently on display in his *Defence of Usury*, originally a series of letters written to Adam Smith. In contrast to earlier writers from the Middle Ages onwards, Bentham does not distinguish between usury and interest. Instead Bentham takes the two to be synonyms, as we can see when he suggests that the main strength of the argument against usury lies in the very sound of the term itself (Bentham 1787, 130). But his failure to distinguish clearly between usury and interest perhaps makes it more difficult to explain adequately the meaning of *riba* in English.

Bentham's attacks on usury laws themselves – by which we mean laws that placed limits on the rate of interest that could be charged – involve both a contempt for their supposed intellectual justifications and a genuine horror at what he perceives to be their counterproductive consequences. The contempt for the philosophical criticisms of usury is most notoriously on display in his discussion of Aristotle's 'argument from barrenness'. Aristotle had argued that money was incapable of creating more money – for it was barren – and hence any profit made from the mere loaning of money must be based on some fraud. Bentham satirises these views in the following cruel passage:

> with all his industry, and all his penetration, notwithstanding the great number of pieces of money that had passed through his hands (more perhaps than ever passed through the hands of a philosopher before or since), and notwithstanding the uncommon pains he had bestowed on the subject of generation, had never been able to discover, in any one piece of money, any organs for generating any other such piece. (Bentham 1787, 158)

Although the Protestant theologian John Calvin had already criticized the Aristotelian argument, suggesting that money would only be sterile if it were hidden in a box, Bentham's parody was probably more influential in undermining its legitimacy and ultimately condemning it to be an historical relic.

Bentham argues against the laws as well on grounds that they are morally arbitrary. He suggests that there is no reason to think any particular rate of interest provides a marker between the just and the unjust: indeed when we look to the customs of different countries and historical periods, we find no consensus on what the just rate should be. He asks why think that amongst these widely different rates that 'there is one that is intrinsically more proper than another'? (Bentham 1787, 132). This is directed squarely at all those in favour of interest rate ceilings.

Bentham also suggests that it is entirely arbitrary to allow one person who sells a house and makes a 10 per cent gain on it to be free of moral opprobrium whilst the person who makes the same amount of profit on the sale of money should be labelled a usurer. After all, we do not fix the price of horse-flesh. Why should money be different from other assets? 'Why' he asks, should the government legislate against the 'owners of that species of property more than of any other?' (Bentham 1787, 133).

However, Bentham's real concern is with what he takes to be the social harms caused by the laws against usury of the time – laws which Adam Smith had endorsed. He identifies three major grounds for concern, all of which arise despite the stated objects of the laws. Firstly he suggests that although one aim of the laws was to protect the needy (or 'indigent') from exploitation they have in fact produced the equal and opposite harm. They have either driven the needy into the arms of black-market money lenders under far more disadvantageous terms, or alternatively debarred them from access to the funds they need. (We find a similar concern regarding the harms of banning 'desperate exchange' in Margaret Jane Radin's recent work in political philosophy on the 'double bind' – see Radin, 1996). According to Bentham, usury laws preclude people from 'getting the money they stand in need of, to answer their respective exigencies' (Bentham [1801] 1952, 142).

Secondly, he suggests that although part of the motivation for the existence of usury laws was to prevent 'prodigality' or wasteful consumption, in this 'they have failed spectacularly'. The prodigal is pushed towards even more disadvantageous conditions.

> Instead of stopping or diminishing the waste which the prodigal is committing, they have accelerated the progress of it, by driving him into expedients whereby future money is exchanged for present upon terms more disadvantageous than those of an ordinary loan (Bentham [1801] 1952, 285).

Once again it would appear that the laws bring about the opposite of what they set out to achieve. Bentham argues that given there are so many ways that the prodigals (or spendthrifts) might come to waste their resources, why should we focus solely on moneylending? Why pick moneylending out from the variety of ways in which one might waste one's money? Bentham could not see the point of 'stopping the current expenditure at the fossett (the tap in English), when there are so many unpreventable ways of letting it run down the bung-hole' (Bentham 1787, 137).

Thirdly, Bentham argues that these laws have 'nipped in the bud' and 'destroyed outright' inventive industry. The argument here is simply the utilitarian one that we wish to encourage those with initiative to develop projects for their own enrichment if these are the kind of projects which ultimately benefit society as a whole. Adam Smith had claimed that only prodigals and 'projectors' (whom we would now refer to as 'entrepreneurs') would accept loans at high rates or interests. We have already noted his repudiation of the concern with prodigals, but his defence of projectors bears further examination. According to Bentham, projectors have been responsible for the progress of humanity and the usury laws, by placing impediments in their path, have only hindered that progress (Bentham 1787, 172). Against those who would say that usury has ceilings he responds that ceilings provide no mechanism for distinguishing between prudent and imprudent projects. All that they manage to achieve is to stymie the kinds of new projects that provide us all with great benefits.

One striking feature of all of Bentham's criticism of the usury laws is his failure (or perhaps his unwillingness) to distinguish between those who would abolish the institution of lending at interest entirely and those who are simply opposed to usurious lending practices. The position of Aristotle is treated equally as harshly as that of Smith who advocated a rate of 6 per cent. In effect, for Bentham no moral concerns were to be found in the practice of lending at interest and only benefits could come from deregulation. But this wilfully ignores the many injustices to which these financial transactions can give rise and, furthermore, it overlooks the possibility (of which we are now all too aware) of the negative social consequences that can arise from unregulated lending. With Bentham we lose the ability to distinguish between vicious and acceptable forms of money lending.

5.0 CONCLUSION

The influence of Bentham on Western thinking was substantial and as a consequence we find little discussion of just rates of interest amongst subsequent philosophers and economists. In the 20th century normative discussions about how the taking of interest might be justified are almost non-existent; certainly when one looks through most standard economic textbooks, the question of what might legitimate making profit on the loan of money does not appear.

We do not wish to give the impression in all of this that Bentham's critique was without its merits. There were many reasons to be critical of the anti-usury laws of his time. The imposition of complicated and unwieldy regulation was clearly something worth opposing. Few ideals, no matter how worthy or desirable, remain justifiable in the face of poorly framed or hypocritically administered laws.

Nonetheless Bentham was mistaken in his failure to acknowledge how desperate circumstances could lead borrowers to accept exploitative conditions. While it is obvious there is no particular rate that marks the boundary, across time and space, between the just and the unjust, it is also clear that, within specific economic conditions, there will be rates which are exploitative relative to those conditions. While we would want to encourage productive investment, we would not wish to endorse consumption loans drawn up when the borrower is in financial difficulty. Furthermore his refusal to distinguish between those who wanted to abolish interest altogether and those who wanted usury ceilings led to a loss of an ethical tradition that wished to accept the institution of money-lending at the same time as placing moral constraints upon it.

But it is here we see part of the importance for the West of the recent revitalization of intellectual interest in Islamic finance. In the Islamic tradition there is considerable debate about what constitutes *riba* and what constitutes legitimate compensation to a lender in making a deal. Bentham's defence of usury lies at the basis of the conventional system of finance in the West. Unfortunately, one legacy of his views on the morality of money – and his claims that usury is always legitimate – has been a tendency in financial circles to lose sight of the principles that underpin financial behaviour. Perhaps Islamic reasoning here might reawaken these normative questions amongst Western thinkers about why we behave in the way we do.

REFERENCES

Aquinas, Thomas (1985) *Summa Theologiae*, vol. 38 *Injustice* (IIaiiae.63–79), trans. Marcus Lefébure. London: Eyre & Spottiswoode.

Armstrong, Lawrin (2003) *Usury and Public Debt in Early Renaissance Florence: Lorenzo Ridolfi on the Monte Comune.* Toronto: Pontifical Institute of Mediaeval Studies.

Bentham, Jeremy (1787), *Defence of Usury*, fourth edition 1818. London: Payne and Foss; electronic facsimile Online Library of Liberty, http://oll.libertyfund.org/ToC/0167.php.

Bentham, Jeremy ([1801] 1952), *Defence of a Maximum*, in W. Stark (ed.), *Jeremy Bentham's Economic Writings.* Leicester: Blackfriars Press.

Hollander, Samuel (1999) 'Jeremy Bentham and Adam Smith on the usury laws: A "Smithian" reply to Bentham and a new problem', *European Journal of History of Economic Thought*, 6(4), 523–551.

Iqbal, Zamir and Abbas Mirakhor (2007) *Introduction to Islamic Finance. Theory and Practice.* Singapore: John Wiley & Sons (Asia).

Kaye, Joel (2005) 'Changing definitions of money, nature, and equality c. 1140–1270, reflected in Thomas Aquinas' Questions on Usury' in Quaglioni et al. (2005, 25–55).

Kerridge, Eric (2002) *Usury, Interest and the Reformation*. Aldershot, Hants: Ashgate.

Langholm, Odd (1992) *Economics in the Medieval Schools*. Leiden: Brill.

Mews, Constant J. and Ibrahim Abraham (2007), 'Usury and just compensation: religious and financial ethics in historical perspective', *Journal of Business Ethics* 72(1) (April), 1–15.

Nelson, Benjamin (1949) *The Idea of Usury. From Tribal Brotherhood to Universal Otherhood*. Chicago: University of Chicago Press.

Noonan, John (1957) *The Scholastic Analysis of Usury*. Cambridge, Mass.: Harvard University Press.

Paganelli, Maria (2003) '*In medio stat virtus*: an alternative view of usury in Adam Smith's thinking', *History of Political Economy*, 35(1), 21–48.

Persky, Joseph (2007) 'Retrospectives – from usury to interest', *Journal of Economic Perspectives*, 21(1) (Winter), 227–236 http://tigger.uic.edu/~jpersky/research.html#_ftn3.

Quaglioni, Diego, Giacomo Todeschini and Gian Maria Varanini (eds) (2005) *Credito e usura fra teologia, diritto e amministrazione: linguaggi a confronto, sec. XII–XVI* Rome: Ecole française de Rome.

Radin, Margaret Jane (1996) *Contested Commodities*. Cambridge, Mass.: Harvard University Press.

Smith, Adam (1776) *The Wealth of Nations*. Reprint, Edwin Cannan (ed.), New York: Modern Library, 1937.

Walsh, Adrian J. and Tony Lynch (2008) *The Morality of Money: An Exploration in Analytic Philosophy*. New York: Macmillan-Palgrave.

12. *Riba* and interest in Islamic banking: an historical review

Raquib Zaman

1.0 INTRODUCTION

The origin of Islamic banking is rooted in the belief that interest and usury are synonymous, and that all conventional financial institutions are dealers in usury and that their transactions are usurious. The Islamic concept of *riba*, which should appropriately be translated into usury, is instead proclaimed to be interest by the proponents of 'Islamic' banking and finance. Since *riba* is clearly prohibited in Islam, as will be shown below, they argue that Muslims should not deal with the conventional banking system. Hence, we are now showered with discourses that not only come up with the justification of Islamic banking and finance (IBF), but with the 'theory' of Islamic finance.[1] A number of texts elucidate the claimed rationale behind the creation and operation of IBF,[2] while a number of others[3] question their *modus operandi*. But, for a basic understanding of the concept of *riba* and its interpretation one must start with the *Quran*,[4] Islam's holy book, and then examine the *hadith*[5] literature, followed by the opinions of Muslim jurists, *shari'ah*.[6]

2.0 THE CONCEPT OF *RIBA* (USURY) IN ISLAM

Prohibition of *riba* according to the Holy Quran:

> O you who believe! Devour not usury, doubling and quadrupling (the sum lent). Observe your duty to God, that you may be successful.[7]

> O you who believe! Observe your duty to God, and give up what remain (due to you) from usury, if you are (in truth) believers. And if you do not, then be warned of war (against you) from God and His messenger. And if you repent, then you have your principal. Wrong not, and you shall not be wronged.[8]

> Those who swallow usury cannot rise up save as he arise whom the devil has prostrated by (his) touch. That is because they say: Trade is just like usury; whereas

God permits trading and forbids usury. He unto whom an admonition from his Lord comes, and (he) refrains (in obedience thereto), he shall keep (the profits of) that which is past, and his affair (henceforth) is with God. As for him who returns (to usury) – such are rightful owners of the Fire. They will abide therein.[9]

God has blighted usury and made almsgiving fruitful. God loves not the impious and guilty.[10]

The Arabic word for usury is *riba* (pronounced as rēē'ba). According to the Quran (Chapter 3, Verse 130, quoted above), *riba* is defined as 'doubling and quadrupling (the sum lent)'. This is the only definition of *riba* available from the Quran. All the other verses (all of which were quoted above) admonish the believers to refrain from usury and avoid God's punishment.

Judaism and Christianity, also ask their followers to refrain from usurious transactions to avoid burning in hell fire.[11] The classic commentators of Quran, such as al-Tabari,[12] Zamakhshari[13] and Ibn Kathir,[14] argued that the Quranic verse 3:130 on *riba* essentially talks about *riba-al-jahiliya* (i.e., usury practiced in the pre-Islamic period in Arabia). Al-Tabari in his *Jami* (4:49) points out that *riba* in the pre-Islamic period referred to doubling and redoubling of the principal amount lent in commodities over a period of time. At the due date, if the borrower failed to repay the amount borrowed, the loan was extended for another year but the borrower had to pay double the quantity originally lent. If, at the end of the second year, the borrower again failed to repay the loan, the loan was extended again for double the quantity of the second year to be repaid next year. Thus, in two years' time, the insolvent borrower would owe the original lender four times the quantity lent to him at the outset. Al-Zamakhshari, in his *al-Kashshaf* (p. 234, date of publication unknown), presents a similar interpretation pointing out that even a small debt could consume all the wealth of a debtor because of repeated doubling of the unpaid loan. Ibn al-Arabi[15] also gives a similar interpretation of *riba*, that is *riba al-jahaliya*. Prophet Muhammad in his farewell *hajj*, clearly proclaimed that, '*riba al-Jahiliya* is null and void from this day and that *Riba* of Abbas bin Abdul-Muttalib has been waived.' Ibn al-Arabi states that: 'Riba was well known among the Arabs. A person would sell something on a deferred payment basis and upon maturity the creditor would ask: "Will you pay (now) or add an amount to the bill"?'[16] (see also, Zaman and Movassaghi[17]).

Those who equate *riba* with interest seek support from al-Jassas,[18] who claimed that pre-Islamic Arabia practiced a form of *riba* where money was lent at a predetermined sum over the principal amount. However, there is no historical evidence to suggest that *riba al-jahiliya* also consisted of transactions that were similar to modern loans on interest.[19]

Thus, the basis for equating all forms of interest, whether they double or quadruple the principal or whether they are a small fraction of the principal, must be sought elsewhere. Let us look at the verified traditions or sayings (*hadith*) of the Prophet, which are the second major source of *Shari'ah* (Islamic jurisprudence).

2.1   *Riba* in Hadith and its Interpretation by Muslim Jurists (*Fuqaha*)

The traditions (i.e., *hadith*) of the Prophet on *riba* are essentially confined to *riba al-fadal* dealing with the borrowing or lending of commodities – e.g., gold, silver, etc. – but returned/exchanged at the same point in time. These 'hand-to-hand' transactions do not make any sense – why would anyone borrow, i.e., exchange gold for gold or for silver, unless it is part of a barter transaction, which is a perfectly legitimate form of trade under Islam? A further discussion of this follows shortly.

The *Sahih Al-Bukhari*[20] cites a considerable number of *hadith* dealing with *riba al-fadal*. A very few *hadith* – indeed, if any specific one – can be found in the verified collection of *hadith*[21] on *riba al-nasia*, i.e., collection of fixed and predetermined percentages of return on the amount of money lent, popularly known as 'interest'. Then one wonders what is the basis for regarding all kinds of interest as usurious? Is it the meaning of the Arabic word *riba* itself, which lends to this type of assertion? The word *riba* apparently means 'an excess or addition – i.e., an addition over and above the principal sum that is lent'.[22] If the Muslim jurists are referring to interest as usury on the basis of this literal meaning of *riba*, then naturally one wonders why God Almighty used the terms 'doubling' and 'quadrupling' (the sum lent) as usury in Chapter III Verse 130 (quoted above), and why there was no further clarification of this verse in the Quran, or by the Prophet. Some of the Muslim writers[23] who claim interest is *riba* have no problems in explaining the verses of the Quran and the *hadith*, as they simply translate the term *riba* as interest and then assert it is forbidden. It appears as though they start with an axiom that interest is *riba* and, as such, forbidden.

It is instructive to note here that while the Quran refers to *riba* in the context of loan (debt), the *hadith* literature cites it in the context of sales, and there is no mention of loan (*qard*) or debt (*dayan*). One such *hadith* that is often quoted, and is known by the epithet 'six commodities *hadith*', relates to the time around the Khyber Expedition – well before the prohibition on *riba* was imposed[24] – was as follows (it was narrated by Abu Sa'id al-Khudri on the authority of the Prophet):

> Gold is to be paid for by gold, silver by silver, wheat by wheat, barley by barley, dates by dates, salt by salt, like by like, payment being made hand to hand. He

who made an addition to it, or asked of an addition, in fact dealt in usury. The receiver and the giver are equally guilty.[25]

This particular injunction said to have been made by the Prophet to stop the cheating of the Muslims by the defeated hypocrites of Medina who were trying to get back the valuables they had to surrender as part of the Khyber Treaty. Muawiah, the fifth Caliph, a very learned man of his time, questioned the validity of this *hadith* and calling such transactions *riba*.[26]

It is important to note here that, when one borrows one commodity to be returned later, it is no longer 'hand-to-hand' – there is an elapsed time and, as such, it comes under the purview of *riba al-nasia*, i.e., deferred payment. If we were to accept the 'six commodities *hadith*' then all transactions that did not involve the use of money (i.e., barter trade) would be usurious. This is unacceptable from the point of view of rational thinking as well as religious and moral principles. The Muslim jurists, depending on how transactions are worded, consider *nasia* transactions as *salam* sale (instalment payments at a higher price than the original) or *murabaha* transactions (pre-determined mark-up on the original price to be paid over time), and, therefore, permitted. Others contend that all *nasia* transactions are usurious. Ironically, IBF not only considers these transactions to be permissible, but make most of their profit from such!

Two concepts, *illa* (efficient cause) and *hikma* (rationale) need to be considered. The *fuqaha* use *illa* to describe a transaction to be dealing with *riba*. For example the Quranic verse *lakum ru'usu amwalikum* (i.e., 'you shall be entitled to the return of your principal' 2:279) is used for *illa*, ignoring the remainder of the verse, *la tazlimuna wa-la tuzlamun* (i.e., 'you will do no wrong, and neither will you be wronged'), which provides the *hikma.* If the first part of the verse was taken literally, then the IBF policy of profit/loss sharing cannot be accepted. The following excerpt often quoted in legal circles is quite instructive:

> In many case the '*Illa*' approach appears superficial and devoid of moral con-siderations. For example, coins like '*fals*' did not involve *Riba* in Maliki, and Shafi'i schools. Thus 100 '*fals*' (which were used as a unit of currency but were not made of gold or silver) could be exchanged for 200 either on the spot or on a deferred delivery basis. (Why today's fiat money could also be not counted in this category, is a good question to ask.) Commodities which were countable like apples and eggs did not involve *riba*, and hence could be exchanged less for more, according to Hanafis. A piece of cloth could be exchanged for two pieces of the same quality and measure since it was neither measurable, or weighable, or gold or silver, or foodstuff.

Let us now go back to the issue of *riba* and interest. The contention of this author is that the two most important sources of the *Shari'ah* (i.e., the

Quran and the *hadith)* do not provide us with clear guidance as to whether or not interest is *riba* (i.e., usury). Some of the *fuqaha* or Muslim jurists are of the opinion that interest is *riba* and, as such, it is prohibited. This view can be acceptable if it is solely based on the argument that the word *riba* has only one meaning, and that is 'an addition over and above the principal sum lent'.

All other arguments against interest (i.e., rates of interest which are only fractions of the principal sum) such as provided by Muslim writers or scholars are, at best, superfluous and self-serving. If *riba* means any addition over money lent out, then no one can loan out money to someone else or an organization to share in profits or losses. In other words, one cannot be an inactive participant in business or trade ventures and share profit because he/she cannot get back money that is in 'addition to the sum lent'. Just because one is ready to accept losses, does not entitle one to claim a part of the profit because he/she is a partner in capital. If *riba* really meant 'an addition to sum lent', then how did the traders during the life of the Prophet share their profits and losses with their aged and/or female partners who could not physically participate in the long journeys that such trades required?

Mudaraba or joint ownership does not necessarily mean that every single shareholder actively participates in the decision-making process as well as the implementation of the decisions. If Islam permits *mudaraba* then it is difficult to understand how *riba* can mean 'an addition to the sum lent'.

Once *riba* is defined as 'an addition to the sum lent', all arguments for joint enterprises, cooperative ventures (as not all members of the coops can participate in the decision-making process or in implementation of those decisions), interest-free banking and/or Islamic monetary policies become redundant and all these institutions become forbidden for the Muslims. The so-called interest-free banks that operate in some of the Muslim countries are really indirect participants in *riba*, in its literal sense, then. The practice of payments of commissions to the depositors or charging of variable or fixed fees from the borrowers, or lending less than the contracted amount while recovering the full amount, cannot be anything less than *riba* – i.e., 'an addition to the sum lent'. On the one hand, the IBF claim interest is *riba* and, as such, forbidden, while on the other, they are dealing in interest, but calling it profit/loss sharing!

The *fuqaha*, it seems, have developed quite narrow interpretations of the term *riba* to suit their own line of thinking. Some just substitute 'interest' for the term *riba*.[27] There are others[28] who make a clear distinction between *riba* and interest. Some among the former group find support for their arguments from the leftist economic theorists (inspired by Marxist philosophy?) that interest is inherently destabilizing[29] and morally reprehensible. Many of the exponents of the current form of IBF have professionally and financially benefited from the IBF industry and, as such, are not in a position to think critically and, less so, to question their practices in writing. It is heartwarming to see that academicians like El-Gamal, Warde, Vogel and Hayes,[30] among others, have come forward to enlighten the public about the Islamicity of the IBF. It is important to remind the Muslims that Islam is not the only religion that prohibits usury (*riba*); Judaism and Christianity also have similar restrictions.

3.0   USURY IN JUDAISM AND CHRISTIANITY

It appears that Judaism allowed usury to be extracted from non-Jews only. Nelson[31] quotes Deuteronomy Xxiii: 20, thus:

> From him, it says there, demand usury, whom you rightly desire to harm, against whom weapons are lawfully carried. Upon him usury is legally imposed. On him whom you cannot easily conquer in war, you can quickly take vengeance with the hundredth. From him exact usury whom it would not be a crime to kill. He fights without a weapon who demands usury: he who revenges himself upon an enemy, who is an interest collector from his foe, fights without a sword. Therefore, where there is the right of war, there also is the right of usury.

Nelson continues to quote St. Ambrose's interpretation of Deuteronomy, thus, 'The Law forbids you under any circumstances to exact usury from your brother', who 'is your sharer in nature, co-heir in grace, every people, which, first, is in Faith, then under the Roman Law.'[32]

With the beginning of the Crusades, the teaching of Ambrose gave the Christians an excuse to demand interest from Muslims, even though it was against the teaching of Jesus not to extract usury from anyone. The Jews in Europe got the cue from this to charge usury from their Christian debtors.[33] However, Christianity in medieval and renaissance Europe, in general, condemned usury, and started to make a distinction between usury and interest. Homer[34] provides an excellent expose on the history of interest rates. He states that, 'It was from exceptions to the canon law against usury that the medieval theory of interest slowly developed. Compensation for loans was not licit if it was a gain to the lender, but became licit if the compensation was not a net gain, but rather a reimbursement for loss or expense . . . It was often a compensation or penalty for delayed repayment of loan.'[35] This is similar to the *riba* transactions at the pre-Islamic Arabia.

An excellent concise history of the evolution of interest from usury throughout the medieval and renaissance period is presented by Persky[36] in a recent essay. Of special interest to the Muslim scholars of today, who are engaged in the debate over *riba* and interest, is Persky's enunciation of the positions of Adam Smith and Jeremy Bentham on the question of usury. While Smith advocated government control of interest rates to prevent usury, Bentham maintained that any attempt to control this would be thwarted by the 'projector' and the 'prodigal'.[37] Time and again history proves that Bentham was right. While the IBF proclaims that it does not deal with interest, the practitioners working for them have found ways to charge exorbitant fees and mark-ups that are significantly higher than the market rates of interest! A careful analysis of the instruments used by the IBF will bring this point home.

4.0   FINANCIAL INSTRUMENTS USED BY IBF TO 'AVOID' *RIBA*

The financial instruments used by IBF are numerous. According to Raphaeli,[38] the most frequently used ones are: '*wadi'ah* (safekeeping), *mudharabah* (profit sharing), *murabahah* (cost plus), *ijarah* (leasing), *qardh al-hassan* (benevolent loan), and *musharakah* (joint venture)'.

Wadi'ah is a non-interest-bearing demand deposit (checking account) similar to the ones offered by commercial banks around the globe. It is also a non-interest-bearing savings deposit account, but with a promise of giving *hiba* (gift) whenever the bank has 'profits' to share! In practice, though, IBF claim to offer '*hiba*' which are a tad higher than the interests on savings account in conventional banks, to attract deposits. In practice, ordinary depositors get nothing.

A *mudharabah* (profit-sharing) account is a form of time deposit that cannot be withdrawn before the contractual time is elapsed. The bank as the intermediary (*mudharib*) takes no risk when it lends money to the borrowers. The borrowers sign contracts that specify the principal amount borrowed and how much would be paid back, all predetermined. Since usually the 'cost' of the loan is collected when the loan is given, i.e., the amount of the loan minus the 'cost' is advanced, usually such loans are more expensive to the borrower than the ordinary commercial loans offered by conventional banks. If the borrower defaults on the loan, the loss is borne by the depositors to the bank. If the loan is repaid early, the borrower does not receive any part of the 'cost' that the bank collected at the origination of the loan!

Murabaha (cost plus) transactions, a very profitable business for IBF, is no different in character than that of a finance company. The Islamic bank

(IB) buys the merchandise, adds an amount for 'profit' and sells it to the buyer, to be paid back in equal instalments. Even if the borrower would attempt to pay back the loan ahead of time, the payments are not reduced. For all practical purposes, *murabaha* loans have implicit fixed interest rates that are higher than those on instalment loans from conventional financial institutions.

Ijarah (leasing) or *ijarah waqtina* (lease and purchase) is another way of enriching the IB at the cost of the borrower. The lessee cannot refinance or change the contract in view of changes in the market conditions. Any break in the contract goes in favour of the IB. Thus, the lessee can lose the equity in the property after paying payments for a number of years, if for some reason s/he can no longer honour the contract.

Qardh al-hassan (a goodwill loan) is given in good faith – the borrower is obliged to pay back the amount lent only, without any obligation to pay anything extra. It is quite obvious that a financial institution that is open for business to make money would not advance many loans.

Musharakah is a joint venture in which an IB and clients jointly finance a venture by issuing 'participation certificates' that can be bought and sold in the market. This type of joint venture is commonly known as *sukuk*, and the 'participation certificates' are traded like bonds. Apparently, the market for *sukuk* mushroomed to around $41 billion[39] fuelled by Middle Eastern oil money that is being invested in building booms and other infrastructure. It is not clear how returns on such instruments are determined, but the returns are predetermined nonetheless.[40] If the past is any indication, it would be based on returns from similar instruments issued by 'non-Islamic' entities and would simply be labelled as profit-sharing. It would be interesting to watch what happens when an IB fails to meet its obligations on *sukuk* to the investing public.

The IBs, at this period of bounties from oil-exporting countries, seem to be doing financially all right. Hardly a day goes by when Islamic banking does not make it into the pages of financial papers, e.g., *The Financial Times*, *The Wall Street Journal* and *The Economist*.[41]

5.0   ASSESSING THE OPERATIONS OF THE IBF

The brief review of the financial instruments above leads to an obvious question: in what ways do the so-called Islamic Banks and financial institutions qualify to be called Islamic? Apart from the claims that the IBF follow Islamic 'principles', there is no difference in their operations from the conventional financial institutions (CFI), except for the fact that the

IBs' principal thrust is towards maximizing their own coffers at the cost of depositors and the borrowers.

It can be demonstrated that the IBs use religious slogans to convince the common people that they are functioning to promote welfare of the believers. In reality, most of their loans cost a lot more than what the conventional banks charge. While the CFI are subject to regulations and are accountable for their actions, the IBs are prone to corruption and mismanagement (in some countries where these are not centrally controlled); all they need is a review from their *Shari'ah* council, that the transactions do not involve dealing with interest rates. The IBs frequently place their customers' deposits into short-term instruments of conventional banks abroad to earn interests so that they can present their own depositors with shares of their interest earnings as 'profits' and/or, advance *hiba* (gift) to them!

In reality the IBs are deposit-taking finance companies. Herein lies their attractiveness to the major financial institutions of the developed West. It is not that Citibank or HSBC suddenly developed a fervour for 'Islamic' banks and financial institutions. Where else can they find an easy way of making money without any risk or responsibility to their clients, and without being subject to regulations? After all, the IBs have been using their facilities to earn short-term income (read, 'interest') and delve into futures, options and other speculative transactions!

The IBs, as institutions, seem to attract a fraction of the business of financial transactions in countries where CFI are allowed to operate. The total assets of all IBs are minuscule[42] compared to the CFI in the Muslim countries, and compared to some of the regional banks' assets in the US. It will not take long for the Muslims to figure out[43] that the *sukuk* transactions are nothing more than institutional bonds, but with mismatched risk–return relationship. It appears that no matter how the transactions are structured by the IBs, as long as these are made into 'contract' documents, these are termed as Islamic.[44]

5.1   IBF and the use of Contractual Agreements to 'Avoid' Riba

Earlier in the chapter, it was pointed out that Islamic jurisprudence (*Shari'ah*) developed the idea that the way to avoid *riba* is to take recourse to contractual agreements that Muslims have been advised by God in the Quran to undertake in dealing with each other in financial matters. While such a contractual agreement was required to be signed by the lender and the borrower in the presence of witnesses in personal transactions at a time when there were no financial institutions and money-based economies, the Muslim scholars have extended that feature to modern financial institutions and instruments. Vogel and Hayes[45] provide an excellent expose about the development of contractual laws and application in IBF. However, the question remains, why the *Shari'ah* 'experts' are going overboard to stretch the personal 'opinions' of scholars of a different age who had no knowledge of modern financial institutions.

It appears that the modern Western scholars are essentially reporting what the proponents of IBF claim, without critically examining them from both critical religious and logical points of view. The *Shari'ah* 'experts' are rarely cognizant of the operation of modern financial institutions. From the discussion above of the financial instruments used by the IBF, one may tend to agree with Saleem[46] that the title of his book, *Islamic Banking – A $300 Billion Deception*, may not be too far fetched.

5.2 IBF's Venture into Wall Street

This discourse on IBF will be incomplete if there is no discussion, albeit a short one, on the Dow Jones Islamic Market Indexes (DJIM–World). The data were collected from Dow Jones and Company on the composition and the selection of the companies that constitute the DJIM–World[47] and its recent performance. Despite the claim by the founders of the indexes that companies that deal with some 24 areas[48] are excluded from the indexes, in reality 18 out of the 30 Dow Jones Industrial Average (DJIA) companies are in the DJIM–World, and the top 8 out of 10 companies in the latter are from the DJIA. And these companies deal directly or indirectly through their various divisions and affiliations with the list of 'excluded' products and services. Securities issued by corporations are not separated by products – these are issued in the name of the parent companies. Agro giant Monsanto, for example, produces a number of products that are used as feed grains by animals, including pig farmers. Most chemical, engineering, pharmaceutical, energy and electronics companies provide raw materials, intermediate and final products that are defence- and weapons-related. Inclusion of such companies in the DJIM–World is nothing short of astonishing.

It is not surprising that the market performance of this so-called Islamic market index is not significantly different from the DJIA. Again, we have no choice but to conclude that the so-called Islamic financial institutions, the instruments they use, and the claims they make, have little to do with Islamic injunction about the separate nature of usury and interest. In reality there is very little difference between IBF and the modern financial institutions, except for the fact that the former tries to use religious slogans and symbols to do business.

NOTES

1. See, for example, Iqbal, Z. and Mirakhor, A. (2007), *An Introduction to Islamic Finance: Theory and Practice*, Singapore: John Wiley & Sons (Asia) Pte Ltd.
2. Vogel, F.E. and Hayes III, S.L. (1998), *Islamic Law and Finance: Religion, Risk, and Return*, London: Kluwer Law International; Warde, I. (2000), *Islamic Finance in the Global Economy*, Edinburgh: Edinburgh University Press; Venardos, A.M. (2006), *Islamic Banking & Finance in Southeast Asia: Its Development and Future* (2nd Edition), Singapore: World Scientific Publishing Co. Pte. Ltd.
3. El-Gamal, M.A. (2002), *Islamic Finance*, Cambridge University Press (available through *e brary* 2007); Saleem, M. (2005), *Islamic Banking – A $300 Billion Deception*, Xlibris Corporation, www.Xlibris.com.
4. The Quran, the holy scripture of Islam, was revealed by God to Prophet Mohammed through the angel Gabriel over a period of 23 years. The text is in Arabic and it has been memorized by millions of Muslims across the globe since its revelation. Every attempt to tamper with the text by the enemies of Islam came to naught because of its unique composition and the memorization by the devotees. A Muslim must believe in the message and the integrity of the Quranic text to be considered a Muslim. The Quran has been translated into various languages, and some translators added their own commentaries.
5. *Hadith* literature consists of collections of the Prophet Mohammed's sayings, exhortations, and his practices that were narrated by the disciples of the Prophet and their descendants and compiled into volumes by collectors at around the second century of Islam and later. Depending on the number of narrators and the chain of transmission, some *hadiths* are more authentic than others, while some are not considered as true *hadiths* at all.
6. *Shari'ah,* which is commonly referred to as Islamic law, has evolved out of interpretations of the Quranic verses and *hadiths* and mainly opinions of various scholars – agreeing or disagreeing among themselves – about them. Originally, *Shari'ah* was considered as a set of moral guidance and norms and not laws, but over the centuries some schools of thought elevated them to the status of rigid laws.
7. The Holy *Quran*, Chapter 3, verse 130.
8. The Holy *Quran*, Chapter 2, verses 278–279.
9. The Holy *Quran*, Chapter 2, verse 275.
10. The Holy *Quran*, Chapter 2, verse 276.
11. Homer, S. (1977), *A History of Interest Rates* (Second Edition), New Brunswick, New Jersey: Rutgers University Press, pp. 69–80.
12. Al-Tabari, A.J.M. [d.923 AD] (No date), *Jami' al-bayan 'an ta'wil ay al-Quran*, English translation of the abridged version by J. Cooper, New York: Oxford University Press, 1987.
13. Al-Zamakhshari, M.I.U. [d. 1144 AD] (No date), *al-Kashshaf 'an Haqa'iq al-tanzil wa-'uyun al-aqawil fi wujuh al-ta'wil*.
14. Ibn-Kathir (d. 1373 AD). Quoted by Omar Afzal (see reference shortly) and others.
15. Ibn al-'Arabi [d. 1240 AD] (No date), *Ahkam al-Quran*, Beirut: Dar-al-ikzat al-'Arabia, 1968, V. 1:24.
16. Ibid. p. 241.
17. Zaman, M.R. and Movassaghi, H. (2002), 'Interest-free Islamic Banking: Ideals and Reality', in D. Ghosh and M. Ariff (eds), *Regional Financial Markets: Issues and Strategies*, Westport, CT: Praeger Publishers, Chapter 14.
18. Al-Jassas, A.R. [d. 981 AD] (No date), *Ahkam al-Quran, V. 1*, Istanbul, Turkey: 1916, p. 465.
19. Suhail, I. (1936), *Haqiqat al-Riba* (no other information available); Tantawi, M.S., et al. (1989), *Arbah al-bunuk baina al-Halal wa al-Haram*, Cairo: Dar al-Ma'arif; and Afzal, O. (1996), 'Riba: Usury or Interest or Both', a Conference paper for the Islamic Chamber of Commerce and Industry (ICCI), San Jose, California, November 7–9.

20. *Sahih Muslim*, Vol, III (1976). Translated by Abdul Hamid Siddiqi, Lahore, Pakistan: Sh. Muhammad Ashraf.

21. This author checked *Sahih Al-Bukhari*, *Sahih Muslim* (*Sahih Muslim*, Vol, III, 1976, translated by Abdul Hamid Siddiqi, Lahore, Pakistan: Sh. Muhammad Ashraf); *Mishkat al-Masabih* and *A Manual of Hadith* (Ali, Maulana M., *A Manual of Hadith* [no date of publication], Lahore, Pakistan: The Ahmadiyya Anjuman Ishaat Islam), for various *hadith* related to usury, debts and general business transactions.

22. Ali, Maulana M., *A Manual of Hadith* (No date of publication), Lahore, Pakistan: The Ahmadiyya Anjuman Ishaat Islam, p. 323. The author quotes this explanation from Lane's *Arabic English Lexicon.*

23. Afzal-ur-Rahman (1976), *Economic Doctrines of Islam*, Vol. III, Lahore, Pakistan: Islamic Publications, Ltd.; Iqbal, Z. and Mirakhor, A. (2007), *An Introduction to Islamic Finance: Theory and Practice*, Singapore: John Wiley & Sons (Asia) Pte Ltd.

24. Afzal, O. (1996), 'Riba: Usury or Interest or Both', a Conference paper for the Islamic Chamber of Commerce and Industry (ICCI), San Jose, California, November 7–9, p. 3.

25. Muslim, I. (1990), *Sahih Muslim* (Volume III), translated into English by A.H. Siddiqi, Lahore, Pakistan: Sh. Muhammad Ashraf, p. 834.

26. Suhail, I. (1936), *Haqiqat al-Riba* (no other information available).

27. Among them are: Siddiqi, M.N. (2006), 'Islamic Banking and Finance in Theory and Practice: A Survey of State of the Art', *Islamic Economic Studies*, 13(2), 1–48; Siddiqi, M.N. (1976), *Banking without Interest* (2nd Edition), Lahore, Pakistan: Islamic Publication, Ltd.; Siddiqi, M.N. (1986), *Model of an Islamic Bank*, Chicago: Kazi Publications; Chapra, M.U. (1985), *Towards a Just Monetary System*, London: The Islamic Foundation; Naqvi, S.R. (1993), *History of Banking and Islamic Laws*, Karachi, Pakistan: Hayat Academy; Faridi, F.R. (1991), *Essays in Islamic Economic Analysis*, edited volume, New Delhi: Genuine Publications (P) Ltd.; Wohlers-Scharf, T. (1983), *Arab and Islamic Banks: New Business Partners for Developing Countries*, Paris: OECD Development Centre Studies; Anwar, M. (1987), *Modeling Interest-Free Economy: A Study in Macroeconomics and Development*, Herndon, Virginia: The International Institute of Islamic Thought; and Iqbal, Z. and Mirakhor, A. (2007), *An Introduction to Islamic Finance: Theory and Practice*, Singapore: John Wiley & Sons (Asia) Pte Ltd., who argue that IBF cannot deal with interest, whereas, Sanhuri (1954–1959), al-Saud (1985); Tantawi (1989), Salus (1991), Suhail (1936), Yousuf Ali (1946), (in his commentaries on Quran 2:275 and 2:324), Shah (1967), Rahman (1980) and Afzal (1996) make a clear distinction between *riba* and interest.

28. Sanhuri, A. (1954–1959), *Masadir al-Haq fi al-Fiqh al-Islami*, 6 parts in 2 volumes (No other information available); al-Saud, A.M. (1985), 'Bain al-Faida wa al-Riba', *Al-Shuruq al-Islami*, April 18–20; Tantawi, M.S., et al. (1989), *Arbah al-bunuk baina al-Halal wa al-Haram*, Cairo: Dar al-Ma'arif; Salus, A.A. (1991), *al-Rad'ala Kitab Mufti Misr*, Cairo: Dar al-Manar al-Hadithah; Suhail, I. (1936), *Haqiqat al-Riba* (no other information available); Ali, A.Y. (1946), *The Holy Qur'an: Text, Translation and Commentary*, Washington, DC: The American International Printing Company (no printing date), see Ali's commentaries on Quran 2:275 and 2:324; Rahman, F. (1980), *Major Themes of the Quran*, Chicago: Bibliotheca Islamica; and Afzal, O. (1996), 'Riba: Usury or Interest or Both', a Conference paper for the Islamic Chamber of Commerce and Industry (ICCI), San Jose, California, November, 7–9.

29. See pages 16–22 of Iqbal, Z. and Mirakhor, A. (2007), *An Introduction to Islamic Finance: Theory and Practice*, Singapore: John Wiley & Sons (Asia) Pte Ltd.

30. See endnotes cited above.

31. Nelson, B. (1969), *The Idea of Usury From Tribal Brotherhood to Universal Otherhood* (Second Edition, Enlarged), Chicago: The University of Chicago Press, p. 4.

32. Ibid., p. 4.

33. Ibid., p. 6.

34. Homer, S. (1977), *A History of Interest Rates* (Second Edition), New Brunswick, New Jersey: Rutgers University Press.

35. Ibid., p. 73.
36. Persky, J. (2007), 'Retrospectives – From Usury To Interest', *Journal of Economic Perspectives*, 21(1), Winter 2007, pp. 227–236.
37. Ibid. pp. 231–233. 'Prodigals generally have property to run down, and where security exists, prodigals are likely to get the customary rate. Hence, usury laws won't stop the greater part of prodigality . . . Prodigals are not done in by interest rates that are a few percentage points higher, but by their pattern of excessive spending and much borrowing' (p. 232). According to Bentham 'projectors are the very fount of "invention" and "improvement" . . . lending to investors may well be the best of market transactions, rather than the one that should be limited or prohibited, precisely because lending carries with it a substantial externality, that of technological advancement and change' (p. 233).
38. Raphaeli, N. (2006), 'Islamic Banking – A Fast-Growing Industry', *Inquiry and Analysis Series – No. 297*, The Middle East Media Research Institute, September 29.
39. Ibid.
40. Siddiqi, M.N. (2006), 'Islamic Banking and Finance in Theory and Practice: A Survey of State of the Art', *Islamic Economic Studies*, 13(2), 1–48.
41. Prystay, C. (2006), 'Malaysia Seeks Role as Global Player After Nurturing Islamic Bond Market', *The Wall Street Journal*, 9 August, pp. C1 and C4; Diwany, T.E. (2006), 'How the Banks are Subverting Islam's Ban on Usury', *The Financial Times*, 14 July, p. 11; Bokhari, F. and Oakley, D. (2006), 'Islamic Finance Gets Ready to Spread', *The Financial Times*, 24 November, p. 29; Bokhari, F. and Felsted, A. (2007), 'Insurance: Takaful Cover Worth Billions Set to Take Off', *The Financial Times*, 18 January, p. 17; Johnson, S. (2006), 'How to Hedge and Abide by Sharia', *The Financial Times*, 16 August, p. 14; Lane, K. (2006), 'Islamic- Bond Market Becomes Global by attracting Non-Muslim Borrowers', *The Wall Street Journal*, 16 November, pp. C1 and C6; Oakley, D. (2007), 'Pioneer Islamic-compliant Tracker Launched', *The Financial Times*, 9 January, p 31; Oakley, D. (2007), 'Sukuk: Shock Fades as Deals Break Records', *The Financial Times*, 18 January, p. 17; Saigol, L. and Tett, G. (2006), 'Investors Tap into Wave of Islamic Bonds', *The Financial Times*, 18 September, p. 17; Tett, G. (2006), 'Secondary Trading in Islamic Bonds Promise Earthly Riches', *The Financial Times*, 14 July, p. 20; Tett, G. (2006), 'Shariah-compliant Finance: Banks Create Muslim "Windows" as Islamic banking Expands its Niche', *The Financial Times*, 2 June, p. 6; Tett, G. (2006), 'London Gains Greater Role in Expanding Sharia Market', *The Financial Times*, 2 June, p. 6; and *The Economist* (2006), 'Islamic Finance: Calling the Faithful', *The Economist*, 9 December, p. 77.
42. Islamic Development Bank (2006), *Annual Report 2005–2006*, Jeddah, Saudi Arabia, 1 November.
43. Saleem, M. (2005), *Islamic Banking – A $300 Billion Deception*, Xlibris Corporation, www.Xlibris.com.
44. Siddiqi, M.N. (2006), 'Islamic Banking and Finance in Theory and Practice: A Survey of State of the Art', *Islamic Economic Studies*, 13(2), 1–48.
45. Vogel, F.E. and Hayes III, S.L. (1998), *Islamic Law and Finance: Religion, Risk, and Return*, London: Kluwer Law International.
46. Saleem, M. (2005), *Islamic Banking – A $300 Billion Deception*, Xlibris Corporation, www.Xlibris.com.
47. *Dow Jones Islamic Market Indexes*, Dow Jones and Company, May 2008 (supplied to the author by the company through e-mail attachment).
48. The 24 listed (in Section 3.2) are: defence, brewers, distillers and vintners, food products, tobacco, food retailers and wholesalers, broadcasting and entertainment, media agencies, gambling, hotels, recreational services, restaurants and bars, banks, full line insurance, insurance brokers, property and casualty insurance, reinsurance, life insurance, real estate holding and development, consumer finance, specialty finance, investment services, and mortgage finance.

13. Tensions in Christian financial ethics: an historical overview

Ibrahim Abraham

1.0 INTRODUCTION

In his study of faith and finance 'in a world without redemption', Taylor (2004: 122) observes that '[i]n their long and tangled histories, it is often impossible to know whether money represents God or God represents money'. Semantics aside, what this observation points to is the long and tangled history of finance and faith in Christianity, a religion founded on the teachings of an impoverished Jewish preacher who once instructed a wealthy man to 'sell what you own, and give the money to the poor . . . then come, follow me' (Mark 10:21), that proclaims 'the love of money is the root of all kinds of evil' (1 Timothy 6:10).

Rather than attempting to conclusively untangle this difficult relationship, this chapter will illustrate that the tension evident in Taylor's statement is a recurrent theme in Christian approaches to money and financial ethics from the pages of the Bible, through to the early church, the Reformation and today. As in other religions, Christian approaches to financial ethics are diverse. Taken as a whole, Christian financial ethics is a quarrelsome and contradictory body of thought. However, one can distinguish distinct approaches and recurrent tensions in this area, especially in the contemporary context wherein Christian financial ethics is embedded within the broader field of Christian approaches to capitalism and its attendant political and cultural forces.

To understand the various vectors of this discussion, let me use the contemporary example of the so-called 'sub-prime crisis', the most significant financial event of recent years. As financial actors of considerable wealth and reach, Christian churches have been involved in multiple aspects of this crisis. Firstly, the availability of cheap credit, partially blamed for the crisis, facilitated the building of many new churches in the USA, in the same areas of suburban growth heavily hit by the crisis (Hudnut-Beumler 2007: 201–202). Further, it has been revealed that Australian churches have lost millions of dollars in the sub-prime crisis, particularly through their investments in collateralised debt obligations (West 2008).

Finally, as a result of the financial crisis and other ill-timed economic problems, the charitable activities of churches have been in heavy demand in dealing with the disastrous effects of hundreds of thousands – and potentially millions – of mortgage defaults, particularly in the USA, and the effects of increasing individual and household indebtedness, as the culture of cheap credit comes into question. In Australia, churches and Christian charities such as the Brotherhood of St Laurence, the Salvation Army and the Uniting Church are offering financial counselling services that are in heavy demand. Further, the Brotherhood of St Laurence has begun to offer small loans as an alternative to the high-interest 'pay day loans' low-income earners are increasingly reliant on to meet everyday expenses: this harkens back to what happened in Venice several centuries ago.

Of course, the challenges of indebtedness are not unique to our late capitalist era. This chapter will present, as evidence of the recurrent nature of debates and challenges in Christian financial ethics, a potted overview of historical approaches to financial ethics within Christianity, beginning with the Biblical text itself, through to the early church, the medieval age, the reformation, modernity and some contemporary developments. Perhaps the main historical issue in Christian financial ethics from a contemporary perspective has been the question of usury.

As with Islamic financial ethics, the question of lending at interest and debt-based financial products is a topic of such interest given the dependency of readily available debt in late capitalism and the inconceivability, to some, of a financial system functioning without lending at interest. Conscious that it is being studied in detail elsewhere in this book, and that it has been studied in relation to Islamic finance elsewhere (Mews and Abraham 2007), I will not linger on the issue of usury, however, since it is just one of the tensions running through the history of Christian financial thought. Accordingly, in the extended conclusion, I will explicitly draw out some of the tensions and contradictions running through Christian financial ethics, focussing on the tensions in the uses of scripture and history, the tensions in utilising economic theory, and the contradictions of culture and capital itself.

2.0 SCRIPTURE

The Bible would seem the best place to start from exploring Christian approaches to financial ethics, multivalent though the text obviously is, not least because many of the financial prohibitions in the Bible are repeated in Islamic scripture and practice. The Hebrew Bible (or the 'Old Testament') contains a number of legal prohibitions and instructions, as well as prophetic denouncements of injustice linked to the failure to obey God's commandments. The best-known prohibition is, of course, on the lending of money at interest. Exodus 22:25 insists that one 'shall not exact interest' from a fellow Jew, nor may one 'wrong or oppress a resident alien' (Exodus 22:21). Nehemiah 5 condemns the state for violating these rules and extracting interest from its people. One of the more interesting financial arrangements in the Hebrew Bible is its insistence that contracts and debts are finite (see generally Veerkamp 2007: 171–174), with Deuteronomy 15 declaring all debts to be cancelled on the seventh year, similar to the Year of Jubilee every fiftieth year that sees the cancelling of debts, the freeing of slaves and return of property (Leviticus 25). This law functioned as an instrument of redistribution and is central to the contemporary Jubilee debt-cancellation movement.

It is not just the hoarding of wealth or charging of interest that is condemned in the Hebrew Bible, but unjust business practices, too. In Ezekiel (28:11–19) the King of Tyre is condemned for 'the unrighteousness of [his] trade'. Similarly, Micah 2:1–2 condemns those who 'covet' and 'seize' fields and homes 'because it is in their power'. Amos 8:4–14 condemns exploitative and dishonest business practices that 'trample on the needy'. On the other hand, the Hebrew Bible has passages that describe wealth as reward for obeying God's instructions, such as Deuteronomy 28. Just as the Jubilee tradition of economic redistribution has been picked up in contemporary theology, so too has this tradition of divinely-endowed financial reward. These approaches to religion and wealth are a feature of the contemporary 'prosperity gospel' or the 'health and wealth gospel' (Barron 1987), preached by some conservative churches, particularly large Pentecostal churches in North America and Australia called 'megachurches', as well as growing Pentecostal churches in the developing world.

Now, by the time of Jesus and the events depicted in the New Testament (or Greek Bible), Yoder (1994) notes tensions emerged around the application of the Jubilee laws, with various legal schemes emerging for the wealthy to avoid the remission of debts. The gospels pick up the notion of the Jubilee, with Jesus quoting Isaiah 61:1–2 in announcing his ministry (e.g. Luke 4:14–30), linking it both with the Prophetic tradition, and with material outcomes. The New Testament generally, and the gospels in particular, are acutely concerned with issues of money, and broader economic and political questions. One of the best-known New Testament stories, included in all four gospels, is Jesus throwing moneychangers and traders out of the Temple in Jerusalem. Mark 11:15–19, has Jesus quoting Isaiah 56:7, that the Temple should be a house of prayer, not the 'den of robbers' the moneychangers and traders have made it.

Other elements of the Hebrew Bible's financial ethics are reasserted in the gospels, too. Notably the prohibition on usury, albeit put in a broader context. In Luke 6:34–36, Jesus asks:

> If you lend to those from whom you expect to receive, what credit is that to you? Even sinners lend to sinners, to receive as much again. But love your enemies, do good, and lend, expecting nothing in return. Your reward will be great, and you will be children of the Most High; for he is kind to the ungrateful and the wicked. Be merciful, just as your Father is merciful.

As seen here, the gospels' view of financial risk and reward is entirely counter to the norms of conventional economics, ancient or modern. A reversal of the wealth, status and respectability of society is offered, along with financially irresponsible generosity – as both metaphor and instruction – common examples of God's economy of abundance and grace. For example, in the parable of the vineyard in Matthew 20:1–16 workers who work one hour are paid the same as those who work loyally all day. These notions are picked up in contemporary anti-capitalist Christian approaches to finance and its alternatives.

Evidently then, the gospels include many statements, often subversive parables and nuggets of mocking wisdom aimed at the wealthy and respectable in society that, as Luke 6:34–36 and Matthew 20:1–16 above show, go counter to social norms and common sense. Included amongst these are various statements of Jesus condemning the rich. In contrast to the poor, who are 'blessed' and for who exists the Kingdom of God, Luke 6:24 reads 'woe to you who are rich, for you have received your consolation'. And, of course, Matthew 19:24 offers one of the most well known surrealist images, 'it is easier for a camel to go through the eye of a needle than for someone who is rich to enter the Kingdom of God'. In further contrast to the financial norms of their society (and ours), Jesus and his disciples, we are told in John 12:6 and 13:29, kept a common purse, unfortunately overseen by Judas, with some predictable results. Further, one of the integral statements of Christian belief, the Lord's Prayer, says 'forgive us our debts, as we have forgiven our debtors' (Matthew 6:12) although 'sins' (Luke 11:4) is often used instead and the text is usually given a highly personal tone. Crossan (1993), however, reasserts the material element in Jesus' teaching, arguing that the substance of his teaching, particularly the alternative socio-economic order, the Kingdom of God, was primarily concerned with two things: bread and debt.

Striking a similar note to Crossan, concerned with drawing out the financial and broader political and economic aspects of the gospels, Gay (2007), in his reflection on the theology of credit unions, and the financial lives of the poor, draws attention to Mark 12:41–44 wherein Jesus 'sat down opposite the treasury, and watched the crowd putting money in'. He observes:

> Many rich people put in large sums. A poor widow came and put in two small copper coins . . . Then he called his disciples and said to them, 'Truly I tell you this poor widow has put in more than all those . . . who are contributing out of their abundance . . . she out of her poverty has put in everything she had, all she had to live on'.

Sometimes interpreted in a way as to approve of the widow's giving in faith – megachurches would likely take such an approach – the passage is better understood as an acute observation of the financial burdens of the poor.

3.0 THE EARLY CHURCH

Such situations should be contrasted to the economic arrangements of the early church, depicted in the New Testament. The early church, as depicted in Acts 2:44–45 is said to have held 'all things in common; they would sell their possessions and goods and distribute the proceeds to all, as any had need'. Acts 4:32 continues, 'no one claimed private ownership of any possessions, but everything they owned was held in common'. Thus, as Viner (1978: 14) summarises the early church, its 'ideal was in the political field anarchic in character and in the economic field communistic'. However, this went beyond a mere saintly ideal, as many contemporary conservatives insist, and certainly beyond the current vogue on the scholarly left for a return to utopian thinking, for these ideals were actually lived out (see generally Gonzalez 1990).

Accordingly, one also encounters a variety of statements about money in the depiction and documentation of the early church in the New Testament. It is in this context that Timothy 6:10 offers one of the best-known aphorisms, that 'the love of money is the root of all kinds of evil'. Similarly, the epistle of James condemns one Christian community's apparent reversal of Jesus' teaching that 'God [has] chosen the poor in the world', by instead privileging the wealthy (2:1–5). 'Is it not the rich who oppress you?' James asks (2:6). Similarly James, at 5:1–6 tells the wealthy to 'weep and wail for the miseries that are coming to you . . . The wages of the labourers who mowed your fields, which you kept back by fraud, cry out, and the cries of the harvesters have reached the ears of the Lord of hosts.'

Of course, as the church develops, we soon encounter the issue of the interpretation of Jesus' message. Not only was the early church – actually, churches – extraordinarily diverse, so was its interpretation of Jesus' preaching. A good example of where this leads is the Church Father Clement of Alexandria's interpretation of Jesus' instructions to a rich man in Mark 10:21 to 'sell what you own . . . then come, follow me'. For Clement, this was a warning for the rich man not to get overly attached to his wealth, not actually abandon it. As McGuckin (1987: 1) notes, this early example shows the problem of holding up scripture as a universal ethical code. This does not stop latter interpreters from attempting to distinguish between statements of the early church to create one, however. Ernst Troeltsch, for example, insists that Christian ethics, must 'ignore all statements which ascribe private property to sin, and which describe Paradise as the home of communism', since admonitions of this sort were, apparently, only rhetorical gestures towards the pure heart of the individual (cited in Viner 1978: 10).

The usual approach of the early church, after the Apostles depicted in the Bible, is to condemn wealth's *misuse*. Viner (1978: 15–17, 20–26) observes the abiding concern of the Church Fathers was the ethical questions of rich and poor living alongside each other, typically resolved through almsgiving, elevated to a functionalist system by Augustine who saw the need for rich and poor to exist so as the former could experience generosity, the latter patience (Wilson 1997: 77). However, for many Church Fathers, possessing and misusing wealth are often synonymous. John Chrysostom, for example, responded to the claim that 'I am often reproached for continually attacking the rich' with the retort that, 'yes, because the rich are continually attacking the poor. But those I attack are not rich as such, only those who misuse their wealth' (cited in McGuckin 1987: 13).

The economic question framing all of this is how finite wealth is distributed. This attitude is expressed by Jerome, who says '[a]ll riches come from inequity, and unless one person suffered loss another would not make gain. Hence the popular saying seems to be to be very true: A rich person is either wicked himself or the beneficiary of someone else's wickedness' (in McGuckin 1987: 14). Understandably, many contemporary conservatives, from Viner onwards, dismiss these attitudes, since the notion of finite wealth and its zero sum implications run counter to capitalism's self-understanding of infinite growth. Hence, individual wealth does not deprive others of it; if that wealth is productive capital, one individual's wealth inevitably trickles down to the rest of society.

4.0 SCHOLASTICS AND REFORMERS

Given that the Scholastics, important medieval scholars whose work has profoundly shaped contemporary Christianity, are discussed elsewhere in this book, I want to briefly note a few contemporary takes on their innovations, which illustrate some of the tensions and inherent problems in the discipline of Christian financial and economic ethics. Woods (2005) argues, from a neo-liberal, pro-capitalist Catholic position, that the Scholastics thoroughly refuted any arguments against usury, only to see Luther come along and revive them – reversing the usual (mis)understanding of the reformation and financial ethics.

Similarly, Pecquet (2005) views the development of Scholastic teachings on money – thoroughly anachronistically, of course – as akin to the Soviet Union's *Perestroika* reforms. That is, the Scholastic innovations developed a theology friendlier to emerging forms of business. This is certainly the normative position, and given this book's broader consideration of Islamic and Christian thought, it is worth mentioning the profound role that the Crusades played in this. European intervention in the Muslim-majority Middle East, then as today, required enormous outlays of capital. Had strict prohibitions on lending at interest been observed, the Crusades would have proved far more difficult. The significance of this, then, is to illustrate the extent to which theology is shaped by prevailing political and economic concerns and changes.

The best historical example of this tension is, of course, the reformation. For Martin Luther, the rise in the commercial orientation of the church and its followers and its changing financial practices – including the rise in lending at interest – went hand-in-hand with its other spiritual sins, such as the selling of indulgences. Just as Luther saw the emergent capitalist exploiting the peasant, so the papacy exploited believers (Tawney 1998). 'Under the papacy,' Luther said, 'the Devil has established a market for souls' (Taylor 2004: 78). Accordingly, in his eschatology, Luther associated money with excrement, all to be swept away by the Second Coming of Christ (ibid.: 79). The result of the Lutheran reformation and the resulting religious violence was the *de facto* nationalisation of religion in Western Europe.

It is entirely wrong, therefore, to view the reformation as somehow disentangling religion and the state, as various commentators advocating an Islamic reformation these days sometimes do. Although the era of the reformation saw the development of all manner of Christian radicals, from violent peasant revolutionaries to pacifists intent on recreating the early church, the second major part of the reformation emerged with the Calvinist intervention. Just as the Lutheran reformation placed religion under the yoke of the emerging modern state, the Calvinist reformation saw the subordination of Christianity to the emerging logic of capital, proving the old adage that revolutions always strike twice.

The difference between Luther and Calvin was also evident in the perspectives each brought; Luther worked from within the ideology of a peasant, Calvin from within the ideology of the nascent urban bourgeoisie. Thus, as Weber's (1976) famous thesis argues, Calvin developed a theology with an affinity to capitalism. Although he still condemned usury as the charging of excessive interest that harmed a neighbour (Kerridge 2002), lending at interest was allowed in Calvin's totalitarian 'Godly Republic' of Geneva. This more restrictive definition of usury largely holds to this day, legally, morally and theologically, outside of the Islamic financial market. Now, no one is arguing that Calvinism itself was responsible for the 'capitalist spirit', not least because similar ideologies emerged independent of Calvinism. Rather, Calvinism was one aspect of the overdetermined origins of capitalist ethics.

The precise influence of Calvinism on the development of capitalism, moreover, is impossible to determine. To illustrate this, Marshall (1980: 252) imagines a 17th century Scottish Calvinist businessman explaining in his diary that, because of his profound Calvinist conviction, he will conduct his life according to the values of the new ideology of capitalism. On the other hand, Marshall can also imagine the same Scottish Calvinist confessing in his diary that he has adopted the Calvinist religion to justify his financial interests. Moreover as many, including Yinger (1957, 1970) argue, focussing too much on the influence of Calvinism in the development of capitalism runs the risk of neglecting the extent to which the religious morality in question was itself fundamentally shaped by emergent capitalism and the nascent bourgeoisie who developed it and who had an intimate relationship before Calvinism entered the scene (Tawney 1998). Equally, one must appreciate the partiality of the particular reading of Calvin at the hands of the urban bourgeoisie that led to its reputation that carries on today. As Boer (2009) illustrates, in different hands Calvin's theology produces a very different economic and political morality.

5.0   MODERN DEVELOPMENTS

As we move into the modern era, the financial issues Christians had to deal with become more recognisable to us today. For example, the latter-day reformer, the 18th century English priest, theologian and founder of Methodism, John Wesley, was often caught up in the financial and economic questions of his day, especially given Methodism's initial base in the working class in the era of the Industrial Revolution. Late in his life, Wesley (1788) had to deal with a financial scandal of the day, what he called the 'execrable bill trade', essentially the rampant passing of fraudulent cheques. 'In London I expel every one out of our Society who has anything to do with it,' Wesley wrote. 'Whoever endorses a bill (that is, promises to pay) for more than he is worth is either a fool or a knave.' Wesley's (1995) general approach to money was to honestly work to 'gain all', 'save all' and 'give all' one can, with the concerns of the poor and the hypocrisies of the middle and upper classes always utmost in his preaching (see generally Jennings, Jr 1990; Meeks 1995). For Wesley (1995: 195):

> in the present state of mankind [money] is an excellent gift of God . . . it is food for the hungry, drink for the thirsty . . . By it we may supply the place of a husband to the widow, and the father to the fatherless. We may be in defence of the oppressed, a means of health to the sick . . . it may be as eyes to the blind, as feet to the lame, yea, a lifter up from the gates of death.

While Methodists are encouraged to '[g]ain all you can by honest industry' (ibid.) and with 'unwearied diligence . . . "Save all you can"' (ibid.: 196) Wesley equates self-centred investment (or consumption) with waste, arguing that 'you may as well bury it in the earth, as in you chest, or in the Bank of England' (ibid.), since the third rule for Methodists is to 'Give all you can'. The redistribution of wealth in Acts 4, discussed above, was Wesley's idea of Christian finance in action (Jennings, Jr 1990)

In England, still another Christian development on the edge of modernity was the development of the banking networks of the Quakers, which included banks such as Lloyds and Barclays. Founded in the 17th century, the usually pacifist, mystical and somewhat eclectic Quakers developed sophisticated financial networks and funded missionary and charitable works. Whilst embracing egalitarianism they were ironically often financed by wealthy patrons. Initially violently persecuted, the respectability of latter generations of Quakers was, in effect, purchased by purging the movement of its more extreme elements, from Leveller-style revolutionaries, to would-be miracle healers. Ridding the movement of any sensual pleasures, so the theory goes, they devoted themselves to business, albeit with substantial charitable activities. However, the public image of pious and ascetic Quakers was largely maintained by harsh internal discipline and the exclusion of members considered too worldly, and Quaker businesses were often guilty of the same ill-treatment of workers as their non-Quaker contemporaries (see generally Walvin 1998).

It is not surprising, given the Quakers' oscillating history of entrepreneurship and social justice, that they established the first ethical investment fund in the UK in 1984. The Friends Provident Stewardship Fund avoids investing in weapons or environmentally or socially destructive products such as heavily polluting companies (Wilson 1997: 190–191). Staying with banking, it is worth noting that in the 1860s the notion of the 'credit union' was developed for the modern era by German Lutheran Victor Aime Huber, who saw in credit unions the chance to develop 'a Christian, communal life, based upon economic reforms with the help of associated activity carried on in a spirit of Christian love' (Hume 2007: 98).

Today, Christian investment funds are quite common in North America in particular, ranging from those taking a broadly progressive approach, focusing on workers' rights and the environment, such as the Friends' Fund or the Catholic Aquinas Fund, to those more concerned with advancing a conservative social agenda, such as the Ave Maria Fund, also Catholic, which made headlines when it sold its shares in companies who ceased discriminating against unmarried and same-gender couples (Mews and Abraham 2007). Interestingly, in a comparative study of Islamic, Christian and non-sectarian socially responsible investments, Ghoul and Karam (2007) noted that other than a few niche areas, it was abidingly only the question of investing in conventional finance that separated the three. Indeed, they predicted a great deal of overlap in the investments of the various funds.

The modern era also saw the emergence of new forms of Christian radicalism, typically inspired by socialist politics and the rising labour movement. Europe saw the rise of explicit Christian Socialism, from Britain's Labour Church and Christian Social Union to the League of the Just, the international Christian-centric socialist organisation that commissioned Marx and Engels to write *The Communist Manifesto* shortly after changing its name to the Communist League (Boer 2007a: 130). In the USA, the main vehicle of this theology was the Social Gospel movement that vacillated between advocating the moral reform of capitalism and its overthrow (see generally Hopkins 1940; Atherton 1994; Dorrien 1995). Along the way, the movement played a decisive role in the creation of the American Economic Association, which was quickly divorced from the principles of the social gospel movement and in line with conservative economic thought of the day (Bateman and Kapstein 1999).

On the other hand, the Catholic Church was firmly placing itself, officially at least, within the moral sphere of the modern powers, departing from its early condemnatory attitude towards modernity itself, in defence of feudalism (Holland 2003). This was most evident through Pope Leo XIII's 1878 encyclical *Quod Apostolici Muneris* that defended the institution of private property as 'sanctioned by the law of nature', condemning notions that property should be held in common as 'monstrous views'.

Like many Papal statements, this one proved very unpopular with many Catholics (Viner 1978: 71–72). The Catholic Church's economic teachings and the response of the laity are, therefore, not unlike other areas of social teaching of the Church, which have limited influence on the actual beliefs and behaviour of the billion-or-so Catholics in the world. Whilst the Vatican was continuing into the 20th century to maintain its usually conservative teaching, tempered with concerns for the material and moral implications of unfettered capitalism, largely forgotten sections of the Catholic world were developing their own theological approach to economic and financial issues, combining Christian scripture and tradition with contemporary social sciences.

6.0 CAPITALISM AND CONTEMPORARY DEVELOPMENTS IN CHRISTIAN FINANCIAL ETHICS

What I am referring to here is so-called liberation theology that, whilst certainly not exclusively Catholic, gained most prominence in Catholic theology through its influence in Latin America and the Vatican's opposition to it, with liberation theology particularly attracting the ire of Cardinal Ratzinger (1984), better known these days as Pope Benedict XVI. The concern of liberation theologians was economic and political injustice, from poverty and inequality, to dictatorships and other forms of undemocratic politics, gender inequality and various demands for cultural recognition. Demands for economic justice are at the heart of liberation theology, which usually advances a strong theological critique of capitalism and often a preference for socialism.

Financial issues are important to Latin American liberation theologians, particularly debt. The debt the continent owed to the wealthy 'north' was viewed as a result of the collusion of the ruling classes of Latin America and wealthy countries, resulting in unjust burdens on the poor. In contrast to the regime of global financial capitalism, Mexican priest and theologian José Cárdenas Pallares (1997: 71) is representative of Latin American liberationists in calling for a system that embodies 'the scandalous mercy of God that explode[s] all logic and calculation', embodied particularly in the miracles of Christ that evince his 'identification with the weakest . . . Jesus, the parable of God's love, reveals the limitlessness and generosity of the justice and love of God'. The consequence is, for Cárdenas Pallares (ibid.), 'that if I believe in Jesus' proclamation of the reign of God, there is no way I can accept the reign of that devouring idol which is money, the cause of genocide called the foreign debt'.

Focussing particularly on parts of Luke 6, many liberation theologians insist that the Kingdom of God belongs exclusively to the poor; the idolatry of the rich excludes them (Fitzgerald 1999). As Uruguayan liberation theologian Juan Luis Segundo (1985: 107) wrote, 'the dividing line between joy and woe produced by the reign [of God] runs between the poor and the rich'. The concern is that the alternative socio-economic reign (or 'Kingdom') of God is a necessity for the poor and must have a material element, that is, political and economic change. Thus, Gustavo Gutiérrez (1991: 118–120) views Christian economic ethics as embodying a dialectic of divine gifts and human work for justice.

Accordingly, whilst for the most part keeping within Vatican teaching, Catholic liberation theologians reject the idealist – that is, the moralist – approach of the Vatican to economic and financial ethics, insisting that material changes to institutional structures are necessary, including debt structures and the institutions that oversee the creation and distribution of financial resources (Fitzgerald 1999). Accordingly, an option for socialism is often advanced, although the authoritarianism and atheism of Soviet-style regimes is axiomatically rejected. As Fitzgerald (1999: 222) notes, since actual existing capitalism and socialism in Latin America have both failed the poor, Latin American liberation theologians have been understandably more inclined to side with socialism, given that its ideals are preferable to capitalism's.

However, whereas Latin America's liberation theologians see Christianity as necessitating the development of an alternative to capitalism, in the institutions of global financial capitalism a thoroughly different theology emerged. Beginning in the 1960s, conservative think-tanks such as the American Enterprise Institute started to promote pro-capitalist theology (Hinkelammert 1997: 36), particularly the work of Catholic conservative Michael Novak. This has expanded to Australia, with the conservative think-tank the Centre for Independent Studies also publishing theology (e.g. Gregg and Preece 1999; Novak 1999). Novak was particularly deployed against liberation theologians in the Americas, with his work distributed in Latin America via the USA's embassies (Hinkelammert 1997: 36).

In a similar, but still thoroughly bizarre manner, the International Monetary Fund (IMF) developed its own pro-capitalist theology. In 1992 Michel Camdessus, Secretary General of the IMF, invoked the Bible to justify his institution's work. The IMF's mandate is that same one which, Camdessus argued:

> resounded at the synagogue at Nazareth . . . the realization of the promise made in Isaiah (61:1–3) *beginning with our present history*! It is a text of Isaiah which

Jesus explained; it says (Luke 4: 16–23) 'The spirit of the Lord is upon me. He has anointed me in order to announce the good news to the Poor, to proclaim liberation to captives and the return of sight to the blind, to free the oppressed and proclaim the year of grace granted by the Lord.' And Jesus only had one short response: 'Today this message is fulfilled for you that you should listen.' *This today is our today and we are part of this grace of God, we who are in charge of the economy . . . It is we who have received the Word.* This Word can change everything. *We know that God is with us in the work of spreading brotherhood.* (Cited in Hinkelammert 1997: 40, my italics).

In this astounding public statement, Camdessus perversely insists that the IMF is doing God's work and is equal to Christ as an agent of God.

This is not the only example of capitalism and the will of God being merged in contemporary theology. The late 20th century saw a rise in the corporate mentality of many churches, especially in North American Protestantism, and especially in regard to fundraising and the analogous question of financial rewards (Hudnut-Beumler 2007). This is most prominent amongst preachers of the 'prosperity gospel' who insist that faith, positive thinking and donations to the church will be repaid by God with financial and material rewards. Aside from its dubious scriptural base, one of the concerns about the prosperity doctrine is its obvious conflict of interest, insofar as churches or individuals may solicit funds by telling congregations that their charitable gifts are akin to conventional financial investments. For example, tele-evangelist Kenneth Copeland told his followers they could expect a 'hundred-fold return' on money given to his church (Copeland 1974; Hudnut-Beumler 2007: 225). In a stranger, apocalyptic vein, the appropriately named tele-evangelist Creflo Dollar insists that believers must financially repay the debts of the church, since Christ refuses to return 'to an indebted church' (ibid.: 226). The prosperity gospel is also part of the theology of high-profile Australian mega-church Hillsong, as developed by its founder Brian Houston (1999). Like some contemporary 'new age' and 'self-help' literature, Houston's 'Bible economics' is largely based on an individual developing a positive attitude to attracting wealth, albeit with God playing His part.

Falling short of the wholesale embrace of capitalism are a variety of contemporary Christian financial and economic ethical approaches which would be more familiar to scholars of Islamic finance. The normative position of the Catholic Church is representative of this approach that advocates the moral regulation of capitalism. Rejecting socialism, the Church opines that '[t]he free market is an institution of social importance because of its capacity to guarantee effective results in the production of goods and services' and that 'the free market is the most efficient instrument for utilizing resources and effectively responding to needs' (Pontifical Council 2005: 176). However, the concern of the church is that left to its own devices, *laissez faire* capitalism may not be able to deliver the outcomes the church wants. This is distinct from a variety of neo-liberal pro-capitalist Christian scholars, often associated with secular or religious think-tanks, who embrace capitalist ethics such as self-interest within their Christian ethics.

For the Catholic Church, accordingly, a key concern is that '[e]conomic activity and material progress must be placed at the service of man and society' (ibid.: 166). Accordingly, 'efficiency and the proper care of "capital" cannot be the sole concern of businesses' (ibid.: 175). The Church insists that 'economic activity and moral behaviour are intimately joined one to the other' (ibid.: 169). Accordingly, the Church raises the question of whether qualitative changes in the economy are 'morally correct' (ibid.: 170), an especially acute issue given the Church's deep concern about the increasingly secular consumerist culture of many societies (Pontifical Council 2005: 182). This approach was well exemplified by Pope Benedict XVI's statements on his 2007 tour of Brazil when he condemned the gap between the rich and the poor, Marxism and capitalist globalisation, focussing on the moral problems the latter created through 'drugs, alcohol and deceptive illusions of happiness' (Associated Press 2007).

The late 20th century also saw a rise in critical theological attitudes towards capitalism and dominant financial ethics. As well as the global proliferation of various forms of liberation theology, arguably the highest profile development was the Jubilee movement that drew inspiration from the financial laws of the Bible to argue for the cancellation of debts owed by highly indebted poor countries, developing a (wary) relationship with the broader anti-capitalist movement that rose to prominence around the turn of the millennium. Smaller developments also occurred in wealthy Christian majority nations, often in reaction to the expansion of market logic into the church. Two interrelated movements are the emerging church (see generally, Gibbs and Bolger 2005; Jones 2008) and new monasticism (see generally, Wilson-Hartgrove 2008). Largely based in urban and suburban contexts, these movements have sought to recapture practices of the early churches by focussing on building community within or alongside the poor.

A significant financial development within these movements is the 'relational tithe', which emerged in part as a reaction against wealthy churches, particularly evangelical churches. Rather than donate money to an already wealthy institution, churches and communities involved in the relational tithe movement donate their money into a common pool which other members of the community may request funds for. Sometimes this money goes to basic income support, health or education costs, and sometimes to specific projects run by associated communities in developing economies. The desire of such movements is to develop an economic system that embodies a different logic to capitalism. As Long (2000: 269) writes, 'rather than constructing an economic vision for a global empire, the task of the church is to produce countless alternatives to the marginalist domination of rationality . . . Constant alliances must be made to produce alternative economic formations that bear witness to the expressive character of God's exchanges with us'. In other words, Christian theology and faith manifests in materially different economic systems and financial relationships.

7.0 CONCLUSION: THE TENSIONS IN CHRISTIAN FINANCIAL ETHICS VS SECULARISM

My initial argument in this chapter was that Christian financial ethical thought has always been full of tension, conflict and contradiction. As I have shown in the previous sections, history has seen diverse and antagonistic developments, and the contemporary field of Christian financial and economic thought is as diverse as any time in history. From the Christian celebration and identification with capitalism and its culture, to wary moral critiques and outright anti-capitalist radicals, it is hard to draw any common themes through all this, aside from the obvious point that financial ethics, the question of the morally correct use of money within a broader economy and culture and faith, has always been an integral part of Christian thought. What is also apparent is the recurrent tensions or contradictions in these various approaches to Christian financial ethics, particularly within contemporary conservative Christian financial ethics, which I will briefly draw out here.

Firstly, there are tensions in the use of Christian scripture and history. As Stackhouse (1987) observes, with various contemporary ideologies used to interpret the world and text of the Bible, self-aware honesty is a necessary (albeit rare) commodity. As Boer (2007b) notes, often the Bible is interpreted through the ideological assumption that capitalism is natural and eternal – part of human nature. Gregg and Preece (1999: 11), for example, although acknowledging the Hebrew Bible's ethical pronouncements are 'neither socialistic or capitalistic' nevertheless read the economic ethics in Leviticus in contemporary neo-liberal language, arguing the text has common values to 'democratic capitalism'. Similarly conservative economists, theologians and biblical scholars (e.g. Halteman 2004, Malina 1987, 1997) seek to neutralise the Bible's statements on money and wealth by differentiating the contemporary capitalist economy, in which wealth in the form of productive capital facilitating the infinite growth constitutive of capitalism's self-understanding is justified, with the ancient world of the Bible wherein wealth in the unproductive form of hoarding finite riches is not.

Malina (1997: 15–16) is refreshingly blunt in this regard; arguing that to return to the economic ethics of the gospels would require a return to the political economy of the time and place. Accordingly, 'what good is the Bible in matters economic? My answer is none!' This is obviously not going to sit very well with Christians – especially conservatives – who believe the biblical text to be ethically instructive, if not binding. Accordingly, some sections of the Bible are read quite 'literally' by pro-capitalist scholars, such as the parable of the talents in Matthew 25:14–30 wherein a master entrusts money to his slaves, rewarding those who invest and gain returns. Although the normative view is that this parable concerns obedience to God, or condemns the prevailing economic system, the neo-liberal pro-capitalists read it as explicitly concerning capital investment.

Similar tensions appear in the use of history as with the use of scripture. It is one thing to (re)assert that the capitalist thought of Adam Smith has a strong Christian theology and ontology at its core, but to do the *reverse* with Augustine or Aquinas is something else entirely. For example, Woods (2005: 213) positions his neo-liberal Catholic theology as 'merely extend[ing] the insights of other great Catholics, particularly the late scholastics'. The most melodramatic example is Novak's (1982: 347) characterisation of capitalists as 'Christian soldiers . . . bound to daily combat with the self, inspired to noble competition by the example of the saints who have gone before, hearts burning in emulation of Abraham, Sarah, the good David, Jesus, Paul, Stephen and others'. The common approach is the one identified by Viner (1978: 13), the inconsistent distinguishment between 'texts which are to be accepted literally and texts which are to be interpreted as metaphorical, or insincere, or the products of self-deception and momentary over enthusiasm'.

The second tension I want to look at is the question of culture and capital. Whilst Islamic financial ethics are, arguably, as much about cultural recognition and the public performance of one's faith as religious proscriptions on certain financial transactions, the cultural question in Christian financial ethics must deal with the question of the complete cultural conflation of Christianity with the culture and ethos of capitalism, according to some of its highest profile scholars and preachers, particularly in high-profile and influential mega-churches. On the other hand, the Catholic Church, for instance, views capitalism as potentially undermining Christianity. Their hope is that through the moral regulation of finance and economics in general, an explicitly religious commercial culture can develop, not unlike the piety of the Calvinists. The problem is, of course, that the distinct culture of these pious capitalists was rather short-lived; a particular form of Christianity worked as a 'vanishing mediator' (Jameson 1988) for a full-blown capitalism that soon outgrew any need for religious justification and, with that, any obligation for religiously-derived moral restraint.

What ultimately informs these approaches to economic and financial ethics is the question of how politically proximate the dominant economic theory, neo-liberal capitalism, is to one's theological perspective and project. Those who see a cultural and political affinity between capitalism and Christianity endorse the language and ideology of neo-liberal economics whilst those who oppose the neo-liberal order advocate various Christian alternatives subtly or wholly distinct from market logic. What this augurs for is a downgrading of the significance of theology in the determination of financial ethics – much like the approach to Calvinism must be tempered by the understanding of the effect that capitalist culture had on the very formation of normative Calvinism itself. This is not to argue that theology is wholly subservient to economics.

Even if one wished to suggest that prevailing economic systems frame cultural discourses such as theology, one of the benefits of theology's integral leap of faith is its ability to reason beyond the boundaries of prevailing economic categories, evident in both the reversal of the social and economic order of the parables of the New Testament and in the lives of latter-day radicals such as the emerging church, seeking to live beyond the logic of capital, within the belly of capitalism. What this chapter argues, then, is that Christian financial ethics, precisely the same as Islamic financial ethics, exists within an over-determined field wherein scripture and history at times comes to work upon contemporary politics and economics at the same time as it inevitably gets worked over in the process. Faith, culture, politics and capital are often quarrelsome partners in dialogue, but they are constitutive of contemporary Christian financial ethics, which is all the more predictably diverse a field for it.

REFERENCES

Associated Press (2007) Pope assails Marxism, capitalism at end of Brazil tour. *International Herald Tribune*, May 17. Online: http://www.iht.com/articles/ap/2007/05/14/america/LA-GEN-Pope-Brazil.php?page=1.

Atherton, John (ed.) (1994) *Social Christianity: A Reader*. London: SPCK.

Barron, Bruce (1987) *The Health and Wealth Gospel*. Downers Grove, IL: InterVarsity Press.

Bateman, Bradley W. and Ethan B. Kapstein (1999) Between God and the Market: The Religious Roots of the American Economic Association. *Journal of Economic Perspectives* 13(4): 249–258.

Boer, Roland (2007a) *Rescuing the Bible.* Oxford: Blackwell.

Boer, Roland (2007b) The Sacred Economy of Ancient 'Israel'. *Scandinavian Journal of the Old Testament* 21(1): 29–48.

Boer, Roland (2009) *Political Grace: The Revolutionary Theology of John Calvin.* Louisville, KY: Westminster John Knox.

Cárdenas Pallares, José (1997) The Kingdom of God and the Kingdom of Money. In Leif A. Vaage (ed.) *Subversive Scriptures: Revolutionary Readings of the Christian Bible in Latin America.* Valley Forge, PA: Trinity Press: 60–74.

Copeland, Kenneth (1974) *The Laws of Prosperity.* Fort Worth, TX: Kenneth Copeland Publications.

Crossan, John Dominic (1993) *The Historical Jesus.* New York: HarperCollins.

Dorrien, Gary (1995) *The Soul in Society: The Making and Renewal of Social Christianity.* Minneapolis: Fortress Press.

Gay, Doug (2007) Embodying 'Divine Economy': Credit Unions as the Practice of Political Theology. *Political Theology* 8(1): 117–122.

Ghoul, Wafica and Paul Karam (2007) MRI and SRI Mutual Funds: A Comparison of Christian, Islamic and Socially Responsible Investing Mutual Funds. *Journal of Investing* 16(2): 96–102.

Gibbs, Eddie and Ryan K. Bolger (2005) *Emergent Churches: Creating Christian Community in Postmodern Cultures.* Grand Rapids, MI: Baker Academic.

Gonzalez, Justo (1990) *Faith and Wealth: A History of Early Christian Ideas on the Origin, Significance and Use of Money.* New York: Harper & Row.

Gregg, Samuel and Gordon Preece (1999) *Christianity and Entrepreneurship: Protestant and Catholic Thoughts.* Sydney: Centre for Independent Studies.

Gutiérrez, Gustavo (1991) *The God of Life.* Maryknoll, NY: Orbis.

Halteman, Jim (2004). Productive Capital and Christian Moral Teaching. *Faith & Economics* 44: 26–38.

Hinkelammert, Franz J. (1997) Liberation Theology in the Economic and Social Context of Latin America. In David Batstone, et al. (eds) *Liberation Theologies, Postmodernity and the Americas.* London: Routledge: 25–52.

Holland, Joe (2003) *Modern Catholic Social Teaching: The Popes Confront the Industrial Age, 1740–1958.* Mahwah, NJ: Paulist Press.

Hopkins, Charles Howard (1940) *The Rise of the Social Gospel in American Protestantism 1865–1915.* Oxford: Oxford University Press.

Houston, Brian (1999) *You Need More Money: Discovering God's Amazing Financial Plan for Your Life.* Castle Hill: Maximised Leadership Incorporated.

Hudnut-Beumler, James (2007) *The Pursuit of the Almighty's Dollar: A History of Money and American Protestantism.* Chapel Hill, NC: University of North Carolina Press.

Hume, John (2007) Credit Union, An International Model of Social Inclusion. *Political Theology* 8(1): 97–111.

Jameson, Fredric (1988) [orig. 1973] The Vanishing Mediator; or, Max Weber as Storyteller. In *The Ideologies of Theory, Volume 2: Syntax of History.* Minneapolis: University of Minnesota Press: 3–34.

Jennings, Jr, Theodore W. (1990) *Good News to the Poor: John Wesley's Evangelical Economics.* Nashville: Abingdon Press.

Jones, Tony (2008) *The New Christians: Dispatches from the Emergent Frontier.* San Francisco: Jossey-Bass.

Kerridge, Eric (2002) *Usury, Interest and the Reformation.* London: Ashgate.

Long, D. Stephen (2000) *Divine Economy.* London: Routledge.

Malina, Bruce J. (1987) Wealth and Poverty in the New Testament World. *Interpretation* 41(4): 354–366.

Malina, Bruce J. (1997) Embedded Economics: The Irrelevance of Christian Fictive Domestic Economy. *Forum for Social Economics* 26(2): 1–20.

Marshall, Gordon (1980) *Presbyteries and Profits: Calvinism and the Development of Capitalism in Scotland, 1560–1707.* Oxford: Clarendon Press.

McGuckin, J.A. (1987) The Vine and the Elm Tree: The Patristic Interpretation of Jesus' Teachings on Wealth. In W.J. Sheils and Diana Wood (eds) *The Church and Wealth.* Oxford: Blackwell: 1–14.

Meeks, M. Douglas (ed.) (1995) *The Portion of the Poor: Good News to the Poor in the Wesleyan Tradition.* Nashville: Abingdon Press.

Mews, Constant and Ibrahim Abraham (2007) Usury and Just Compensation: Religious and Financial Ethics in Historical Perspective. *Journal of Business Ethics* 72(1):1–15.

Novak, Michael (1982) *The Spirit of Democratic Capitalism.* New York: Simon & Schuster.

Novak, Michael (1999) *In Praise of the Free Economy.* Sydney: Centre for Independent Studies.

Pecquet, Gary M. (2005) *Perestroika* in Christendom: The Scholastics Develop a Commerce-Friendly Moral Code. In Nicholas Capaldi (ed.) *Business and Religion: A Clash of Civilizations?* Salem, MA: Scrivener Press: 135–153

Pontifical Council for Justice & Peace (2005) *Compendium of the Social Doctrine of the Church.* London: Burns & Oates.

Ratzinger, Joseph, et al. (1984) *Instruction on Certain Aspects of the 'Theology of Liberation'.* Rome: Sacred Congregation for the Doctrine of the Faith.

Segundo, Juan Luis (1985) *The Historical Jesus of the Synoptics.* Maryknoll, NY: Orbis.

Stackhouse, Max L. (1987) What Then Shall We Do? On Using Scripture in Economic Ethics. *Interpretation* 41(4): 382–397.

Tawney, R.H. (1998) [orig. 1926] *Religion and the Rise of Capitalism.* London: Transaction.

Taylor, Mark C. (2004) *Confidence Games: Money and Markets in a World Without Redemption.* Chicago: University of Chicago Press.

Veerkamp, Ton (2007) Judeo-Christian Tradition on Debt: Political, Not Just Ethical. *Ethics & International Affairs* 21(1): 167–188.

Viner, Jacob (1978) Religious Thought and Economic Society: Four Chapters of an Unfinished Work. *History of Political Economy* 10(1): 1–189.

Walvin, James (1998) *The Quakers: Money and Morals.* London: John Murray Publishers.

Weber, Max (1976) [orig. 1926] *The Protestant Ethic and the Spirit of Capitalism.* London: Allen & Unwin.

Wesley, John (1788) Letter to Thomas Taylor. Online: http://wesley.nnu.edu/john_wesley/letters/1788a.htm accessed August 1, 2008.

Wesley, John (1995) The Use of Money. In Max L. Stackhouse, et al. (eds) *On Moral Business.* Grand Rapids, MI: Eerdmans: 194–197.

West, Michael (2008) Sub Grime. *The Age* (Melbourne), August 16: B24.

Wilson, Rodney (1997) *Economics, Ethics and Religion: Jewish, Christian and Muslim Economic Thought.* New York: New York University Press.

Wilson-Hartgrove, Jonathan (2008) *New Monasticism.* Grand Rapids, MI: Brazos Books.

Woods, Thomas E. (2005) *The Church and the Market: A Catholic Defense of the Free Economy.* Lanham, MD: Lexington Books.
Yinger, J. Milton (1957) *Religion, Society and the Individual.* New York: Macmillan.
Yinger, J. Milton (1970) *Scientific Study of Religion.* New York: Macmillan.
Yoder, John Howard (1994) *The Politics of Jesus*, Second edn. Grand Rapids, MI: Eerdmans.

PART V

Education and professional banking
accreditation

14. Human capital development in Islamic finance: initiatives and challenges

Syed Hamid Aljunid

1.0 INTRODUCTION

The chief of Bank Negara, the central bank of Malaysia, at the ceremony to mark the establishment of the International Center for Education in Islamic Finance in 2006, alluded to the fast growth of the Islamic finance industry during the previous ten years. This observation is all the more relevant as the industry was in the process of being integrated within the international financial system as shown by the increasing demand for *Shari'ah* (Islamic common laws)-compliant products and services that had been designed over some four decades. The establishment of the training centre was aimed at creating a sustainable and competitive growth in the industry by training and certifying programmes/courses on human capital development. A call has been made at least in that country to properly plan both training and certification through the collaborative efforts of the regulators, the industry players and training institutions, including the tertiary institutions.

In order for any country to foster finance industry development, some other countries with majority Muslim populations should take the first steps to develop the Islamic finance industry to the level that will lead to the creation of training and certification institutions in this new form of banking. That requires efforts to train the right kind of professionals who are not only certified in terms of skills and competencies, but must be given exposure to the leadership and ethical aspects for the good governance of managing ethic-based Islamic financial products in competition with the conventional banks, which has alternative set of products with its own legal norms based both on statute and civil laws.

Implementing such a stepped plan of human capital development calls for the involvement of the finance industry and the tertiary training institutions. The initiatives and the regulatory responsibility of the government alone in any such sufficiently developed Islamic banking country environment may not be the best strategy in all cases especially at the nascent stage of the development of the industry or if the scale of operations is such that such training should be done in collaboration with institutions serving large markets. This is especially so if the training provider is seen as respected at the global level because of the esteem of such training facilities.

Governments can facilitate and provide broad-based direction for the development of the Islamic financial industry, but the demand for the skills must exist in the first place in the industry and the industry is keen to co-operate on such schemes of training. At the global level, the Ten Year Master Plan for the Islamic financial industry as formulated jointly by IRTI (Islamic Research and Training Institute) and IFSB (Islamic Financial Services Board) is the case in point. It is specifically mentioned in that plan that there is a need for the financial institutions and tertiary institutions to make a concerted effort to build capacity to develop the combined competencies of finance and *Shari'ah* by way of strategic alliances between training institutions and the industry players.

However this concerted effort is not without its challenges if past experience of collaboration between academic institutions (which tend to be in the public sector domain) and the private-sector-based institutions is of any value. The former are more focused on the educational development of knowledge and competencies expected of a citizen in the exercise of his or her citizenship within the exposure given to some specialized knowledge such as Islamic finance. The latter, on the other hand, are concerned not only with the critical requirements of delivering services that are viable but also have no room for laxity where it involves reputation and risk. They are more concerned with specific expertise or skills that can get the job done. Importantly the private sector training institutions require the fundamental knowledge that is only created by the well established public tertiary institutions, which tend to be largely state-owned in countries with majority-Muslim populations, where the industry is growing fast.

The difficulty of practical training of qualified university students is a case in point. Other than the chance to observe the capacity to learn and adapt to the working environment, practical training of the sort in the banking profession to be done mostly by the private sector is perceived as unsophisticated as it does not attempt to relate the contents of training beyond the application. The lack of references to existing knowledge (alas, in some cases, there is no literature yet developed to base the training on the knowledge base) is seen by professionals under such training as cheap labour training to do the jobs that are not worth paying the high fees charged by the private sector. In the process neither party benefits from the supposed synergy of cooperation between the strictly private sector training in collaboration with the industry players.

In short, professionals under training appear to question the lack of depth that can only come from well-founded training that is based on sound quality publications relating to the knowledge base on the topic covered. Training on the topic of *sukuk* bonds by merely referring to the conventional banking literature to understand the structure of *sukuk* is invalid. It is invalid because the economic principle of safeguarding income streams as consistent with the principle of *gharar* and the legal concepts are still not sufficiently researched in the literature available to trainers.

The same can be said for the attachment of academics at industry and vice versa. This problem is not difficult to understand when we consider the divergent interests of the respective parties. Unlike ordinary exchange, there seems to be no corresponding value within the relevant time-frame that can be considered as mutually benefiting. Of course there are exceptions to the rule such as in the case of specific technical or scientific research collaborations where responsibilities and expectations are clearly defined and monitored. However in general, the state of cooperation between industry and academic institutions in Malaysia as an example requires a careful study to ensure that the tripartite collaboration so essential to deliver quality training and certification is examined carefully. Despite specific shortcomings/challenges, much progress is being made towards training and certification.

2.0 EVOLUTION OF TRAINING AND EDUCATION IN ISLAMIC FINANCE

Development of competencies and skills for the Islamic finance industry covers banking, investment and insurance (some would include capital market) sectors. Thus there are four disciplines where (i) the relevant knowledge base is to be developed and (ii) industry-relevant training materials need to be developed. The tertiary institutions are the ones that help develop the knowledge base needed for the four disciplines. There is already a body of knowledge in each of these areas as developed by the mainstream disciplines. What is needed is to make this knowledge relevant to Islamic finance by extending the literature to include Islamic principles where this is called for. For example, how does one price the mortgage rate to be offered by an Islamic bank when the conventional banking pricing is based on term structure of interest rates? Since profit-share is the basis for pricing financial instruments in Islamic banking, how the mainstream theories and techniques in mortgage financing can be changed/amended to suit Islamic banking is an area that is not yet fully developed. Be that as it may, the current state of training places much emphasis on a mode of training revolving around short courses, often delivered in-house or contracted out, but based on how to turn the conventional principles *Shari'ah*-compliant rather than -consistent. The costs of such training have tended to be built into the cost of providing the services which will later be translated into lower cost of services as the staff accumulate knowledge and experiences (Salim, 1996).

As more conventional banks were given licenses to operate Islamic windows in the 1990s in Malaysia, the training services secured specific versions of Islamic products, their contracts, and developed a list of *Shari'ah* issues for compliance, documentation and financial techniques, among others. In the last few years it has been increasingly felt that because of an acute shortage of competencies and skills, there is a need for moving away from this mode of training design to a more sophisticated one based on the fundamentals of the Islamic finance industry. This pressure has been further exacerbated as the number of full-fledged Islamic banks increased from two prior to 2004 to five in 2005 reaching to six as of 2008 (Natt et al. 2007). With securitization and other aspects of Islamic services gaining prominence, the need to develop high quality manpower must be met by the development of specialized knowledge bases and competencies designed to provide the capacity and the flexibility to lead the industry beyond the current concerns of 'compliance' to 'consistent' status of products.

Another impediment to quality training is the quality of the students enrolling in the Malaysian certification programme by the INCEIF. Most of the Islamic banking and insurance sector employees have overseas educational backgrounds rather than either local or overseas professional backgrounds. Almost all the students have MBAs, BBAs and Economics training with a few from other broad-based tertiary degrees. At the start of the training, it was expected that a bout of short training in new areas will be easily translated into new and relevant skills for the industry.

3.0   TRAINING PROVIDERS, PROGRAMMES AND THE ISSUES OF CERTIFICATIONS

The need to educate future human capital in Islamic finance through the university and training systems had been felt in the early 1990s but was somewhat interrupted by the financial crisis of 1997. In Malaysia, the years following the crisis saw significant expansion of Islamic banking initially through Islamic banking windows which was soon followed by the setting up of new fully fledged Islamic banks, thanks to the determination of the Government to make Islamic banking a significant segment of banking in the country albeit within the dual banking system. Consonant with this policy direction, not only were the financial infrastructure and institutions recreated, but also there was an official stance to encourage institutions of higher learning to provide courses if not programmes at undergraduate and postgraduate levels in Islamic finance.

The same enthusiasm was seen in Pakistan despite the reversal of policies from a fully Islamic financial system to that of a dual banking system in 2001. From then on Islamic branches of conventional banks, Islamic financial subsidiaries and even fully fledged Islamic banks were established. The International Islamic universities that had been established earlier in Pakistan and Malaysia had all this while been offering courses in Islamic economics, business and management supported by courses in *fiqh* (jurisprudence) and related complementary *Shari'ah* courses (Tahir 2008).

In 1996 the Islamic Management Center of the International Islamic University offered the postgraduate diploma in Islamic Banking. The International Institute of Islamic Economics (IIIE) Pakistan launched an MSc Economics and finance programme in 2003 followed by an MSc in Islamic banking in 2005. The same pattern emerged in Malaysia and other countries including Jordan (Yarmouk University launched its bachelor degree in Islamic economics and banking in 2001), Brunei (Master's programme in Islamic banking and finance) and Saudi Arabia (Imam Mohamad bin Saud Islamic University). However, until 2008, no Islamic banking programmes or courses have been offered in the Gulf States as part of the bachelor degree programme with the notable exception of Bahrain (Al Jarhi, 2008).

In the five years of the 2000s there has been a notable increase in courses and programmes offered in Islamic banking and finance among the public and private universities of Malaysia. This can be attributed to the perceived potential demand for human capital in the expanding Islamic financial industry (Natt et al., 2007). The International Center for Education in Islamic Finance (INCEIF) was established by the Central Bank of Malaysia in 2006 as a private university specializing in Islamic finance. Its mission is to produce professionals in Islamic finance with its Chartered Islamic Finance Professional programme which is designed to provide future manpower training and such trainees are ready to be absorbed into the Islamic finance industry. This is further elaborated below. Programmes with similar orientation to the professional dimension of training have been on the rise. These are usually offered by universities, institutes and related professional accounting associations (for example, the Chartered Institute of Management Accountants United Kingdom, CIMA) and even standards-setting bodies (for example, the Accounting and Auditing Organization for Islamic Financial Institutions, AAOIFI (see http://www.aaoifi.com/cipa2.html)) in face-to-face mode as well as in the online mode of teaching. Online mode is being designed to provide opportunities for working executives in the financial industry to advance their career with such certifications.

The duration, entry requirements and assessments of these qualifications vary in accordance with the competencies their examinations are designed to provide. A number of these certifications are based on collaboration with standards organizations or universities either through the services of tutors or through endorsement by the collaborating universities or standards organizations (AAOIFI). In the latter case, the certification called Certified Islamic Professional Accountant (CIPA) is awarded after completing a three hour examination; 75% of the exam paper comprises multiple-choice questions and students are required to attain a score of 75%. On average, this certification is based on a four months' programme where tutorials and study packs are optionally provided. The certification is awarded to those who meet the requisite technical understanding and professional skills on accounting for the Islamic Financial Institution. The specific requirements for enrolment into this programme are not available. General reference is made to those who are currently involved in accounting, auditing and finance especially for the international Islamic banking and finance industry. There are also diplomas and postgraduate diplomas in the area of Islamic banking, Islamic insurance or both offered by institutes of banking and finance which may or may not be part of a university (Appendix 14A.1). Aside from Islamic universities mentioned above, most religious institutions and universities have not proceeded to introduce basic understanding of and insight into Islamic finance from the economics and *Shari'ah* perspective. This is rather unfortunate as they represent the bulk of the population that will eventually be major stakeholders of these Islamic financial institutions.

A recent study conducted by INCEIF by surveying the industry players, that included the *takaful* (mutual Islamic insurance) institutions, found that this state of affairs of mixed input quality of incoming trainees has its shortcomings, and this is still the case (Natt et al., 2007). It was also found that the skills or competencies required of new recruits vary from one institution to another, but most tend to go for generic skills rather than professional skills, which is what are needed for the industry. It was also discovered that where training is provided on the job, such training effectiveness is measured by the key performance indicator of the individual staff. It can be inferred that training of this nature is expected to lead to immediate outcomes rather than outcomes concerning the future capacity to develop new and innovative ideas on the services provided by the industry. In other words, an emphasis on the cost aspect of training rather than the investment aspect of human capital development has been the norm of some local-based institutions. To be fair to these institutions, as recently as 2006 there have been no professional qualifications launched in the area of Islamic finance or accounting, something similar to the central-bank-influenced training offered for the industry workforce to qualify as professional certified bankers and insurance personnel. It is to be expected that, thus far, prior to the 2006 advent of INCEIF with a long-term plan for human development, Islamic finance professional certification was absent in this country. The lack of orientation toward professional qualifications is attributable to many factors, but one factor that stands out is the unanticipated growth of the Islamic financial industry.

Given the unprecedented growth of the Islamic finance industry at around 15 per cent asset growth per annum, the opportunities for the financial sector to seize the opportunity move towards professional human development to increase the shareholder value of the players and also to ensure sustained growth of the industry has become urgent. One of the necessary conditions for this is the strategic orientation of manpower planning and investment to include the role of Islamic finance professional training. It is to be expected that the risk of untrained human capital development is high; that the investments may not yield the expected return and it may not be easy to retain the best talents in a global environment of the industry with capital markets in places such as Bahrain, Dubai and Singapore, willing to pay good money for good quality professionals. Handy (1993) has alluded to the paradox of intelligence, now commonly labelled as human capital.

The paradox, as an observer sees, is that the product of training is both sticky and leaky. Unless documented by the employer who pays for the training by outside private bodies, the knowledge of the professionally-trained employees leaks from the organization once the staff leaves. It sticks with the person who leaves to seek better jobs elsewhere. We are witnessing this phenomenon today where the monetary attraction from different parts of the world is creating a pull factor that cannot be matched by the local employers. As companies recoil from investing in human capital training to avoid such losses, the industry equally loses the trained professional human capital. This creates the perverse incentives for INCEIF and also others to train more than the needs of the country, in fact go global in training.

4.0 NOTABLE INSTITUTIONS INITIATED BY THE CENTRAL BANK

It is in this context that the effort of the central bank of Malaysia in facilitating the growth of the training and certification of human capital is worth noting. To provide the short-term but targeted specific training for the industry, the Islamic Banking and Finance Institute of Malaysia (IBFIM) was established in 2001 as an industry-owned institute which is a joint effort among the Islamic financial institutions in Malaysia. The training courses were short-term in nature and often took the form of being customized to the needs of the clients. They were meant for practitioners in employment who intended to broaden their skills and competencies in the specific areas of Islamic finance (banking, investments and insurance as well as capital markets). IBFIM also undertakes certification programmes that include the following: Islamic certified credit professional; *Shari'ah* scholars induction programme; Islamic financial planner certification programme. These are examination-based and are designed as modules of subjects supported by optional tutorials for the students to participate. Candidates are normally expected to complete these programmes within six months, but are given two years for completion failing which they are required to re-register for the examinations. It is worth noting that the *Shari'ah* scholars' induction programme is an important initiative especially since most *Shari'ah*-trained practitioners lack foundational knowledge of economics and finance, and also the Islamic perspectives on the issues to be able to understand the context in which they are required to offer their views on *Shari'ah* compliance. This course is endorsed by the central bank as a prescribed course for *Shari'ah* officers and advisors before they can practice in their respective institutions. The courses offered have significant industry input and this provides the credibility in terms of meeting the skills set and competency requirements of the industry.

IBFIM also provides advisory services in *Shari'ah* and project management services to other institutions in several Muslim-majority countries. Countries such as Brunei, Indonesia and Sri Lanka have gained from sharing the experience through the services of IBFIM. Future collaborations under action include Thailand, the Philippines and Kazakhstan as well as the D-8 countries especially in the area of *takaful*.

The practical and industry-related training of IBFIM is one significant approach to filling in the gap of manpower in the ever-increasing demand for qualified practitioners who have the skills to contribute to deliver the specific aspects of the financial services to their clients, especially when the issue of *Shari'ah* compliance is utmost in the minds of all parties to the transactions. One comment on this is appropriate. Targeting compliance as the sole objective of Islamic finance has been criticized by scholars because that limits Islamic finance to becoming a clone of conventional finance. Instead a focus on how to operate the industry players on the basis of *Shari'ah* consistency is likely to develop in the future which will be a welcome change for freeing the mindset to think in terms of Islamic finance as an ethics-based operation which in sum total is more than the conventional banking, investment and insurance. Just to quote an example: *takaful* insurance is akin to mutual insurance, and it also requires governance rules that would make the insurance institutions shy away from many practices that are in conventional insurance. Similar comments may be made on other institutional operations merely as a copy of the conventional operations.

5.0 PROFESSIONAL QUALIFICATIONS AND THE ROLE OF INCEIF

For the strategic development of the Islamic financial industry as a whole at the national and international levels, a complementary approach taken by the central bank is to create institutions that can develop the quality of professionals for the industry at the global level. Such a strategic plan calls for professional training to appreciate the micro, meso and macro perspectives on the work demands in the industry. Such training also calls for the trainees to possess the theoretical as well as the practical competencies to qualify themselves as professionals in the field of Islamic finance. Such lofty yet realistic training could only be done at tertiary institutions. As indicated earlier, thus far there are universities that are providing the specialized courses in Islamic finance at the Masters level as well as the final year of the undergraduate programme. It is hoped that there will be academic programmes designed to provide strong theoretical foundations to the discipline that will enable future research to be conducted in moving the industry forward into the future. Those who had completed a first degree and are wishing to become Islamic finance professionals may have to look for an alternative path to their career development. Such persons will need a reputable institution to get this training.

This demand had been anticipated by the central bank, which moved in 2006 to establish the International Center for Education in Islamic Finance (INCEIF). The gap to be filled is not just manpower in the Islamic finance industry, but also to create the wealth of literature and certification capacity to meet the educational needs of Islamic finance professionals. Necessarily this effort was seen as internationally recognized certification programmes that are based on the Islamic finance competency model, complemented by research-oriented postgraduate programmes.

The missions of INCEIF are as follows:

- To develop high quality and internationally recognized professionals for the development of the Islamic finance industry imbued with an understanding of the worldview of Islam and competent in interfacing with *Shari'ah* experts in diagnosing and solving complex financial transactions and models.
- To offer recognized certification such as Chartered Islamic Finance professional that will reflect the international qualifying standards of the Islamic finance profession in terms of quality process, delivery of programmes, examinations, assessments, articleship, industry participation and continuing professional education and development.
- To buttress the content and delivery of the professional qualification with relevant research programmes whether on its own or in collaboration with other research institutions for the sustained value contribution of the programme to the future of the Islamic finance industry.

It can be seen that the timeframe involved is longer than the training courses described earlier. It is also pertinent to note that this is a unique institution funded by the central bank as a private institution of professionals for higher learning specializing in customized training to meet the need of the Islamic finance industry, not just one entity. INCEIF is equally unique in the sense that it is an academic-cum-industry venture fused into one to deliver a professional programme.

To cement its integrated approach to the development of manpower and human capital for the industry goals, the central bank also established the International Center for Leadership in Islamic Finance (ICLIF) as the centre that is responsible for developing, among others, the Islamic finance competency model to be employed by INCEIF and sister institutions. Its core mission is to build a high quality human resource pool of top management for the financial sector corporations that will contribute to the global environment.

Its training activities are centred on leadership programmes for Directors and CEOs, based on ICLIF's Leadership Competency Model which has recently metamorphosed into the Breakthrough Leadership Model centring on ethics, equity, fairness, integrity and the drive for excellence as core values of leadership as well as on innovation, execution and transformation as core interpersonal qualities of leadership. 'The model depicts the leader as one who exists within a broader institutional environment that has its unique mix of organizational capabilities, such as risk management, talent management, or customer orientation that defines the drive for operational excellence in the institution' (www.iclif.org). The model also has its Islamic perspective and is known as the ICLIF Islamic finance competency model (Al Attas and Wan Daud, 2007). INCEIF's educational framework is guided by this model. The core components of INCEIF's training model is the emphasis on moral and ethical values, complemented by the higher order thinking skills as depicted by cognitive taxonomy formulated by Bloom (1956). In the course of the training, candidates are expected to share and diagnose the entrepreneurial and innovative experiences of those in the finance industry through various modes of discourse and learning.

5.1 The CIFP Programme Perspective

The CIFP programme is designed to produce professionals with knowledge, skills and competencies who can create value through their ability to understand the expectations of bankers and *Shari'ah* scholars in developing the institutions and the industry. The professional is not only knowledgeable in the affairs of banking and finance, but is imbued with sound knowledge of the worldview of Islam and the economics and financial concepts therein. This requires sufficient understanding of primary as well as secondary sources of knowledge. This knowledge is useful in assisting practitioners to collaborate with *Shari'ah* scholars to create new financial products and services in mobilizing funds for economic growth and development. Among the offshoots of this knowledge is the awareness of ethics if not immersion of values from the Islamic perspective. The Islamic Finance Competency Model of ICLIF centres on strong ethical values being imparted throughout the various levels or parts of the programme. Other areas of knowledge include theoretical and industry-related practical knowledge. Modules in this knowledge component include *Shari'ah* and its applications, Islamic Economics (or Economics from the Islamic perspective), Ethics and Governance, Financial Institutions and Markets, Capital Markets and Wealth Planning.

Upon completion of building knowledge modules, students are required to take modules designed to build practical skills in the management and practices of Islamic banks and insurance, as well as structuring financial products.

Students who have completed the knowledge and skills modules are required to be attached to an Islamic financial institution for a period of six months under the articleship programme. This is a kind of internship programme where students will not only learn to be part of the practice, but also will have their interpersonal and decision-making skills evaluated. Students from the financial industry are not required to undergo the articleship programme, but must instead submit a paper that requires them to reflect on how the modules have influenced their perception of the practice (see Appendix 14A.2: INCEIF model).

How the graduates of the CIFP programme satisfy the needs of Islamic financial institutions will be known in time. Feedbacks on the performance of internship students will be useful in gauging the relevance of the programme to the manpower requirements. Another area of study to determine the quality of CIFP graduates to these institutions is whether current industry linkages and inputs are sufficient to provide relevant and current materials such as cases for a balanced approach to learning and evaluation. This is all the more critical for online students overseas who have no opportunities to attend industry talks or even tutorials.

5.2 Critical Success Factors for Education and Training for Islamic Finance

Notwithstanding the above, the critical success factors for these institutions include the following:

- Its ability, capacity and pace to develop theoretical and applied/discretionary knowledge with strong fundamentals in Islamic finance and related disciplines, and in the process build stable careers for members.
- Recognition in terms of quality of professional work in respect of diagnosing, inference and treating problems, attitude and innovativeness accorded to its graduates by industry over and above the recognition by the regulatory authority. The requirement of continuing professional education after graduating and becoming members in order keep up to date with the development of markets, policies and regulatory developments.
- The recognition of the profession as a body that (1) can protect its standard, (2) has global networking and alliance, (3) can move up the value chain by transforming the industry through intellectual engagements and in the process contribute to economic development as well as make a difference to the cause of social justice.

The critical role of INCEIF and its professional staff is to embody the ethical components of the Islamic worldview to enjoin good work processes such as commitment to quality in its vision, ethical governance and activities that are reflected in its work style processes and values and staffing. Of late the perception of the public is that there are too many unethical activities in the financial industry despite regulations and laws, thus arguing the need for highlighting in the training the upholding of high ethical considerations. The trust that has been the cornerstone of the finance industry has been betrayed by unscrupulous individuals and opportunists have been bent on taking advantage of flaws and cracks in the system. The business of finance without trust will be a destructive force in a market-based economy.

Considering the phenomenal growth of the financial sector in the world economy, it is imperative that the finance industry's integrity is restored at any cost. It is in this regard that the Islamic finance profession is being sought to give a new perspective to ethics and justice in managing the finance industry. For the profession of Islamic finance to remain relevant and useful at the micro and macro levels it must address its processes, structure, values, leadership, system and strategies so as to deliver and control its services in the interest of the public. Therefore self governance and leadership based on a highly developed sense of fairness and justice embodied in Islamic values ought to underpin the conduct of its training, examinations and assessments, code of ethics, peer review and sharing and dissemination of knowledge.

6.0 CHALLENGES AND STRATEGIES FOR MUSLIM COUNTRIES TO TRAIN PROFESSIONALS

The total solution approach to the establishment of the training and certifying institutions mentioned in the last section is one example of an integrated approach to training involving the central bank of a country, the country's industry and the training institutions. However, with any newly established framework, there will always be the risk that the goals may not be fully achieved due to factors within or beyond the control of the institutions concerned. Over time, the institutions would remove shortfalls. We proceed to discuss some of the challenges that ought to be considered by the relevant parties when dealing with change and execution.

Unlike the case of IBFIM which is entirely industry-driven for training as required by its mandate, the collaboration between INCEIF as a training institution on Islamic finance is still in the early stage of learning. There are activities that have taken off: industry talks for staff and students; inputs from industry in terms of moderation of examination questions; the presence of industry leaders; and intellectual discourses organized by both parties. Despite all these positives, there is still room for greater synergistic collaboration. Ideally members of the profession, when they form their association, would comprise those from the industry and regulators. These would be one major source of input into the curricula as well as in the delivery of courses. Hence the formation of a professional association when there are sufficient numbers of certified professionals will lead to this. Joint teaching or lectures where the practical dimensions of issues are discussed will be meaningful to the students. A sense of ownership to the body of knowledge being imparted will go a long way in promoting the quality of the programme.

As in the case of most professional qualifications, the involvement of practitioners and academics in the writing of modules and examination questions review are intensive and substantive. What is generally missing in academic questions is the practice and application aspects of knowledge. Acceptable in an academic and theoretical environment, this exclusion is not acceptable in professional training. The analogy to this can be made in the case of golf. A student can be taught a golf swing, how it is done, the principles behind a good as opposed to a bad swing. However, without the ability to choose the right club, the end result is unachievable. Not only must questions test the ability to apply the knowledge in simulated situations, but there must be periods of certified experience in the industry that can qualify the individual as a member of the profession. The articleship requirements of the accounting profession seem to emphasize this practical aspect strongly, and may serve as the model for future adoption for Islamic finance.

Even if existing practitioners are interested in assisting, they may not have sufficient time to give to this project. Besides, not all practitioners can relate to the academic components of the examinations, especially those who are at the high end of Bloom's taxonomy. What is required is a mechanism that will be mutually beneficial where it is in the interest of each party to be involved in the collaboration. One such option is for the institution to be recognized by the central bank as fulfilling its social responsibility by allowing its personnel to be substantively involved in the project. At the same time the employer can reward the practitioner for the knowledge he has acquired while cooperating in the project.

The profession of Islamic finance is finance within the Islamic worldview. As such the core knowledge of finance and *Shari'ah* ought to be the mainstay of the profession. In the absence of this combination, there is a likely possibility that the recognition will be accorded to other professions in the area of finance and accounting that provide Islamic finance certification as a value added qualification. The example of CIMA and its certification in Islamic finance is a case in point. Otherwise, the certification does not confer authority either in finance or in *Shari'ah*.

It is hoped that the curricula and entry requirements of these professional certifications will be reviewed by the professions so that they will remain competent to deal with newer versions of financial models in Islamic finance.

There will soon be a need to have international education or qualifying standards as a benchmark for the varying certifications that are being awarded to participants. As of today there are many training organizations providing certifications from within and from outside the national borders through online or virtual modes of teaching and learning. The problem here is the monitoring and evaluation of the quality standards of such providers so that trainees are getting valued commensurate with their investments. As indicated earlier, their standing and recognition by the authorities in the countries in which they are registered may not be known to the candidates registering for those qualifications. Those pursuing such qualifications do so with the assumption that the standards of certification are good and recognized globally. They hope that they will be able to improve their career and at the same time have greater mobility within and across boundaries. Without properly defined standards and scope of 'authority', this benefit of qualification may not be realizable. The potential benefits to employers will be illusionary and qualifications will be nominal rather than real.

The issue of *Shari'ah* harmonization can be considered as another facet of this challenge. When we consider this issue, the absence of harmonization will mean another break in the mobility of these employees. One potential solution is for the standard to require competent knowledge of different schools of thought in the curriculum. The effort of INCEIF to establish the centre for *Shari'ah* research is in line with this effort towards harmonization.

Even institutions of good standing will have to deal with the issue of reaching candidates located in different parts of the world. The online mode of learning is acknowledged as a bridge to learning, giving opportunities for those where such institutions are not available to improve their knowledge and careers. With recent technological advances, it is possible to bring them close to the face-to-face environment that is available for local candidates. However, there is a need for real rather than virtual discourse if we are to do justice to the certification programme. Strategic alliance with institutions of higher learning or training institutions overseas is a realistic option to achieve this. However, logistical and technological issues must be properly managed for the model to succeed. Unless there is a central accrediting agency for Islamic finance education that can guide the choice of partners, the reputational risk to all parties can be very high, especially for the certifying party. This issue needs to be considered seriously in the light of the numerous certifying bodies being registered and offering certification to candidates all over the world.

As industry recognition and acceptance are critical in evaluating qualifications and certifications, it is imperative that professional associations be formed that include key officers of institutions as fellow members. Their role will be to guide the profession in moving forward and in facilitating industry-wide involvement to develop the activities of the profession including examinations, attachment/articleship and dissemination and sharing of knowledge.

This can start at the national level and the international association can be included in the process. For a start there has to be a sharing of information and knowledge, as well as collaboration in terms of recommending regional partners. Industry and training institution collaboration can start on a specific project basis. A database on the institutions interested in taking students for attachment and their areas of interest will help planning for attachment. This can be further enhanced by urging the regulatory institutions to acknowledge attachment assistance as part of Corporate Social Responsibility projects.

Because a professional qualification in Islamic finance is *Shari'ah* and finance competence, the curricula must reflect these competencies. Entry requirements should emphasize basic proficiency in finance at least at the undergraduate level. Candidates without such qualifications should be required to enrol in a prerequisite course before being fully admitted to a programme. Without this foundation, the qualification may not portray the right image of the graduates as Islamic finance professionals. A workshop on the categories of professions and certification would help in clarifying the core ingredients of Islamic finance curricula that are acceptable globally.

7.0 CONCLUSION

Some of the pertinent issues that warrant the serious attention of policy makers and industry players have been discussed in this chapter. The integrated approach to the recognition and accreditation of certifications, benchmarking of educational standards, and the role of professional bodies in Islamic finance ought to be deliberated, initiated and implemented urgently through the cooperation of industry representatives of member countries of the Islamic Development Bank or any such body recognized by the industry. At the same time, various proposals have been made as initial steps in moving the profession forward. The key task before us is to categorize and delineate the varying types of qualifications offered and define their roles in the development of the profession.

REFERENCES

Al Attas, S.M. and Wan Daud, W.M. (2007). *The ICLIF Leadership Competency Model: an Islamic Alternative*. ICLIF, Kuala Lumpur, Malaysia.

Al Jarhi, Mabid Al. I. (2008). 'An Overview of Human Resource needs for the Islamic Financial Services Industry for the Next Ten Years'. Paper presented at the Joint Symposium on Islamic Finance, Kuala Lumpur, April 2008.

Bloom, B.S. (1956). *Taxonomy of Educational Objectives, Handbook 1: The Cognitive Domain*. David McKay Co. Inc., New York.

Handy, Charles (1993). *The Empty Raincoat-Making Sense of the Future*. Arrow Business Books.

Natt, Agil, AlHabshi, S.O. and Zainal, M.P. (2007). 'A Proposed Framework for Human Capital Development in the Islamic Financial Services Industry'. Paper presented at the Knowledge Economy and Management Congress, Istanbul, Turkey, 26–28 December, 2007.

Salim, Rafiah (2006). *Development of Human Capital to Support the Envisaged Growth of the Industry*, ICLIF, Kuala Lumpur, Malaysia.

Tahir, Sayyid (2008). 'Islamic Finance, Undergraduate Education'. Paper presented at the Joint Symposium on Islamic Finance, Kuala Lumpur, April 2008.

The Holy Quran, <http://www.usc.edu/dept/MSA/quran/> at 23 October, 2008.

APPENDIX 14A.1: LIST OF INSTITUTIONS OFFERING ISLAMIC FINANCE CERTIFICATION

A.   CIMA – The Chartered Institute of Management Accountants (United Kingdom)

Link: http://www.cimaglobal.com/cps/rde/xchg/live/root.xsl/islamicfinanceindex.htm

Programme
CIMA Certificate in Islamic Finance (Cert IF) with four compulsory modules: Islamic commercial law, Banking and Takaful, Islamic capital markets and instruments, Accounting for Islamic financial institutions.

B.   Islamic Banking & Finance Institute of Malaysia (IBFIM) (Malaysia)

Link: http://www.ibfim.com/index.php?option=com_content&task=view&id=1386&Itemid=201

Programme

- Islamic Certified Credit Professional (CCP-i) Certification programme for credit officers to practice Islamic financing.
- Islamic Financial Planner (IFP) Certification programme for individual to market/ promote Islamic financial planning services.
- *Shari'ah* Scholars Induction Programme (SiSIP) Specialized programme to equip *Shari'ah* scholars with necessary knowledge on the operational aspect of Islamic finance.

C.   International Institute of Islamic Finance Inc. (IIIF) (Malaysia)

Link: http://www.iiif-inc.com/iiif/certification.php

Programme
Certification programme is meant to certify relevant human resource sectors in the industry of Islamic Finance according to a certain standard. This programme in collaboration with relevant regulators/authorities will certify personnel in the following areas: Islamic Accounting (Accountant), Islamic Auditing (Auditors) and *Shari'ah* Certification (*Shari'ah* Advisers).

D.   Centre for Islamic Management Studies (CIMS) Pte. Ltd. (Singapore) (In collaboration with IIUM)

Link: http://www.cimss.com.sg/CIBF.htm

Programme
Certificate in Islamic Banking & Finance (CIBF) a 6-month programme.

E.   Institute of Islamic Banking and Insurance

Link: http://www.islamic-banking.com/index.php

Programme
Post Graduate Diploma in Islamic Banking and Insurance – distance learning.

F.   Accounting and Auditing Organization for Islamic Financial Institutions (AAOIFI)

Link: http://www.aaoifi.com/Latestnews.html

Programmes
Certified Islamic Professional Accountant (CIPA).
Certified *Shari'ah* Adviser and Auditor (CSAA).

G.   International Institute of Islamic Business and Finance

Link: http://www.netversity.org/programs.html

Programme
Certified Islamic Banker[SM] (CeIB[SM]).
Certified Islamic Insurance Professional[SM] (CeIIP[SM]).
Certified Islamic Investment Analyst[SM] (CeIIA[SM]).

H.   Markfield Institute of Higher Education

Link: http://www.mihe.org.uk/html/shortcourse_IslamicFinance.htm

Programme
Certificate & Diploma in Islamic Finance.

I.   Bahrain Institute of Banking and Finance

This body is perhaps the oldest offering rigorously designed professional training courses both as in-house training and as publicly offered courses leading to recognized diplomas in Islamic finance. Based in Bahrain, it has developed courses in collaboration with CMA, DePaul University and central banks in the region.

J.   Securities & Investment Institute

Link: http://www.sii.org.uk/SII/WEB5/sii_files/Qualifications/IFQ/IFQ%20Factsheet%20Oct06.pdf

Programme
Islamic Finance Qualification (IFQ).

K.   GARP Risk Academy

Link: http://www.garpriskacademy.org/certification_overviews.html

Programme
Certificate in Risk Management for Islamic Financial Institutions.

L.   The American Academy of Financial Management

Link: http://www.aafm.org/certification.php?cat=21

Programme
MIFP – Master Islamic Financial Professional.
RIFP – Registered Islamic Finance Professional.

M.   Five Pillars Associates Pte Ltd, in collaboration with the Society of Financial Services Professionals

Link: http://www.fivepillarsassc.com/courses/courses.php

Programme
Islamic Finance Certificate (IFC), a 6-month basic Islamic Finance certification course.

APPENDIX 14A.2:   INCEIF MODEL

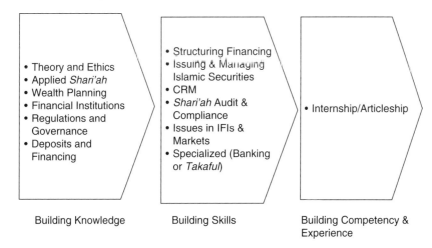

- Theory and Ethics
- Applied *Shari'ah*
- Wealth Planning
- Financial Institutions
- Regulations and Governance
- Deposits and Financing

- Structuring Financing
- Issuing & Managing Islamic Securities
- CRM
- *Shari'ah* Audit & Compliance
- Issues in IFIs & Markets
- Specialized (Banking or *Takaful*)

- Internship/Articleship

Building Knowledge

Building Skills

Building Competency & Experience

Figure 14A.1   INCEIF's Model of Certification

Index